W9-AKC-619

THE MAN THAT GOT AWAY

MUSIC IN AMERICAN LIFE

*A list of books in the series appears
at the end of this book.*

THE MAN THAT GOT AWAY

The Life and Songs of Harold Arlen

WALTER RIMLER

UNIVERSITY OF ILLINOIS PRESS

Urbana, Chicago, and Springfield

© 2015 by the Board of Trustees
of the University of Illinois
All rights reserved
Manufactured in the United States of America
C 5 4 3 2 1
♾ This book is printed on acid-free paper.

Library of Congress Cataloging-in-Publication Data
Rimler, Walter, author.
The man that got away : the life and songs of Harold Arlen / Walter Rimler.
pages   cm — (Music in American life)
Includes bibliographical references and index.
ISBN 978-0-252-03946-1 (cloth: alk. paper)
ISBN 978-0-252-09757-7 (e-book)
1. Arlen, Harold, 1905–1986. 2. Composers—United States—Biography.
I. Title.
ML410.A76R56   2015
782.42164092—dc23 [B]   2014049421

For Vivian Wills

CONTENTS

INTRODUCTION

In October 1984, Harold Arlen was in his eightieth year, a widower, sick with Parkinson's disease and prostate cancer and unable, without assistance, to leave his apartment in the San Remo building on New York's Central Park West. Formerly lively and gregarious, he was spending these last days—and sometimes nights, as well—watching TV from a lounge chair, his social life limited to visits from his friend and biographer Edward Jablonski, his brother Jerry, and Jerry's wife, Rita, and phone conversations with Irving Berlin. Berlin, in his nineties, placed a daily call to check up on him, commiserate with him about aging, cheer him with jokes, let him know which Arlen songs he'd heard on the radio and television, and complain about the fact that their careers had been upended by a generation of rock and rollers—the Beatles in particular—whose songs had pushed theirs off the airwaves.

At the beginning of that month, he'd received an invitation from Paul McCartney to attend a party in celebration of the purchase by McCartney's company MPL Communications of the publishing rights to Arlen's songs. In his reply he wrote, "I deeply appreciate your invitation to sit at your table, but regret that my health at the moment makes that impossible. However, I send sincere personal best wishes. Your work over the years has fascinated and excited me. And I would like you to know that 'Michelle' is one of my favorite songs."[1] After the event, McCartney wrote back saying he wished Arlen had been there, and added, "It means a lot to me to be appreciated by people like yourself, as I am a great admirer of your work."[2]

Arlen hadn't been dissembling when he praised McCartney. But he hadn't been pleased when blues-based rock and roll replaced the amalgam of jazz and European operetta that had been the Tin Pan Alley style—his style. In an interview in the early 1970s, he'd referred to current popular music as "that *farkakteh* stuff."[3] On the other hand, he'd also said that rock and roll was "good for the kids. They have a good beat. If this makes the kids happy that's great . . . the public somehow selects some good music right in the eye of the hurricane of every passing tornado of a fad. Don't worry about it. Music somehow grows on people who can improve their taste."[4] He was correctly predicting that what had happened in the 1920s, which began with "Yes, We Have No Bananas" and ended with "More Than You Know," would happen again in the 1960s, which began with "Itsy Bitsy Teeny Weenie Yellow Polka Dot Bikini" and ended with "Let It Be."

McCartney's admiration for Arlen was also genuine. He'd gotten into music publishing when told he could buy the rights to "Stormy Weather"—a song Arlen had written with lyricist Ted Koehler in 1933. His father, James McCartney, had been a musician with his own group, Jim Mac's Jazz Band, that played standards from Arlen's era, and McCartney knew and loved those songs. He wrote something in that vein himself when he was sixteen, a time when Arlen's style was still in vogue. This tune later appeared on the *Sgt. Pepper* album as "When I'm Sixty-Four." After that, each Beatles album featured one of what he called his "Astaire songs." And the other Beatles had a similar fondness for this music. George Harrison would pass the time playing Hoagy Carmichael songs on his ukulele. John Lennon, as he penned the group's first number-one single, "Please Please Me," drew on wordplay from "Please" ("Please lend your little ear to my pleas"), written by composer Ralph Rainger and lyricist Leo Robin in 1932. After the Beatles broke up, McCartney put out a feeler to Arlen's old lyricist, Johnny Mercer, asking if they might work together. Mercer had never been comfortable with the music of the new generation and he said no, citing his wife's health problems. Had he said yes, McCartney would have found himself right at home working alongside a great poet with a Jekyll-and-Hyde personality.

Because Mercer was not only a songwriter, but a successful singer and a cofounder of Capitol Records, he, like McCartney, was a well-known man. Arlen wasn't. No other songwriter so accomplished was so unfamous. The reason for this lies in the history of twentieth-century song—a history that Arlen and McCartney, between them, encompassed. For Arlen, playing, singing, and arranging for a band had evolved into a songwriting career, which in his time meant being a garret artist—if one substitutes the word *penthouse* for garret. He composed at a piano, either alone or with his lyricist beside him, and when a number was finished, it was given to performing artists who made the commercial product. Lennon, McCartney, and Harrison evolved within their band, so as they wrote they continued to perform and arrange, and when they found themselves with free rein in Abbey Road studios, they combined their writing, singing, instrumental, and arranging skills to capture on record definitive performances of their songs. "Stormy Weather" was associated with Ethel Waters and later with Lena Horne, but "All You Need Is Love" was the Beatles, and if anyone else wanted to top their version—well, good luck.

In his 1979 book *Yesterdays*, Charles Hamm wrote about the change that came to popular music in the mid-1950s when rock and roll ended the long dominance of Tin Pan Alley.[5] Hamm points out that the difference wasn't simply two different musical wellsprings. It was also the change from notes on a page to sounds in a recording studio. In a studio, the new writers did their own instrumentation. They learned to think in terms of sound—a job that had previously been left to specialists who could write orchestral scores. The stunning guitar chord that introduces the Beatles' "A Hard Day's Night," like the opening clarinet whoop of Gershwin's *Rhapsody in Blue*, proclaimed Here I am! in a way unavailable to composers working under Tin Pan Alley constraints.

No one who records an Arlen standard uses the piano arrangement he created for its sheet music. Arrangers fashion the score and in doing so become co-composers. There isn't any Arlen counterpart to "Yellow Submarine," where the song is its sound and the sound comes from its composers—with each goofy ad lib integral to the whole. The Beatles ushered in an era that still continues, where popular songs are works of performance art created by groups making use of electronics in studio recordings. It will be up to future generations to decide if the music of today measures up to the Beatles and if the music of the Beatles, Bob Dylan, Brian Wilson, Carole King, and Marvin Gaye measured up to what Arlen and the writers of his era accomplished. If the Tin Pan Alley style imposed limits on songwriters, it also concentrated their gifts. Instead of orchestrating his songs or creating them as studio performances, Arlen zeroed in on melody, harmony, and rhythm—ingredients that are always the heart of pop composing—and he became a very great songwriter, perhaps the best.

In this book we will see him at work in his era, composing "Over the Rainbow," "Stormy Weather," "It's Only a Paper Moon," "Between the Devil and the Deep Blue Sea," "Let's Fall in Love," "Blues in the Night," "One for My Baby," "My Shining Hour," "That Old Black Magic," "Come Rain or Come Shine," "Ac-cent-tchu-ate the Positive," "The Man That Got Away," and "A Sleeping Bee," to name a few. We will come to know a man whose work was in the public eye while he himself was not. Even among the musicians, singers, fellow songwriters, and aficionados who venerated him, his personal story was and still is barely known. He didn't have the fame of his predecessor and contemporary Irving Berlin, or his successor Paul McCartney. But his work affected people just as much. The story of his life, which he led with humor and dignity against a backdrop of tragedy, helps us understand what it was like to create timeless songs in the age of the great American songbook.

CHAPTER I

BUFFALO, NY

He came to music through his father, Samuel Arluck, who was a cantor in
Buffalo, New York. The elder Arluck thought enough of his son's singing
to give him a spot in the synagogue choir, where the boy made his debut
at age seven. Shortly after that he performed his first solo, which he nearly
botched due to an attack of stage fright—a problem his father solved by
stepping on his foot.

Samuel Arluck was a no-nonsense fellow. By the age of twenty he'd already
begun his career, singing in a small congregation in Louisville, Kentucky.
When another job offer came his way, he jumped at it even though it was
from the equally small Clinton Street congregation in another midsize town,
Buffalo. It's not clear why he wanted the new job, but he took it even though
that meant rushing into marriage. The temple elders in Buffalo required that
their cantor be a married man, so the twenty-one-year-old Arluck had to
find a wife. He did that by going to Cincinnati, where he knew a woman,
Celia Orlen, who was the same age as he and, like him, an immigrant from
Vilna, Poland—although they hadn't met there but in the United States when
he'd been in Ohio on a cantorial singing tour. There is no evidence they'd
been more than passing acquaintances. Given her illiteracy, they couldn't
have had a correspondence. But he found this dependable Orthodox woman
acceptable, and she was pleased by his offer. Soon they were standing under
the canopy in her home, her rabbi officiating, with none of his relatives
present. Then they went to make a life together in an unfamiliar town.

A year later, on the evening of February 14, 1905,[1] Celia gave birth at
their home on 389 Clinton Street to a boy whom she and Samuel named
Joseph. In the early morning hours of February 15, a twin, Harry, arrived.
Harry was injured by a forceps delivery and lived just eight hours. When
he died, Joseph was renamed Hyman (the H in memory of his brother) although his parents often called him Chaim—Hebrew for "life"—or Hymie.

He would be Hyman Arluck for twenty years until, as he began making a name for himself in music, he made his name literally, by changing Hyman to Harold and joining the first syllable of Arluck with the second of Orlen, his mother's maiden name, to get Arlen.

Six years after his birth, the family became complete with the arrival of another son, whom the Arlucks named Nathan but called Julius and nicknamed Udie. These name changes were never explained, but it wasn't uncommon for Eastern European Jews, especially those who had lost infants, to superstitiously switch names around in order to fool evil should it be stalking their children.

The cantor did well at the Clinton Street shul and by the time of Udie's birth had moved to the larger Pine Street Synagogue and bought a duplex within walking distance of it, at 65 Pratt Street. The Arlucks lived downstairs and rented the upstairs to Anderson and Minnie Arthur and their three children, a black family. The neighborhood was mostly Jewish, but African Americans were moving in, and goodwill prevailed between the groups. The Arluck and Arthur children were in and out of one another's homes and attended the same school, Bennett Park #32, which had been the first in the city to integrate. To her dying day, Minnie kept a mezuzah on her door, given to her by the cantor. It was a friendship that, according to George K. Arthur, a grandson, "made Arlen feel at home among African Americans and with their music."[2]

As a boy Arlen collected dance band records. When he was a little older he went downtown to hear live jazz. His father wasn't pleased by these musical choices but was himself at least partly to blame. "I hear in jazz and in gospel my father singing," Arlen later recalled.

> He was one of the greatest improvisers I've ever heard. Let me tell you a story about him. I brought home a record of Louis Armstrong, I don't remember now which it was. My father spoke in Yiddish. And you have to remember, he was brought into this country originally to Louisville, Kentucky, so he must have picked up some of the blacks' inflections down there. Anyway, I played him this record, and there was a musical riff in there—we used to call it a "hot lick"—that Louis did. And my father looked at me, and he was stunned. And he asked in Yiddish, "Where did *he* get it?" Because he thought it was something that *he* knew, you see.[3]

Young Arlen was attracted not only to jazz, but to show business. He and a neighbor, Hymie Sandler, showed up at vaudeville houses on amateur nights to compete for prize money—as comedians. They did pretty well, too. Arlen also earned money on his own as a pianist at the Gayety Theatre burlesque house on Pearl Street, which featured a troupe called Billy

Watson's Beef Trust ("Beef" referred to the size of the female strippers, who were advertised as weighing between 170 and 225 pounds). And he played piano in movie theaters. One of them had a pipe organ, whose pedalboard was a mystery to him, which meant he could play no bass notes. But he pleased the audience anyway. "I loved to walk up the aisle after I'd finished my playing," he recalled, "or to sweep off the bench to take a bow."[4] That this theater also featured a troupe of vaudevillians made him enjoy the job all the more, especially as he'd become infatuated with one of the singers. "She was a little above burlesque," he recalled. "And she reeked of the most glorious perfume—cheap perfume, maybe—but it was wonderful! What a thrill when she took me around backstage and introduced me."[5] It was at around this time that he became a clothes hound, spending much of his money—and he was earning a fair amount—on silk shirts and bell-bottomed trousers. He would iron the pants himself to make sure the cuffs had perfect edging.

He was amiable, fun-loving, and well liked. His cheeks still had their baby fat, his thick black hair rose in successive waves, and he had blue eyes and a slim, wiry build. He was attractive to girls. While still in grade school he had his first romance—with a dark-haired beauty named Lily Levine. They were still going together when they moved on to Hutchinson High. This bothered her parents because he was, he said, determined to become a musician—not the respectable kind with a dependable income like his father, but the sort who ended up playing piano in joints. Moreover, music was making him ignore his homework and cut classes.

His parents were no less concerned and didn't hesitate to tell him. This, plus their problems with each other, caused him to spend less and less time at home. The cantor considered Celia "a naturally nervous and sick woman . . . You have to know or guess how to answer her in order not to get her excited because after all, *she is always* right."[6] According to Arlen's friend and biographer Edward Jablonski, Celia felt dominated by Samuel and in turn dominated her sons and others. Once, when she was visiting her next-door neighbor, Mrs. Sandler, one of the Sandler boys was so engrossed in his comic book he failed to return her greeting, so she retaliated by giving him and all the Sandlers the silent treatment. It went on for weeks until the cantor told her to stop it.[7]

These family difficulties made Arlen decide at the age of fifteen to run away from home. One Friday evening as his mother was lighting the Sabbath candles, he slipped out of the house and headed to the waterfront, where he and a friend had arranged to board a ship and work as galley hands. A couple of hours later, choppy seas made his friend seasick, leaving Arlen to do both their jobs. That was enough for them. They jumped ship the next day, and after wandering aimlessly and penniless for a few hours in Detroit they gave up. With the help of a sympathetic train conductor they made their way back to Buffalo, where Arlen faced more recriminations. For the next five years he stayed put, but all that time he was working on a more realistic getaway—forming and joining bands, making his way up the musical ladder until he could get to New York City.

The way there began with his first group, the Snappy Trio. He was its singer, pianist, and booking agent. Hymie Sandler became the drummer. Another friend, Teddy Meyer, played violin. Of the three, Arlen was the only real musician. He hadn't had much formal training—some classical piano lessons, which he quickly abandoned—but he was a fine instinctive pianist and a gifted singer, and he had a real feel for jazz. Because of him, the group always had gigs. The first was at a tavern called the Maple Leaf Cafe, where they earned $35 a week plus tips. This went on for six weeks until the new year, 1920, ushered in Prohibition—causing the Maple Leaf and places like it to shut their doors. Undeterred, the trio got work in downtown vaudeville houses where they made even better money—as much as $60 a week plus tips—doing four shows a day, seven days a week. One job was in the town of Gowanda, ninety miles to the south, where they played at a Grange Hall dance. The promoters had insisted that the band include a saxophone, a problem Arlen solved by borrowing a clarinet, inserting a kazoo into the mouthpiece, and producing a sound good enough to fool—or charm—his audience. To keep the jobs coming, he joined the Buffalo Musicians' Union, Local 43. It was a white union, blacks having been relegated to their own Local 533. Still, whites and blacks sat in with each other's bands, and there was a lot of musical cross-pollination. Work was plentiful; there were speakeasies and theaters all over town in the early 1920s. "If you couldn't get along with the leader or members of one band," a current union official says of those days, "you could kiss them off, go across the street, and get another job."[8] Arlen and Sandler quit Hutchinson High, and while their friends who'd remained were getting by on allowances in the twenty-five-cents-a-week range, Arlen was buying the first Model T Ford in his neighborhood.

This was his life in the early 1920s as he approached his own twenties—a pianist, singer, and bandleader who was becoming well known in Buffalo. The Snappy Trio turned into a foursome when they added a real saxophonist. That made a name change necessary, and they became the Se-More Jazz Band. With two more members, they renamed themselves the Southbound Shufflers—with no imminent plans to travel south, only a job on a summer excursion boat, the *Canadiana*, that sailed east to Crystal Beach, Ontario. When Sandler left the group to join the New England Six, another of Arlen's friends, also named Hyman, entered the picture. This was Hyman Cheiffetz, whose ambition was to become a song lyricist. He talked Arlen into writing the music for his first song—the self-published "My Gal, My Pal (Won't You Come Back to Me)." It's an old-fashioned waltz with old-fashioned words ("My Gal My Pal life's not the same dear without you / I pray for you each day and never again will I doubt you"). On the cover Arlen identifies himself as Harold Arluck, using his new first name for the first time. The lyricist also made a name change, spelling his first name "Hymon."[9]

Not a single copy was sold. So Arlen didn't feel he'd found his calling. It seemed to him that improvisation was where his creative talent lay—in his own solos and in those he wrote for the rest of the band. He made his living playing popular songs but played them as a jazz musician, paying little attention to the fact that Jerome Kern and Irving Berlin were turning pop song composing into an art form. He was more excited by the singers, instrumentalists, and arrangers who were also taking artistic flight. His favorite group was the Original Memphis Five, whose personnel included the Dorsey Brothers and pianist Frank Signorelli. He made his first trip to New York City to hear them in a Brooklyn dance hall, and "when they came off the stand," he recalled, "I stood there with as much awe as if the president of the United States had just finished speaking."[10] Shortly after that he accepted an offer to join the Yankee Six, an up-and-coming group favored by Buffalo's college crowd. When five new musicians were added, one of them, Dick George, teamed with Arlen to become the ensemble's featured duo-piano team. The Buffalodians, as they renamed themselves, were now the city's premier group, heard often in its poshest nightclub, Geyer's Restaurant and Ballroom.

Arlen's parents watched all this with foreboding. To stop his son's slide, the cantor asked a friend, Jack Yellen, to talk sense into him. Yellen was a Polish-born member of the Pine Street congregation and, as a journalist for the Buffalo *Courier*, a respected citizen of the community at large. But he had another occupation, one that took him downstate to Tin Pan Alley, where he wrote song lyrics. He'd already had one hit, "A Young Man's Fancy," and before long he and composer Milton Ager would write "Happy Days Are Here Again" and "Ain't She Sweet." It would seem that the cantor had made a curious choice in asking Yellen to be his intermediary, but if anyone could tell the boy about the pitfalls ahead of him it was this man—who knew the business well and who was called "Napoleon" around Broadway because of his gruff, bullying personality. Yellen tracked Arlen to a roadhouse named Minnie's, heard him at the piano, and immediately phoned the cantor to say, "It's all your fault. He's going to be a musician."[11]

CHAPTER 2

New York, NY

In 1924 Cantor Arluck was offered a position with a prestigious synagogue, Temple Adath Yeshurun in Syracuse, New York, and he, Celia, and Udie moved to a house near Syracuse University. Not long afterward, the Buffalodians were booked by their agent into a restaurant in Cleveland, Ohio, and then it was on to Pittsburgh, Pennsylvania, and, in the spring of 1925, New York City.

Harold, who had only recently been excited by downtown Buffalo, was now playing the Palace Theatre in Times Square. The Buffalodians were booked there for two weeks and then moved to Gallagher's Monte Carlo Restaurant at 51st and Broadway, which had a downstairs cabaret featuring a gangly comic dancer named Ray Bolger. Bolger and Arlen had already met when they shared the bill at Geyer's in Buffalo. Now they became good friends. Each was intent on remaining in New York and making it big, so they chipped in on the rent for an apartment in a rooming house on West 57th Street.

In later years, Bolger would talk about how Arlen kept him up at night as he worked at the piano on band arrangements and how, rather than being bothered by this, he'd been fascinated to hear the man thinking aloud musically. The two stayed up late discussing their ambitions. Bolger had been intent on a stage career going back to 1917, when he saw Fred Stone leap "out of a haystack looking just like a scarecrow" in a play called *Jack O'Lantern*.[1] But Arlen was still pondering his ultimate goal. Did he hope to make it as a pianist in a city glutted with virtuosos? Or did his future lie in creating dance band orchestrations? He certainly had a gift for instrumentation—one that had already led to a friendship with one of his heroes, Fletcher Henderson, whose recordings he'd collected and who was leading his band at the Roseland Ballroom, not far from the Monte Carlo. When

Henderson heard the Buffalodians, he asked Arlen to do an arrangement of "That's Dynamite" for him, which Arlen gladly did. But Arlen wasn't looking to make a career out of such work. It was laborious and kept him in the shadows, out of the spotlight. Nor did he want to be a bandleader like Henderson; while heading the Southbound Shufflers he'd grown tired of handling their bookings, scheduling, and payroll—jobs he wasn't especially good at. He told Bolger his goal was to make it as a singer.

The decision crystallized one night at the Silver Slipper nightclub. After finishing a show with the Buffalodians, he'd headed there for some after-hours entertainment, and when the orchestra struck up "I'm Coming Virginia"—a song he loved because of Bix Beiderbecke's cornet solo on the recording by Frankie Trumbauer and His Orchestra—he impulsively took the stage, grabbed a microphone, and sang the vocal. Then, to his amazement, he saw that Beiderbecke himself was in the audience; not only that, this musician, whom he idolized, crossed the dance floor, walked to the bandstand, and said to him, "Great, kid!"[2] "Holy Jesus, that meant so much to me!" Arlen later recalled.[3]

In May 1926 the Buffalodians recorded six songs for Columbia Vita-Tone, and Arlen was the featured vocalist on two: Irving Berlin's "How Many Times?" and "Baby Face" (music by Harry Akst, lyrics by Benny Davis). These and later recordings leave no doubt that he was a first-rate singer. Music critic Will Friedwald has written that, while his voice would sometimes go very high, making him sound like "one of the stratospheric tenors of the era," it could also be "warm and deep" and "sizzling and lusty." He was, Friedwald, concluded, "ahead of the curve," along with Bing Crosby, Cliff Edwards, and Hoagy Carmichael, "as an early example of a white vocalist influenced by black jazz styles."[4] Crosby himself was a fan, writing in a 1947 letter, "I've always considered him one of the best stylists I've ever heard."[5]

He certainly would have recorded more with the Buffalodians had the group not suddenly imploded. The end came because of an incident one night in May 1926 while they were playing a gig at the Monte Carlo in Manhattan. There are two differing accounts of this event, given by Arlen to different people at different times. The first was a contemporaneous letter that he wrote to his bandmates under the heading "Happening's [sic] of the Day." Affecting a Yiddish-style Brooklyn accent, he recounted the evening's events. A fight broke out onstage between the band's leader, violinist Jack McLaughlin, and Arlen's co-pianist, Dick George. "Von void led to anoder," Arlen wrote, "un d Dickey says to Mackey, 'Vot do you know about direction' and Mackay says like a brave leader, 'Oh, shut up.' The great part about it was he said it at the same time that he was playing, dat's what I call marvelous. Den Dickey not being afraid of catching cold says, 'Come on outside.' And the boys from the band at dat time could say that Mackey was even hotter there than he was when he played Columbia Records."[6]

More than thirty years later when he told Ed Jablonski about the incident, he put its location not in Manhattan but at the Monte Carlo in Rockaway, New York. In this version the dispute was between McLaughlin and himself. He'd done something to tick McLaughlin off. He couldn't remember what it was, but it might have been his onstage capering—maybe he'd taken too many bows after a vocal or done some unwelcome singing during McLaughlin's violin solo. Whatever it was, McLaughlin gave him a withering look, Arlen responded with more jokes, and when the bandleader, enraged, charged him, Arlen ran offstage, out of the hall, and into the streets, where McLaughlin cornered him—and here is where this account becomes less believable than the other one—only to knock himself out by running face-first into Arlen's two upraised defensive fists. What isn't in doubt is that McLaughlin quit the Buffalodians soon after and that Arlen declined a request by the others to take over. The band was finished.

But he wasn't out of work for long. Arnold Johnson asked him to join his orchestra. They were a step up from the Buffalodians, working at higher-class clubs and sometimes as the pit band for Broadway shows. Johnson wanted Arlen as an arranger, but Arlen had joined so he could take the microphone during the Johnson Orchestra's weekly radio broadcasts from the Park Central Hotel. Singing over the airwaves allowed him to reach a wide audience, one that included his parents and brother, who tuned in regularly from Syracuse. He also did the entr'acte singing in a Broadway revue. He'd rise from his piano in the orchestra pit and croon "I'm on the Crest of a Wave" (his own arrangement of the DeSylva, Brown, and Henderson song) while the audience, ignoring him, returned noisily to its seats for the second half of *George White's Scandals of 1928*. This was not to his taste, so he left Johnson to become Frances Williams's onstage accompanist in a vaudeville act at the Palace. She was one of the stars of the *Scandals* and had become his girlfriend. When that job ended, he auditioned for Broadway producer Jake Shubert. Jake and Lee Shubert were feuding brothers who spoke to each other only through an intermediary, yet they managed to work together to produce musicals that appeared in the theaters they owned on Broadway and all over the United States. Shubert ignored Arlen as he sang and played, so he walked out. After that there was a job in another vaudeville revue—but he realized he was spinning his wheels.

He had never entirely given up composing after "My Gal, My Pal." He wrote two more songs the following year, 1925. In 1926 he composed a piano piece called "Minor Gaff (A Blues Fantasy)" in collaboration with fellow Buffalodian Dick George. It achieved some success: the Tennessee Tooters (aka the California Ramblers) recorded it, and it was published by Mayfair Music Corp., which credited Harold Arluck on the cover. Another piano piece, "Buffalo Rhythm," came out in 1927, written jointly with two fellow Buffalodians. It was published by Landmark Music, Inc. and recorded by bands led by Jack Hylton, Ted Wallace, and Johnny Ringer. In 1928 came a song, "Jungaleena," and a third piano work, "Rhythmic Moments," which was composed solely by Arlen (again as Harold Arluck) and published by Shapiro, Bernstein and Co. Music. The pace picked up in 1929. In February of that year he was at a party when he met Lou Davis, a wholesale meat dealer who wanted to get into show business and talked Arlen into a songwriting partnership. One of their efforts, "The Album of My Dreams," was recorded by superstar Rudy Vallée, which brought in good royalties. Encouraged, he teamed with a more experienced lyricist, Charles Tobias. When their song "Can't Be Bothered with No One but You" failed, he moved on to lyricist Jack Ellis, with whom he wrote four songs, none successful, although one, "Rising Moon," gave the first hint of his way with a bluesy ballad. But these were desultory efforts; he wasn't thinking of himself as a professional songwriter. He hadn't paid attention to, much less studied, the evolution that had been going on in songwriting during the decade that was now coming to a close. Nor had he noticed the new ideas that were changing the structure, content, and ambitions of the American musical.

Then, in May 1929, he was hired by one of America's great songwriters for a role in what promised to be a landmark musical. The play's tentative title was *Louisiana Lou*, and its composer was Vincent Youmans. The craggily handsome Youmans was from a well-established, well-to-do New York family. He'd grown up in Larchmont County and studied engineering at Yale before the lure of a career in music became irresistible. He was a fine pianist. At a party in New York he was introduced to Sergei Rachmaninoff, who, upon hearing Youmans at the keyboard, asked to be taught his style. Youmans was pleased by the prospect of giving those lessons, although they never came off, and grateful for Rachmaninoff's praise for his songs. By 1929 those songs had achieved a remarkable sophistication. He'd helped pioneer a composing style that became a model for the emerging American songbook: taking a brief melodic phrase and building a succession of variations on it, each supported by its own distinctive harmonization. He used this technique to create up-tempo songs like "Tea for Two" as well as heartfelt ballads such as "More Than You Know"—the latter a song he had just written for this new show.

When Arlen met Youmans, American popular songwriting was in its liftoff moment. Some prodigious new talents, inspired by Jerome Kern and Irving Berlin, had come on the scene. Not that Kern and Berlin were relics. Berlin, at forty, had recently penned "Blue Skies" and "Puttin' on the Ritz," while Kern, three years his senior, had, with Hammerstein, created *Show Boat* in 1927—the best musical then yet written. Now the field included the Gershwin brothers, Richard Rodgers and Lorenz Hart, Duke Ellington, Cole Porter, Jimmy McHugh and Dorothy Fields, Harry Warren, Vernon Duke, Arthur Schwartz and Howard Dietz, Hoagy Carmichael, Burton Lane, and E. Y. "Yip" Harburg. "Our tribe of songsmiths," Harburg later called them.[7] They socialized, tried their songs out on each other, and cheered one another along. Ira Gershwin staked Harburg—his onetime school chum—five hundred dollars to get him started in the business. Berlin gave Cole Porter's stalled career a boost by taking out a newspaper ad to praise one of his shows. Porter would later send Johnny Mercer "little encouraging notes and telegrams when he admired something new I had written."[8] George Gershwin took many fledgling songwriters under his wing, including Ann Ronell, Kay Swift, Burton Lane, and Vernon Duke. Duke also received encouragement from Kern, who could be fearsome but who, in their publisher's office, walked over and said, "You may think it odd and I'm not in the habit of saying such things, but I'm crazy about your music—it's new and it's fresh. Believe it or not, I'm under your influence. Good day to you."[9]

It seemed that everyone was in everyone else's corner—the exception being Youmans, especially when it came to Gershwin. They'd been born within a day of each other in September 1898, and when they got together Gershwin, the elder, would affectionately call Youmans "Junior," while Youmans referred to Gershwin as the "Old Man." Despite all his success, Youmans was envious of Gershwin, who was held in awe by musicians and the public alike, not just as a songwriting wonder but as a composer of concert music. When asked in the 1970s if there was any jealousy among the great songwriters, Arlen said, "Yes, Vincent Youmans. Every time he heard a new Gershwin song, he said, 'So the son of a bitch thought of it.'"[10]

Youmans, too, had concert hall ambitions, but his current aim was to become top man on Broadway. *Louisiana Lou* would be his answer to *Show Boat*. He assumed complete control over it. He was the producer, publisher, librettist, and composer. He even bought his own theater. Unfortunately, he wasn't cut out to be a manager. Even when sober he had a tough time getting along with people, and his drinking excesses were amazing even to other alcoholics. A recent marriage had done nothing to lessen his womanizing. Nor did his feverish ambition bring him joy as it did for his nemesis Gershwin—only bitterness, mistrust, and anger.

Youmans hired Arlen to play a black singer-pianist called "Cokey Joe" and perform a song titled "Doo-Da-Dey." For this Arlen had to darken his face with burnt cork, Jolson-style. When the show, renamed *Great Day!*, developed problems during tryouts in the summer of 1929, Youmans gave him a second assignment: notating the score, which was constantly changing. Arlen did this without complaint and was also amenable when Youmans sent him as an emissary to his lyricists, Billy Rose and Edward Eliscu. Youmans's usual method of collaboration was to hand his writers a lead sheet and walk away. But Arlen stayed in the room with them, playing the tunes over and over again, as many times as they wanted. Since his stage role was minor and required little preparation, he could take on yet another task. In July, during rehearsals for the New York premiere, Fletcher Henderson, who was the show's rehearsal pianist, fell ill and asked Arlen to substitute for him. Arlen obliged. This meant repeatedly playing a song while the choreographer and dancers worked out the steps. Arlen would cue the assembled with a conventional two-bar piano vamp—the customary da-da-d'-dah-dah-DA!—but it became so boring to him that he began improvising variations on it. One variation took the music into a dip that created a melodic twist that caught the attention of the dancers and members of the chorus. They gravitated toward the piano as Arlen continued to toy with the phrase. It was as if they wanted to be present at an event—a blessed event, as Arlen later came to see it.

He would always believe that this, his first great tune, had been given to him—a gift that included not just the music, but the fortuitous circumstances surrounding its arrival. After all, if others hadn't recognized what he'd happened on, he might have let the idea slip by. And those others included not only the dancers and singers, but two composers whose opinions counted a lot with him. One was Will Marion Cook, who had composed "I'm Coming Virginia" and was *Great Day!*'s choral director. The other was Harry Warren, a Brooklyn-born son of Italian immigrants (his birth name was Salvatore Antonio Guaragna), now in his midthirties, who'd composed the hit "Nagasaki" and was about to produce one of the great catalogs in American popular song. Warren encouraged Arlen to finish the tune, saying he knew just the man to write the lyric. That man was paunchy, balding, easygoing Ted Koehler, a thirty-five-year-old former vaudeville and movie theater pianist. Koehler met Arlen at the offices of Warren's publisher, where he listened to the now completed tune, asked Arlen to play it again, and then said, simply, "Get Happy."

CHAPTER 3

"Get Happy"

"Get Happy" was accepted by Koehler's publisher, who offered Arlen fifty dollars a week if he would bring his future songs to them. This money allowed him to get a place of his own—a first-floor apartment in the fifteen-story Croydon Hotel on East 86th Street. It also let him bow out of *Great Day!*, which had received terrible reviews in Philadelphia and more bad notices on Long Island. After a rocky start on Broadway, it would be finished off by the Wall Street crash.

Arlen, in contrast, was doing well. Each day he'd take a two-mile walk from 86th Street to his office, which was a small room upstairs in the Strand Theatre on Broadway. There, as the summer of 1929 waned, he and Koehler went to work on new songs as they waited for "Get Happy" to make a splash.

Songwriting, it turned out, was going to be his career. But it was an uncertain profession, more so than performing. He could always count on being able to sing and play the piano, but would he always be able to write great songs? For the first time in his musical life, he wasn't sure he could do what was required. If good ideas came along, he knew he could make something of them. That had happened after the initial inspiration for "Get Happy" when he wrote the bridge—or release—with its dreamy harmonies ("We're headin' 'cross the river"). But what if the inspirations didn't come? He had no idea where they were from, except that it was someplace beyond his control, maybe outside himself. Still, the experience of writing a great song was so exciting that this had to be the way to go. "When he gets to the piano," said lyricist Yip Harburg, "it's a feeling of witchcraft. He'll spit three times and almost talk to the chords, talk to God. He does it humorously, but behind the humor are all sorts of superstitions and beliefs."[1] According to theater critic John Lahr, Arlen invoked "his unconscious through prayer. Before he began his day's work at the piano, he lowered his eyes, brought his hands together, and put himself in a worshipful state of mind."[2] Ira Gershwin said that Arlen "had an almost supernatural belief in inspiration."[3] He took to carrying a folded sheet of music manuscript paper with him wherever he went. If an idea came, he'd stop what he was doing and notate it. He called these notations *jots*, and always set his jot book in front of him on the piano when getting to work.

Songwriting changed his life in other ways. For the first time he thought analytically about his work. He studied the compositions of contemporary songwriters, looking into their stylistic conventions and innovations, how they constructed and harmonized their melodies, how they tailored their work for specific purposes and performers. He took lessons in theory and harmony from Simon Bucharoff, a Russian-born composer of opera and orchestral works. He gave thought to the nature of the creative process and what philosophers had written about it and about the lives of artists. He wanted to know how to comport himself with dignity given the environment he'd be working in. He would be creating commercial products for a commercial market, he knew, but he had no doubt that his music would be art. Late in life, when asked by writer Gene Lees if he'd been aware in the 1930s that he was writing art music, he "looked at me for what seems in memory a long moment and then said, softly, 'Yes.'"[4]

As he read, he copied meaningful passages and quotations into a journal. "When your daemon is in charge," one entry reads, "do not try to think consciously." "Drift, wait, and obey" is another.[5] From Marcus Aurelius: "Let every action be directed to some definite object, and perfect in its way." From Arnold Bennett: "Mind control is the first element of a full existence" and "Self respect is the heart of all purposefulness." From Rilke: "Nobody can counsel and help you, nobody—there's only one single way—go into yourself." From Einstein: "Imagination is more important than knowledge." From Aristotle: "No excellent soul is exempt from a mixture of madness." On a scrap of music paper he counseled himself: "The less a man says whose [sic] admired by the public the longer will he be admired." And: "I do not like the spirit of competition. There is something very uncomfortable about it." He tried in his reading to give himself the education he had missed when he quit school. In one notebook he listed vocabulary words to learn: *poignant, seductive, incomparable, atrocious, exquisite, exotic, exhilarating, bombastic, neophyte.*[6] His readings, however, did not include fiction; he showed no interest in stories or their construction—an omission that would eventually affect his ability to choose worthy Broadway projects.

But the two big questions that confronted him at the moment were where his song ideas would come from and how they could best reach an audience.

He himself had always gotten jobs and landed on his feet. But now he had to worry about his creations, and that was different. Would "Get Happy" find success? Would it do okay?

Once again, Ted Koehler stepped in. He was able to place the song in a show called *Nine-Fifteen Revue* through his connection to singer Ruth Etting. Earlier in the decade he'd championed Etting as she made the transition from costume designer to singer, and then she had become a star in the *Ziegfeld Follies of 1927*. Now, as the headliner of *Nine-Fifteen Revue*, she was happy to return the favor and sing the new Arlen–Koehler song. The revue's producer was twenty-four-year-old Ruth Selwyn, a singer and dancer who was, with this show, becoming the first woman producer on Broadway. Not that she was new to the business; she had appeared in several *George White's Scandals* revues and was the wife of veteran Broadway producer Edgar Selwyn. Thus she was able to attract some big names to the project. Ring Lardner was one of the writers. George and Ira Gershwin contributed a song.

But the show did badly. It lasted just seven performances. In reviewing it, the *New York Times* overlooked "Get Happy" and summed up the revue by saying: "General Sherman was wrong. There are worse things than war."[7] On opening night, February 11, 1930, two members of the chorus stumbled and fell to the floor. Etting premiered the gospel-style "Get Happy" wearing a bathing suit in front of a beach backdrop—an incongruous set devised by choreographer Busby Berkeley. So Arlen's inspired melody, which was his first to be performed on Broadway, had a disappointing debut.

But its publishers had faith and rushed it into print, making sure the attractive Etting was on the cover, and it caught on with jazz and dance bands and became a source of substantial royalties for Arlen and Koehler. It also brought Arlen face-to-face for the first time with the Gershwin brothers. They'd contributed a song, "Toddlin' Along," to the *Nine-Fifteen Revue*, and their musical *Strike Up the Band* tried out in Boston side by side with it. When George heard "Get Happy," he told Harold it was "the most exciting first-act finale I ever heard."[8] This was the beginning of a close friendship between Arlen and both Gershwins, as well as the beginning of George Gershwin's fascination with Arlen's music—heady stuff for Arlen.

And "Get Happy" had yet another result. During the Boston tryout of *Nine-Fifteen Revue*, a producer named Earl Carroll came to see the show. At the time, Carroll was one of the three most successful producers of Broadway revues. Florenz Ziegfeld Jr. worked the high end, spending whatever it took to make his shows opulent and, once in a while, thought-provoking (he had produced *Show Boat*). The middle ground was held by George

White, a former Ziegfeld dancer who had formed his own long-running series of revues. He was a good talent scout and had helped start the careers of Helen Morgan, W. C. Fields, and Bert Lahr, among others. As with Ziegfeld, his bread and butter was the chorus line. The George White Girls were not as elaborately outfitted as the Ziegfeld Girls, but they *were* dressed. Earl Carroll, on the other hand, took the low road. He was a tall, gaunt, and ascetic-looking man, described by one writer as looking "like a Methodist preacher,"[9] who enticed audiences into his theater with young women who were barely clothed. He'd opened his own theater at 50th Street and 7th Avenue in 1922 but tore it down in 1931 to replace it with a much grander place, designed to resemble an Art Deco skyscraper. His credos about feminine beauty were everywhere, even on the backs of sheet music. The measurements he favored were height: 5'5"; weight: 118; neck: 12"; bust: 34½"; and wrist: 6". He also attracted customers with publicity stunts. The most famous occurred in 1926 when he threw a lavish party in his theater for a paroled murderer and potential backer, Harry Kendall Thaw. The highlight was an ingénue sitting naked in a bathtub filled with contraband champagne. It made headlines, as did Carroll's subsequent trial and six-month incarceration for perjury.

Upon hearing "Get Happy," Carroll offered Arlen and Koehler a contract to write songs for his upcoming revue *Earl Carroll's Vanities of 1930*. They gladly accepted the assignment, and it was during the run of this show that Samuel and Celia Arluck came to New York City to visit their son. Already taken aback by his name change (the cantor, in letters to his son, would always sign them, simply and hugely, "Arluck"), they now found themselves sitting in the *Vanities* audience at the New Amsterdam Theatre[10] as an Arlen–Koehler waltz, "One Love," accompanied a fan dance by the otherwise naked Faith Bacon. They also saw a scene that tried to pass off nude women as mannequins (a ruse that did not fool the vice squad). If this weren't enough, they learned about Harold's romance with Frances Williams—a non-Jew. Arlen did as he had done as a boy: he weathered their displeasure, avoided a confrontation, waited the situation out, then returned to what he'd been doing. And the Arlucks, as always, stopped short of rejecting their son. They could tolerate flings such as this, as long as there was no talk of marriage. Marriage was the important thing. It was essential that he marry within his faith and raise his children as Jews. At the moment there was no need for them to worry. The romance with Williams was cooling down.

CHAPTER 4

THE COTTON CLUB

By 1930, the days when Tin Pan Alley publishers sold their songs to traveling entertainers were coming to an end. Vaudeville was nearly finished. Radio wasn't yet a dependable hit-making medium—in fact, writers and publishers were wary of broadcasting, believing it adversely affected record sales by giving away what the audience should have been paying for. Hollywood musicals had been a passing fad and, although their second heyday was coming, it was still several years away. So the best chance for a song's success was to be in a well-received stage show. From there it could make its way into band repertoires and onto recordings.

Stage shows were either revues or book musicals. Revues sometimes had unifying themes, usually topical satire, but mostly consisted of unrelated sketches. Book musicals, on the other hand, had plots and characters and told stories through music and lyrics. In the 1910s Jerome Kern teamed with writers Guy Bolton and P. G. Wodehouse to create a series of literate, witty musicals for the little 299-seat Princess Theatre, and those shows pointed the way to what was gradually becoming the modern American musical. By 1930 the strongest push in that direction was from Rodgers and Hart.

Unlike Arlen, Richard Rodgers hadn't started off playing in a band. Nor had Gershwin, Porter, Kern, Berlin, or Youmans. From the outset they were songwriters, each focused on writing for the stage. At the age of nine, Rodgers traveled alone by subway to the Standard Theatre at Broadway and 91st Street, where fifty cents got him a seat in the balcony. At thirteen he saw *Very Good Eddie* at the Princess Theatre and became "a Kern worshipper."[1] A year later he talked his older brother into taking him to Columbia University's annual Varsity show, which was where he met Lorenz Hart and Oscar Hammerstein II. In 1919, at seventeen, he teamed up with Hart, who was seven years his senior and had already given a lot of thought to the future of the musical. Rodgers and Hart were ambitious not just for themselves and their songs, but for their shows. "When I get an idea for a song," Rodgers told an interviewer, "I can hear it in the orchestra; I can smell the scenery; I can see the kind of actor who'll sing the song and the audience sitting there listening to it."[2]

Arlen was different. He'd given no thought to Broadway musicals or their future. He'd been content in the vaudeville and burlesque houses on Pearl Street in Buffalo and even happier in the nightclubs of Broadway and Harlem. He and Koehler didn't present themselves as a Rodgers and Hart–type team. They were a couple of jazz-loving songwriters and were pleased to take as their next assignment a floor show called *Biff-Boom-Bang* at the Silver Slipper—a saloon whose principal proprietor was Owney "Killer" Madden.

Composer Jimmy McHugh described Madden as "a lean, hard, quiet man with black hair, piercing blue eyes and a rather cute Irish face" who possessed a "bear-trap mind' and "flintlike executive ability."[3] Madden had gone into the business of purchasing nightclubs and using them as fronts for the sale of bootleg liquor made by his Phoenix Cereal Beverage Company. He bought several nightspots in addition to the Silver Slipper. One was the Club Deluxe in Harlem at Lenox and 142nd Street, which he renamed the Cotton Club and decorated as a southern plantation, complete with "white columns and a backdrop painted with weeping willows and slave quarters."[4] The black waiters wore red tailcoats and served an upper-class white clientele. African Americans were not permitted through the front door—W. C. Handy, known as "the Father of the Blues," was turned away as his music was playing inside. But blacks were welcome as entertainers, and the Cotton Club's roster of performers was at least the equal of anything Broadway had to offer: Cab Calloway, Duke Ellington, Ethel Waters, Fats Waller, Louis Armstrong, Billie Holiday, Dorothy Dandridge, the Nicholas Brothers, Bill "Bojangles" Robinson, Lena Horne, and on and on. Not that Caucasian performers were excluded. The shows were produced, directed, and emceed by a white vaudevillian, Dan Healy, and most of the songs were written by whites. For a time McHugh and lyricist Dorothy Fields provided the numbers, but they quit when Fields balked at having to write material of a requisite raunchiness. With their departure, the proprietors looked to Arlen and Koehler. Their score for the Silver Slipper hadn't produced anything big, but one song from that show, "Shakin' the African," made the owners think they would do a credible job writing the next Cotton Club revue.

There were two productions a year at the Cotton Club, one in the spring, the other in the fall. And there were two shows a night, the first at midnight and the second at 2:00 A.M., timed to accommodate theatergoers looking for cabaret fun after Broadway shows had let out. *Brown Sugar* (subtitled *BlackBerries of 1931*) was the fall 1930 offering. It featured fifty chorus girls who could sing and dance, were at least 5'11" and had "high yaller" or caramel-colored skin. The headliners were singer–tap dancer Cora La Redd, singer Leitha Hill, and the Duke Ellington Orchestra, which had been resident there since 1927. Arlen and Koehler's job was to supply torch ballads, rhythm numbers, comedy material, and specialty songs with lots of sexual innuendoes and drug references. The Cotton Club paid Arlen $100 a week plus free meals. This, when added to the $50 a week he was getting from his publishers as well as royalties from "Get Happy" and other songs, made for a comfortable income at a time when many were being sucked into the quicksand of the Great Depression.

Arlen was embarrassed by a lot of the material he had to write for this show, especially one double-entendre song called "Pussy."[5] Although Koehler didn't mind having his name attached to the song, Arlen, probably thinking of his parents, insisted that it and others like it not be published. Yet he enjoyed his Cotton Club work—and was especially glad to hang out with the performers in their subterranean dressing rooms, singing and laughing with them, entertaining them with impersonations of the mobsters who ran the place. Then he'd go back upstairs and take advantage of the privileges afforded him as a white man: the front entrance, the restaurant, the bathroom. It wasn't difficult for him to get along with the gangsters. He didn't spend a lot of time with them but was amiable in their presence and pleased to say yes whenever Madden offered him a lift home in his luxurious—and bulletproof—Duesenberg.

Nothing much came of the *Brown Sugar* score, although Arlen recorded one of its songs, "Linda," with the Red Nichols Band and it was, as composer-critic Alec Wilder observed, the first to use what would become an Arlen trademark—the sudden octave jump. Because it and the other songs fit the Cotton Club's style, the team was invited to return to write the next production, due in the spring of 1931.

In the meantime Jack Yellen—the man who at Cantor Arluck's behest had followed Harold to Minnie's Roadhouse—heard "Get Happy" on the radio as he was taking a shower in his Manhattan apartment, and he found the song so insistent he bought the sheet music. On the cover was the name Harold Arlen, which his intuition told him was the boy Hyman Arluck, who couldn't be talked out of a musical career. Yellen and Arlen were both habitués of Lindy's Deli, a restaurant on Broadway near 51st Street that attracted notables from show business, journalism, the underworld, and politics. It was particularly favored by people who wrote and promoted songs. Singer Dolly Dawn recalled: "When you came in to the left there was a bar where all the song pluggers would stand, their foot upon the rail and one elbow crooked, and they'd be watching for what celebrities came in. They'd pounce on them and go right into their pitch."[6]

At Lindy's, Yellen buttonholed Arlen and told him—he didn't ask—that they were going to write a Broadway show together. Arlen demurred. He already had a lyricist, he said, and they were set to write another Cotton Club revue. But Yellen kept at it. He'd been thinking about a show that would feature his own lyrics and the comedy of Broadway veteran Lou Holtz. Yellen and Holtz would be co-producers, and Yellen and another comedian, Sid Silvers, would write the script. He urged Harold to come to his nearby office and sign a contract to write the music. Arlen got out of it by making an appointment for a later date, which he didn't keep. But his affection for Lindy's made it easy for Yellen to find him again. And by that time the lyricist had heard another Arlen song—"Hittin' the Bottle" from the Earl Carroll show as recorded by Duke Ellington—that made him all the more eager to work with him. This time Yellen got Arlen to sign the contract. Harold may not have wanted the job, but he recognized the opportunity. Yellen's "Happy Days Are Here Again" had just been introduced in a lavish MGM musical called *Chasing Rainbows* and was becoming popular. A Broadway production with his name on it would attract notice.

When Koehler learned that Arlen had a new partner, he didn't make a fuss. He was a rarity in show business: a calm and happy man. During Cotton Club rehearsals he liked to help the carpenters build sets. In the evenings when others were nightclubbing, he was home in Brooklyn with his wife and daughter. Unlike Arlen, who kept himself trim and fit and dressed fastidiously, Koehler was rumpled, pudgy, and exercise-averse. When writing lyrics he would flop onto a sofa and lie motionless for hours, pen in hand. But he was, Arlen knew, a gifted lyricist who, when presented with a good melody, could find the words inherent in the notes.

Yellen wasn't in Koehler's league as a lyricist and not at all like him in personality. Jumpy, always in motion, never comfortable, he'd summon Arlen to his apartment and pace about proposing and discarding ideas as if he were chain-smoking them. He'd leave the bathroom door open so he could call his thoughts out from the john. Incessantly, he urged Arlen to work harder, faster. Harold, he said, "would write a tune, then stand in the corner and pray for the next one!"[7]

When the show, *You Said It*, tried out in Philadelphia, Yellen realized it wasn't very good. It had an unoriginal plot about college life (a rich student and a poor one vie for the dean's daughter) and a weak script. But his assertiveness saved the day. On a trip home to Buffalo, he and his wife went to a vaudeville show that featured Lyda Roberti, a pretty and dynamic immigrant from Poland whose way of pronouncing the "h" sound as "ch" (as in chutzpah) struck audiences as very funny. Yellen told her she had to be in his show, and when she said she preferred her current success to the iffyness of Broadway, he gave her the same treatment he'd given Arlen and got the same results. She joined *You Said It* and saved it. The way she sang "hot" in the song "Sweet and Hot" brought down the house. It became such a showstopper that it kept the play afloat for a respectable 168 performances—this despite poor reviews. Brooks Atkinson of the *New York Times* belittled the production and, of Arlen's music, said only that it kept "Louis Gress's 'rhythmonic orchestra' blowing hard."[8] Years later Yellen would dismiss *You Said It*, calling it "a lesson in what not to do." As for his brief collaboration with Arlen, he admitted: "I could see he was destined for better things than I could give him."[9]

Then, in the spring of 1931, came the premiere of Arlen and Koehler's second Cotton Club production, *Rhyth-Mania*, and with it, Arlen's takeoff as a songwriter. Two of the new songs were every bit as good as "Get Happy." One was the up-tempo "Between the Devil and the Deep Blue Sea." Arlen later recalled its genesis: "One day I kept thinking of the steady beat of Bill Robinson's tap-dancing at the Cotton Club, for whom I was composing songs at the time, and before I knew it I was myself tapping out the melody of 'Between the Devil and the Deep Blue Sea.'"[10] The song is a wild musical ride filled with melodic leaps and key changes as Koehler's lyric compares being in a romantic relationship to life aboard a shaky boat.

The second great song from *Rhyth-Mania*, like "Get Happy," began with a eureka moment. One day during the winter of 1930, Koehler was at work in Arlen's apartment in the Croydon Hotel when Arlen became restless and decided to take a walk—first to Lindy's and then to the offices of the Cotton Club's music publisher, Mills Music, on West 46th. He'd developed what would become a lifelong habit of walking from his residence (wherever it happened to be) to the offices of his publisher (whoever that happened to be) so he could, as he liked to put it, "schmooze with the boys."[11] He loved to walk in New York City, no matter the season or the weather. If he was caught in a downpour he'd hurry with childlike glee from awning to awning. In summers he'd cool off by standing under theater and hotel marquees to get blasts of chilled air from their lobbies. On this occasion he urged Koehler to come with him. The lyricist, however, was not interested in walks, especially not when it was cold, and certainly not for two miles. Somehow Arlen prevailed, and as they headed downtown he teased his partner by picking up the pace, turning the walk into a march, and playing an imaginary trumpet. Then he hummed a tune that sprang from the rhythm of his steps. Intrigued, the lyricist suggested words to go with the new melody. By the time they reached their destination they had "I Love a Parade," which quickly became a standard. Every subsequent Cotton Club show was called the *Cotton Club Parade*.

In the summer of 1931, a pianist friend of Arlen's, Roger Edens, offered him a gig as an accompanist in a vaudeville show. It was at the prestigious Palace Theatre and featured an up-and-coming star, Ethel Merman. A year earlier she'd made her Broadway debut in the Gershwins' *Girl Crazy*, wowing everyone by holding a note in "I Got Rhythm" for sixteen bars. Now, just prior to opening at the Apollo Theatre in the 1931 edition of *George White's Scandals*, she had time to try a vaudeville act. She began the show by singing to the piano accompaniment of Edens and composer Johnny Green (who had recently written "Body and Soul"). Then Lyda Roberti and Arlen took over for a set that included "Sweet and Hot." And then Merman returned with Edens and Arlen as her accompanists.

She loved to make "a stylish entrance to open her act," Edens recalled. "She always had a cape or a jacket that matched her gown and would sing the first song wearing this cape. During the applause she would take the cape off and place it on top of Harold's piano. Before one matinée performance Harold and I decided to liven up the proceedings by leaving a little memento for Ethel when she left her cape on the piano."[12] That memento was a note that read, "Your left tit is hanging out."[13] This sent Merman into a gale of laughter that puzzled the audience as she didn't let them in on the joke, although they must have realized it was a good one when, after she'd gained control and finished her set, they heard her laughing again, this time backstage. She retaliated the next day by putting a message of her own on Arlen's piano: a single red rose threaded neatly through a jock strap. Then she upped the ante by giving Arlen an over-the-top introduction to the audience, telling them that this young man was about to play some of his many "immortal" songs. For a few days Arlen was stumped for a comeback, but then he and Edens figured out how to respond: they went ahead and played a selection of immortal songs—by Kern, Berlin, Romberg, Youmans, Rodgers, and Gershwin, ending with Merman's signature "I Got Rhythm." As Arlen later recalled, "The audience didn't know the difference; they applauded."[14] This show, which they did four times a day, was so popular it went into a second edition at the Hollywood Theatre.

Arlen continued as a performer for a while, getting together with violinist Joe Venuti, guitarist Eddie Lang, and clarinetist Jimmy Dorsey to sing eight songs for the Parlophone label. His performances on "Pardon Me, Pretty

Baby" (composed by Vincent Rose) and "Little Girl" (music and lyrics by Francis Henry and Madeline Hyde) have, according to Will Friedwald, "all the amorous energy that both songs require, in a way that has less in common with pop singers of the time and more with jazzmen like Armstrong and Red Allen."[15]

By the end of the summer of 1932 he was back to composing. He and Koehler went to work on the fall edition of the *Cotton Club Parade*. But they were interrupted when Earl Carroll asked them for a few songs for his upcoming *Vanities of 1932*. The *Vanities* from the year before had introduced "Goodnight, Sweetheart" (music by Ray Noble, lyrics by Jimmy Campbell and Reg Connelly), a song with a sentimental "Auld Lang Syne" quality. Carroll wanted another like it, but instead Arlen and Koehler gave him "I Gotta Right to Sing the Blues"—whose solemn beat, like a New Orleans funeral procession, would make it a mainstay for New Orleans–born Louis Armstrong. As it was sung in the show, Carroll's newest collection of young women undulated in the background. One was a seventeen-year-old blue-eyed blonde who had recently won a high school beauty contest and was also working as a model. She was Anya Taranda, the daughter of Russian immigrants and a member of the Russian Orthodox Church. Arlen, ten years her senior, fell in love with her.

CHAPTER 5

ANYA

Although Anya appeared onstage in flimsy outfits and modeled for photographers in leopard-skin tops with plunging necklines, she was shy. She dreamed of show business fame but didn't train as an actress or try out for parts. She'd taken ballet but never danced professionally, not even when she was in a chorus line, except to do a step or two or sway back and forth. She liked to sing, but not in a nightclub or to a theater audience. Her best moments as a performer came at parties, when Harold and his songwriter friends listened as she vocalized in a small, if ingratiating, voice. She was beautiful and sweet and the first person who'd ever loved him unreservedly.

She lived with her parents and twelve-year-old brother in an East Harlem apartment. Her father, Frank Taranda, was a machine operator in a shirt factory. Her mother, Mary, cleaned office buildings. Anya's modeling and stage show income helped defray their household bills. We don't know much about this family, except that tensions between Frank and Mary eventually led to their divorce and his remarriage. We do know they were less than pleased by her romance with Arlen, partly because of the ten-year difference in their ages, but mostly because he was Jewish. Anti-Semitism was pervasive in the United States in the 1930s. In New York, where Jews made up a significant portion of the population, universities and professional organizations locked them out or admitted them by quota. Classified housing ads in the *New York Times* specified "Christian only." Harold therefore had to face her parents' antipathy to him while, at the same time, he and Anya were leery of how his parents would react to her—a Russian Orthodox woman who made her living by appearing half naked in public. Would they regard him as an apostate who'd taken up with a harlot? If he married her, would they dismiss him from their lives? In Orthodox Jewish households such reactions were common.

As he considered the problems that would come from his relationship with Anya—an affair that was serious from the start—Harold also had to deal with his brother. Twenty-year-old Udie, who'd adopted Arlen as his surname and exchanged Julius for the more masculine Jerry, appeared at the Croydon late one rainy evening, saxophone in hand, looking for a place to stay. He wanted to play in a band, sing, and write songs like his brother. He was a decent enough musician. He'd sung in the synagogue choir, had taken music lessons, and was proficient on violin, sax and piano. But Harold knew he didn't have a big talent and that he was in for rough times should he try for success in New York. He advised Jerry to go back to Syracuse, where he could look after their parents. Jerry would have none of that. He believed he could make it. He was young, confident, energetic, and handsome—taller than his brother, broad-shouldered and photogenic. They differed in personality, too. Harold shrank from confrontation. Jerry was volatile. Each was a drinker, but alcohol made Harold silly, while Jerry was liable to lash out.

Harold took him in. Improved finances had made it possible for him to move into a posh apartment on the Croydon's tenth floor, and he had plenty of room. Anya was often there, too. Being underage, just seventeen, she had to be careful. She would sometimes enter the Croydon accompanied by a chaperone who'd then slip away. Because she and Jerry were unable to establish a friendship, the atmosphere became strained. More tension came when a fourth person arrived on the scene. This was a friend Jerry had made during a brief stint at the University of Syracuse. Born Edward Chester Babcock, the young man was now calling himself Jimmy Van Heusen—having picked his new name as he watched a shirt manufacturer's truck pass by. He and Jerry had become a songwriting team. Jimmy was a gifted composer, but he let Jerry write the music while he handled the words.

As these people were getting acclimated to their new living and work situations and to one another, Harold got a call from lyricist E. Y. "Yip" Harburg. He and Harburg had met two years earlier when both were at work on the 1930 edition of Earl Carroll's *Vanities*. Now Harburg was in a spot. He'd accepted an invitation from the Shubert brothers to write a revue, *Americana*, with Vincent Youmans. But Youmans preferred book shows to revues and had bailed out, taking his $2,500 advance with him. While the Shuberts were busy trying to get their money back—they filed a case against him with the Dramatists Guild—Harburg took charge of the production. Time being short, he replaced Youmans with three composers. One was Jay Gorney, a refugee from Czarist Russia. Another was Herman Hupfeld, who'd written "As Time Goes By" the year before. The third was Harold Arlen. Since a lot of lyrics needed to be written in short order, he hired a young southerner, Johnny Mercer, to help him out.

Yip enjoyed running the show and was especially pleased that it gave him an opportunity to write scenes as well as lyrics. The idea for one sketch occurred to him as he passed a breadline that was, he recalled, "owned by William Randolph Hearst. He had a big truck with several people on it and big cauldrons of hot soup, bread. Fellows with burlap on their shoes were lined up all around Columbus Circle and went for blocks and blocks around the park, waiting."[1] Harburg turned this into a skit about competing breadlines, one owned by Hearst and the other by a rival newspaper publisher, Ogden Mills Reid.

He, Mercer, and Arlen worked together on one song for the show, "Satan's Li'l Lamb." Thus the first time Arlen worked with either of these men, he worked with both of them. Their song was a blowout production number in the brassy style of the Cotton Club. But it was overshadowed by Harburg and Gorney's "Brother, Can You Spare a Dime?" which became an enormous success and the anthem of the Great Depression. Harburg's lyric was more powerful for being questioning rather than angry. But he *was* angry. He believed the nation had, as presidential candidate Franklin Roosevelt put it, abandoned "the forgotten man."

Like Arlen, he'd grown up in an Orthodox Yiddish-speaking home. The Arluck and Hochberg (Yip's birth surname) households were also alike in the way the parents superstitiously changed the names of their children to protect them from evil. Because six of Yip's siblings died before he was born, his mother asked a visiting rabbi to tell her how to keep him safe from the unseen forces that had taken the others. He advised her to alter the boy's given name, Isidore, which she did by using the letter E which stood for El, the rabbi's first name.[2] The Y came about when, in calling him to dinner one night she shouted, "Yipsel!"—Yiddish for "little squirrel." He is the one who changed Hochberg to Harburg.

Both his parents worked in sweatshops, and he and his siblings grew up in a sixth-floor cold-water flat near the docks of the East River. For a bed he'd push two chairs together. In winters he went to the public library near Tompkins Square to get warm. These privations turned him into a political leftist. When his older brother, Max, whom he idolized, died of cancer at the age of twenty-eight, he became an atheist. As a lyricist he was a polemicist. But he wrote with a gentle touch, humor, and a flair for fantasy. He'd gone to high school at Townsend Harris Hall, where alphabetical seating placed him next to Ira Gershwin, who, as he, loved the work of W. S. Gilbert. One day Ira amazed Yip by telling him that Gilbert's poetry had been set to music. To prove this he took him home—the Gershwins lived in a brownstone apartment on Second Avenue at Fifth Street that Yip considered "swank"—and put *HMS Pinafore* on the Victrola. Yip later recalled hearing "lines I knew by heart. I was dumbfounded, staggered. Gilbert and Sullivan tied Ira to me for life." They became a writing team, signing their high school newspaper articles "Yip and Gersh."[3] At City College they continued to collaborate, working on a newspaper column called "Gargoyle Gargles."

Harburg was nine years older than Arlen, but they began their careers as songwriters at around the same time, when Harburg was well past thirty. For years Yip had watched in frustration as others did what he wanted to do—usher in the era of great American theater music. He was stuck on the sidelines supporting himself and his parents as well as a son and daughter who lived in California with relatives of his former wife. He did this by running his own business, an electrical supply company, which did very well until, as he told it, "that beautiful Depression of 1929 came along and knocked the hell out of my business. I found myself broke and personally in debt for about fifty thousand dollars, my name on all sorts of contracts that I had never read or cared to. All I had left was my pencil."[4] At that point, Ira urged him to write lyrics, gave him five hundred dollars to get started, and introduced him to composer Gorney.

By the end of 1932, after just four years as a lyricist, Yip had worked with twenty-five tunesmiths—as he looked for one who had a quality he'd seen so far only in George Gershwin: a "typically American approach . . . a combination of Hebrew and black music."[5] When he met Arlen, he found the one he'd been looking for. It was more than music; there was also something about the man that touched Harburg. Singer Michael Feinstein, who knew Harburg, described him as "very gentle in how he would treat a soul if he saw they were fragile or tender in some way."[6] And this gentleness came out in his solicitous attitude toward Arlen, who was, Yip said, "always rather on the depressed side . . . although he laughed vociferously as almost a protest to his sadness."[7]

Of the trio who wrote "Satan's Li'l Lamb" in 1932, Harburg and Arlen would write together again later that year. But it would be nearly ten years before Arlen's second collaboration with Mercer. Like Arlen, Mercer was an accomplished singer, and his big goal in life at this point was to become another Bing Crosby. When Crosby left his singing trio, the Rhythm Boys, which performed with Paul Whiteman's orchestra, Whitman asked Mercer to reconstitute the group. Mercer went to Jerry Arlen, whom he knew through Harold, and asked him to join. The opportunity thrilled Jerry, but, as Mercer later explained it, "we were all baritones and our harmony left a lot to be desired. Before one week was up, we had our two weeks' notice."[8]

CHAPTER 6

"Stormy Weather"

In early 1933, Anya, having just turned eighteen, moved in with Harold at the Croydon. It wasn't common in those days for unmarried couples to live together, not even among Arlen's permissive set. There was a greater stigma in this than in marrying, divorcing, and marrying again—the more usual route taken by show people. It seems certain that Anya would have said yes had Harold asked her to marry him. She was devoted to him, and he to her. He would never again fall in love with another woman. Composer Johnny Green "doubted that Arlen ever had a date with anyone else"—something we know to be untrue, given his intense romance with Lily Levine, his affair with Frances Williams, and relationships to come much later in life. But, being a conservative man by nature, he wouldn't have cohabited with Anya had he been able to marry her without fear of his parents' reaction. This seemed the best option, and it was accepted by his friends, although Ira's wife, Leonore, pressured them to tie the knot. As for Anya's friends—she seems not to have had any. Without Harold, she was, except for her parents and brother, alone in the world.

Yip Harburg was also having relationship problems. He'd had fallen in love with Jay Gorney's wife, a fact he openly proclaimed in love poems, including one, "To Edelaine," that was published above his signature in Franklin P. Adams's *New York Tribune* column "The Conning Tower." And he was having problems in a professional relationship, as well. He'd been working with Russian émigré composer Vernon Duke, who, as it turned out, equaled Yip in volatility. Duke was a symphonic composer from Kiev who'd escaped the Russian Revolution and immigrated to the United States. In New York he looked up George Gershwin, who Americanized his name—he'd been born Vladimir Dukelsky—and got him started in the songwriting trade. That Duke and Harburg accomplished anything together is remarkable given what Yip described as "my pumpernickel background and his orchid tunes."[1] Nevertheless, in late 1932 they managed to write "April in Paris."

Yip had set his sights on Arlen. But Arlen and Koehler were still a going concern. A few weeks after *Americana*'s opening came the premiere of the fall 1932 *Cotton Club Parade* (Twenty-first Edition), for which they wrote "I've Got the World on a String"—another Arlen jazz tune loaded with melodic and harmonic surprises. Other songs in the score were tailored to the needs of the Cotton Club and its star, Cab Calloway, who liked his numbers to have call-and-response "hi-de-ho"s and lots of drug references. He'd had a big hit the year before with his own "Minnie the Moocher," so Arlen and Koehler gave him "Minnie the Moocher's Wedding Day" ("a hundred thousand hoppies / Went over to China picking poppies") as well as "The Wail of the Reefer Man."

But Harburg found a way to work with Arlen again when producer Billy Rose asked him to provide a song for a new dramatic production, *The Great Magoo*. This was a play about the seamy, phony side of show business life, and Rose wanted the song for one of its characters—a disillusioned carnival barker who, despite all his cynicism, has fallen in love. The concept and the character appealed to Harburg, as did the fact that just one song was needed. That meant he could turn to Arlen without appearing to horn in on Koehler. Arlen obliged with a frolicsome tune to which Harburg fitted a lyric that was at first called "If You Believe in Me" and later "It's Only a Paper Moon." Here Harburg expressed his worldview: "It's a Barnum and Bailey world / Just as phony as it can be / But it wouldn't be make believe / If you believed in me."

Although it is clear in retrospect that an Arlen–Harburg partnership was starting up, neither man immediately abandoned his other commitments. Harburg was asked in early 1933 to write lyrics for the first *Ziegfeld Follies* to be produced after Florenz Ziegfeld's death, a project that reunited him and Vernon Duke for the last time and resulted in "I Like the Likes of You" and "What Is There to Say?" Arlen returned to Koehler for the Twenty-second Edition of the *Cotton Club Parade*. In this score they came up with an obligatory raunchy song, "I'm Lookin' for Another Handy Man," which was in the same vein as "Pussy" ("He must be handy all around / And know just how to turn my damper down"). But they also wrote two standards. One was "Happy as the Day Is Long," a syncopated up-tempo song with adventurous harmony and cheerful beat-the-Depression slogans ("Just a pocket full of air / feelin' like a millionaire"). The other started off as a three-note riff that seemed perfect for a hi-de-ho until it took a sad turn that made it incompatible with Calloway's jocular style. By the time it was finished—written in a single afternoon—it was a lamentation. Calloway, it turned out, wasn't going to be in the show; he would be on tour. So another vocalist had to be found.

Everyone who heard this new song, "Stormy Weather," remarked on its power. The Cotton Club's producer, Ted Healy, and its manager, Herman Stark, felt that no one on their roster could do it justice, so they looked for someone on the outside. It happened that Ethel Waters was back in town, having quit the Al Capone–owned nightclubs of Chicago, and she was the perfect choice for this sorrowful new song. Born to a teenage girl as the result of rape, raised in poverty in a small Pennsylvania town, married to an abusive husband at thirteen, she'd begun her career singing in a traveling carnival and then made it big in New York as a blues singer who was also effective with popular songs. Healy and Stark arranged for her to hear Arlen and Koehler demonstrate "Stormy Weather," and she listened, loved it, and agreed to do it—so long as the Cotton Club paid her more than they had ever paid any other performer, a stipulation that was granted. Not only was "Stormy Weather" her kind of song, it came at the right time for her. Her second marriage was falling apart, and the words and music struck home. On opening night, the audience demanded twelve encores. Her recording with the Dorsey Brothers Orchestra topped the charts and eventually entered the Grammy Hall of Fame. Arlen also recorded "Stormy Weather," and he did it first, singing with the Leo Reisman Orchestra. This, too, was a best-seller, but Waters's version included the dramatic twelve-bar "Interlude" ("I walk around, heavy-hearted and sad"), which was missing from Arlen's record and is still omitted from many performances. In her autobiography, she explained her success with the song this way: "I was telling things I couldn't frame in words. I was singing the story of my misery and confusion, of the misunderstandings in my life I couldn't straighten out, the story of the wrongs and outrages done to me by people I had loved and trusted."[2]

"Stormy Weather" is loved throughout the world. Many think of it as a folk song—one that's always been around. But musicians tend to see it differently—as an example of artful, even tricky, song construction. The opening (from "Don't know why" to "Stormy Weather") is three bars long, not the usual four, which, according to Alec Wilder, "caused a degree of consternation in the rhythm sections of bands as they had been conditioned by years of playing strict eight-measure phrases."[3] When Wilder asked Arlen about this he was told, "I didn't break away consciously. It fell that way. I didn't count the measures till it was all over. That was all I had to say and the way I had to say it. George Gershwin brought it up and I didn't know

it. He said, 'You know you didn't repeat a phrase in the first eight bars?'
And I never gave it a thought."[4] But there *were* repetitions—not repeated
phrases, but frequent appearances of Arlen's original three-note motif. It is
heard five times in the first eight bars.[5] This is an improvisational style of
composing, one favored by jazz musicians, and by cantors as they chant at
worship services. Arlen presumably absorbed it from both, especially from
his father who was, he said, "the greatest theme-and-variations man I've
ever known."[6] And there was one more unusual feature of this song's construction: its overall length. The line "Keeps raining all the time" repeats,
bringing it in at thirty-six rather than the standard thirty-two bars—forty-
eight if the "Interlude" is included.

Oddly enough, Harold never took much pride in "Stormy Weather." The
most he ever said in its favor was that it was "strong."[7] Decades after it was
written, at a birthday party for him given by composer Burton Lane and
his wife Lynn, when Lane went to the piano and played "Stormy Weather"
Arlen whispered to Lynn, "You know, I never liked that song. I never thought
it deserved to be the hit that it was."[8] He wasn't joking. He said the same
thing to Wilfrid Sheed, calling it a throwaway. It was, he said, "a song I
could have mailed Monday or Tuesday. It wasn't anything special."[9]

But the royalties were special. And another beneficial consequence was
Arlen's friendship with Irving Berlin. The renowned composer-lyricist had
come to the Cotton Club to hear Ethel Waters sing "Stormy Weather" and
scout her for his and playwright Moss Hart's upcoming revue *As Thousands
Cheer*. Waters's recording had provided him with an unexpected windfall
because the flip side had an obscure ballad of his, "Maybe It's Because I
Love You Too Much," sung by Fred Astaire.

Berlin and his wife Ellin now included Harold and Anya in their social
circle. The older composer addressed Anya fondly as Anyusha, and many
years later, in a poem written for Harold and Anya's thirty-third and final
anniversary, he referred to Ellin as their matchmaker. He saw in Anya a
lovely, gentle, and trusting soul. In Harold he saw a decent, convivial, and
kindred man—kindred not only in talent, but because each was the son of
an immigrant cantor, although Berlin's father, Moses Baline, unlike Arlen's,
hadn't been able to adjust to his new surroundings. He ended up, as Berlin's
biographer Laurence Bergreen put it, a lost soul "in a trance of alienation
and drudgery."[10] Israel Baline, the youngest of six children, had to fend for
himself on the streets of the Lower East Side, enduring a depth of poverty
that only Harburg among his songwriting friends could have understood.
But Berlin and Arlen were alike in that each had grown up in a Yiddish-
speaking household, begun his career as a singer, and reached the heights

suddenly and early in life with a big hit—in Berlin's case "Alexander's Rag-time Band," written in 1911 when he was twenty-three.

Another connection was Berlin's knowledge through experience of what could happen when a Jewish man took up with a non-Jewish woman. After the death of his first wife in 1912, twelve years passed before he became serious about another woman, Ellin Mackay, whose father, Clarence, was the wealthy head of the American Postal Telegraph Company and a devout Catholic. To get his young daughter to forget about Berlin, Clarence took her to Europe and got her an audience with the Pope, while Berlin remained stateside writing woeful waltzes—"All Alone," "What'll I Do?" and "Re-member." When the marriage took place, shortly after Ellin's return, she was disinherited—although Berlin's wedding present, the song "Always" and all rights to it, made up for that. A year later the saga took a tragic turn with the death of the couple's infant son. As the tabloids were getting ready to exploit the irony of the fact that the boy had died on Christmas day, Mackay showed up at the Berlin residence to express his condolences and share their heartbreak. A final twist to this Dickensian story occurred when Ellin's father went broke in the 1929 stock market crash and was bailed out by his new son-in-law. Thus Irving and Ellin Berlin understood and supported Harold and Anya.

Arlen wrote more great songs than Berlin or anyone else in the period between "Get Happy" in 1930 and "Stormy Weather" in 1933. His was, in fact, the most spectacular songwriter debut in history. Given that triumph, it seems that he ought to have become a famous man. Yet the public didn't know his name. That spring, a young advertising executive, Robert Wachs-man, arrived in New York from Chicago hoping to enter the music business as a producer. He went to parties where songwriters congregated. At one gathering he met Harburg and learned he was co-author of one of his favorite songs, "It's Only a Paper Moon." He had no idea who the composer was and asked Harburg, who told him about Arlen—a name new to Wachsman, even though he considered himself a pop song connoisseur.

Wachsman went to Arlen's apartment, introduced himself, and proposed a venture: a tour of the Loew's vaudeville circuit with an act featuring Arlen singing "Stormy Weather" backed by an African American chorus. Wachsman would be the producer and get the necessary performers and permissions (the Cotton Club management was at first wary about letting live audiences other than theirs hear "Stormy Weather"). Harold opened on May 19, 1933, at Radio City Music Hall, then went on the road to Baltimore and Washington, D.C., where his parents came to see him. Not long after that, Cantor Arluck began to insert musical quotes from his son's works into his synagogue chants, "Stormy Weather" serving perfectly in that regard. This gesture deeply affected Arlen and established a bond between him and his father that never disappeared, despite the strife to come. But the tour brought no celebrity.

His next move, like the "Stormy Weather" tour, was something he hadn't planned or sought out. On a walk downtown he dropped by the William Morris Agency to chat with friends. While there, the teletype started up and they all gathered around to read the incoming message. It was from Columbia Pictures in Hollywood, asking if Arlen and Koehler would compose the score for a musical to be called *Let's Fall in Love*. As soon as he read this, Arlen had a feeling that he later described as a "charming burning sensation in my stomach."[11] He excused himself and went to the men's room, where he could, in private, jot into his music notebook the theme that had popped into his head. It was one of those rare melodies that seem to have always existed—to have been "found art." When Koehler added words, the notes became "Let's fall in love / Why shouldn't we fall in love? / Our hearts are made of it / Let's take a chance / Why be afraid of it?" It was Arlen's first great love song.

He and Koehler signed a deal with Columbia during the summer of 1933, a time when they would normally have been writing the fall Cotton Club show. So as not to leave his Harlem employers in the lurch, he suggested that his brother take his place. This gave Jerry renewed hope that he was on the verge of success. He went to work with Van Heusen, but their songs made no impression. Only two were accepted for the show, "Harlem Hospitality" and "There's a House in Harlem for Sale." The rest of the score consisted mostly of Arlen–Koehler holdovers, principally "Stormy Weather," although there was one newly minted hit by twenty-year-old singer-pianist Jeanne Burns, who teamed with Calloway to write "Lady with a Fan." For Jerry, the fall 1933 *Cotton Club Parade* (Twenty-third Edition) wasn't the career starter he'd been hoping for, although it did mark the beginning of a relationship with Burns that three years later would result in marriage.

In late September of 1933, Arlen and Koehler went to Grand Central Station and boarded the *Twentieth Century Limited* for a trip to Chicago. From there they transferred to the *Super Chief*, which took them to Los Angeles. Because the Depression had greatly reduced ridership on these luxury trains, the sleeping, dining and observation cars were nearly empty. Arlen saw this as an opportunity to get some work done and took out his jot book. No piano was available, but his idea for "Let's Fall in Love" was so simple it wasn't hard to finish it by borrowing one of the conductors' hand-held four-note dinner chimes. When the train pulled into Santa Fe's Le Grande Station in downtown Los Angeles, he and Koehler had their song.

They spent their first evening in Los Angeles with the man who'd introduced them, Harry Warren. The shy, curmudgeonly, and self-deprecating Warren had been homesick for New York and its community of songwriters and was happy to have their company. Working at the Warner Bros. studio in Burbank was to him "like being on an Indian outpost. You could look out across the San Fernando Valley, through the windows of the music department, and see nothing but empty land."[12] Almost forty now, he'd spent years avoiding Hollywood, hoping to parlay his growing catalog of song hits into Broadway success. That hadn't happened, so he'd accepted an offer from Warner Bros. producer Darryl Zanuck to compose the songs for a movie musical, *42nd Street*. Zanuck teamed him with Warren's New York friend and former collaborator, lyricist Al Dubin; secured the services of choreographer Busby Berkeley; and hired newcomers Dick Powell, Ruby Keeler and Ginger Rogers. Together they created an innovative movie whose success launched a new golden age of movie musicals and introduced the title song as well as "You're Getting to Be a Habit with Me," and "Shuffle Off to Buffalo." Later that year, Warren and Dubin would write the score for another great movie musical, *Gold Diggers of 1933*, which featured "We're in the Money," "The Shadow Waltz," and an extended musical sequence, "Remember My Forgotten Man," that picked up on themes expressed by Harburg in *Americana*.

Prior to these films, movie musicals had been in the doldrums after a period of initial success. But movie music had never stagnated. At the Walt Disney studios, a team of composers, most of them former movie-house pianists, had been creating innovative sounds in animated cartoons in a way that paralleled what avant-garde composer Edgard Varèse was doing in the concert hall. Varèse had originated the idea of creating music out of noise—"multiple streams of sound proceeding simultaneously in a single piece," as music critic Ted Libbey put it.[13] A Disney cartoon from 1929, *The Skeleton Dance*, set animated images to an already written score by a member of that team, Carl Stalling. Musical innovations could also be found in live-action movies. In 1932 a Paramount film, *Love Me Tonight*, directed by Rouben Mamoulian, introduced the technique of prerecording a song (Rodgers and Hart's "Isn't It Romantic") so it could be tossed from singer to singer and locale to locale during the course of a scene. In 1933 Viennese-born Max Steiner, a pupil of Mahler and a pioneer of symphonic film scoring, was writing the music for RKO's *King Kong*. The same year another of Disney's former movie-house pianists, Frank Churchill, composed "Who's Afraid of the Big Bad Wolf?" for *The Three Little Pigs*—the first hit song to come from a cartoon.

Arlen had been a movie-house pianist himself as well as a professional arranger, but he paid no attention to these new roles for composers. He was now what Harry Warren was—a man who lived and breathed songwriting and thought creatively in no other terms. It was a career that had its drawbacks. Opportunities in Depression-era New York were limited, and jobs in Hollywood, although more plentiful, subjected songwriters to the whims of studio moguls who all seemed to lack musical taste. For composers and lyricists, Hollywood was the mirror image of New York. On Broadway, in vaudeville, and in nightclubs, when a song wasn't working songwriters were there to correct the problem, usually by writing something new. In Hollywood they were pushed aside once they'd handed in their songs, and the songs could be summarily rejected. In 1929 Warner Bros. bought the rights to Rodgers and Hart's *Spring Is Here*, threw away most of the score, then hired Warren and others to provide new tunes. Rodgers and Hart had no say. Nor, for that matter, did Warren, whose efforts could just as easily have been jettisoned.

On the other hand, working in Hollywood had its perks. The Gershwins received $100,000 in 1930 for six weeks' work on a film failure called *Delicious*. Arlen and Koehler were getting $20,000 for their six-week stay—still big money. And the workload there was lighter than in New York. Fewer songs were required per show, and there were no frenzied rewrites during out-of-town tryouts. The weather was endlessly—relentlessly—gorgeous. There was no need to go to the studio if one wanted to work elsewhere— which was often the case, given that movie lots were vast walled-in encampments. Instead, Arlen could write at home in Beverly Hills, which was where his paychecks were delivered, always on time, by messengers on motorcycles.

While he was in Hollywood working with Koehler on *Let's Fall in Love*, Anya was in New York appearing in an Earl Carroll musical mystery called *Murder at the Vanities*. She didn't receive individual billing; instead she and the other chorines were presented as "The Most Beautiful Girls in the World." The prior summer she'd made her first movie, *Moonlight and Pretzels*, at Paramount's Astoria Studios in New York. There, too, she'd played an unnamed showgirl and her name had gone unmentioned in the credits.

One of the cast members of *Murder at the Vanities* was twenty-five-year-old Robert Cummings, then a bit player but later a movie and television star. He fell in love with Anya and proposed marriage, but she declined. She only wanted Harold and was constantly on the phone with him, she in New

York, he in California. When he returned to New York in late 1933 they were briefly reunited, but then she headed west. *Murder at the Vanities* was to be a Paramount movie and she was, said Hollywood gossip columnist Mayme Peek, one of the eleven "hand-picked beauties"[14] who'd be in it. Peek wrote that "Anya Taranda would be a fit subject to set poets raving" and that Earl Carroll had described her eyes as "dark limpid pools . . . in which a man could drown." But that wasn't enough to get her name on the screen. In those days newspapers were filled with stories about actors and actresses who'd sought movie success only to end up with nothing but heartache. More recently, author Margaret Talbot described the Hollywood of that era as a town "freakishly overrun with beautiful people."[15] Anya was one of the few who'd managed to get her foot in the door. But when filming was over and no other roles turned up, she became ill. On April 4 the Los Angeles *Times* reported that she was so sick with influenza she'd be unable to return to New York on schedule but would be confined to her Hollywood apartment for at least a month. She finally returned to Harold in New York after a seven-month separation.

The *Cotton Club Parade* (Twenty-fourth Edition) premiered on March 23, 1934, with what would be Arlen and Koehler's final Cotton Club score. Franklin Roosevelt had promised in his 1932 campaign to end Prohibition, and repeal came at the end of 1933, dooming this Harlem nightspot whose allure depended so much on bootleg liquor. Owney Madden sensed this impending end as well as his own—a lot of racketeers were dying violently—so he surrendered voluntarily to the police, pled guilty to a parole violation, served a few months in prison, and then retired to Hot Springs, Arkansas, where he lived peacefully for the remaining thirty years of his life.

This last Arlen and Koehler Cotton Club score produced two more classics. One was "As Long as I Live," which was performed by Avon Long and a newcomer, sixteen-year-old Lena Horne. Its music swings gently and somewhat sadly as the singer promises to remain true to his love if he can manage to stay alive. The other, "Ill Wind," was a follow-up to "Stormy Weather." It was another weather song that used extra bars to restate a recurring phrase, in this case "no good." But where "Stormy Weather" is about misery, "Ill Wind" is about hopelessness. No previous popular songwriter had written with such a tragic feel. A year later, Gershwin would do it in *Porgy and Bess*—and Arlen would be close at hand. In fact, he'd be across the street in Ira's apartment, working on his first major Broadway score.

CHAPTER 7

ON BROADWAY WITH IRA AND YIP

After the January 4, 1934, premiere of the *Ziegfeld Follies of 1934*, Yip Harburg wanted to take some time off. He'd been laboring at a breakneck pace on show after show for nearly five years. Adding to his fatigue was an unsettled and complicated private life. His marriage, which had failed nearly a decade earlier, was only now moving toward divorce. His young son and daughter were living a confused existence far from him on the West Coast, their mother having handed them off to an unenthusiastic aunt and uncle. He and Edelaine Gorney continued their affair, yet she remained with her husband as they raised their son. And, despite his deep bond with Edelaine, he was playing the field.

But there was no time for rest. Lee and Jacob Shubert decided to create a lavish revue for their Winter Garden Theatre, and asked Harburg to take charge. It was too good an opportunity to pass up, but it required more lyric writing than he wanted do on his own, so he asked Ira Gershwin to write it with him.

Ira, he knew, was in the doldrums. Although he and George had been successful in 1931 with their political satire *Of Thee I Sing*—a show that had been Ira's second attempt, after *Strike Up the Band*, to turn his brother and himself into an American version of Gilbert and Sullivan—he'd run into trouble with a sequel, *Let 'Em Eat Cake*, which flopped in 1933. George had willingly signed on to these projects, but Gilbert and Sullivan wasn't his style, and he'd used these shows to test some of the techniques—scene construction, counterpoint, recitative, leitmotivs—he'd need to master if he was to do what he really wanted—grand opera. The stories he favored were nothing like the Marx Brothers–style plots of *Strike Up the Band*, *Of Thee I Sing*, and *Let 'Em Eat Cake*, which were, respectively, about a war with Switzerland over Swiss cheese, a presidential candidate who picks his first lady in a beauty contest, and an ex-president who leads a revolution in order to drum up sales for his wife's shirt manufacturing company. Instead, he was drawn to stories about doomed lovers. One that appealed to him was S. Ansky's play *The Dybbuk*, about persecuted Jews living in a Polish shtetl, but he'd been unable to get the rights. Another was DuBose Heyward's novel *Porgy*, about persecuted African Americans living in a Charleston, South Carolina, tenement. On October 17, 1933, four days before the premiere of *Let 'Em Eat Cake*, he and Heyward signed a contract, which left Ira with nothing to do. That's how things stood when the call came from Harburg in January 1934, and Ira was pleased by the offer. He'd had two unsuccessful musicals in a row (a few months before *Let 'Em Eat Cake*, the Gershwins had flopped with *Pardon My English*) and had been hurt by the stock market crash, so he needed a success to replenish his coffers. But he also relished the idea of teaming again with his old high school friend and fellow word prankster Yip Harburg. It would be Yip and Gersh once more, this time on Broadway. All they needed was a composer, and Harburg had one in mind: Harold Arlen. Ira approved, having known and admired Arlen since 1930 when *Nine-Fifteen Revue* tried out in Boston next door to *Strike Up the Band*. The question was, would Arlen leave Koehler to join them?

He very much wanted to. This was going to be a more mainstream and reputable musical project than his Cotton Club efforts. It was the kind of work that had made Berlin, the Gershwins, Kern, Porter, and Rodgers and Hart public figures. Music critics avoided popular music in all its venues, but newspapers sent their drama critics to Broadway musicals. The problem was Koehler. How could he walk away from the man who'd gotten him started as a songwriter—who'd not only found the ideal words for "Get Happy," but used his connections to get that song off the ground? Although Arlen had strayed from Koehler on occasion to work with Yellen, Harburg, and Mercer, this time he'd really be moving on.

Unable to break the news to his partner's face, Arlen handed him a letter during an evening rehearsal for the spring 1934 Cotton Club show. Koehler didn't read it until the rehearsal was over. Then he approached Arlen, who had his friend Bob Wachsman by his side for support, and said with a genial smile, "You'd be a fool if you didn't do it."[1]

"Harold got loaded that night," Wachsman remembered. "He talked only about Ted—what a fine person he was, what an excellent lyric writer. He even praised the Cotton Club sets that Ted had worked on, how much detail went into them, and other good things about Ted—of which there were many."[2] But the deed was done, and the road was clear.

Ira decided to call the new show *Life Begins at 8:40*, combining the title of a best-selling book, *Life Begins at Forty*, with the show's curtain time. That idea, in turn, inspired the opening sequence, in which the performers made their entrances one by one from inside a mock-up of the Glockenspiel clock of Munich. One of those performers was Arlen's former roommate, Ray Bolger, who'd become well known for his unusual dance routines. Dressed as a bumpkin, he would execute seemingly impossible steps that always threatened a slip or a fall or some other disaster but never quite brought one on. One fan wrote, "It's like his legs are dancing and he's just along for the ride."[3] He could sing well, too, and Yip, Ira, and Harold wrote "Let's Take a Walk around the Block" for him. It was an ingratiating Arlen tune—with extra bars of piano music for some soft-shoeing—and had clever lyrics about a couple too poor to travel very far or in style. The middle of the song, however, assures us that their day will come: "Gangway, we'll begin / When our ship comes in / I'll sit on your lap / All over the map."

Another of the stars was Bert Lahr. Born Irving Lahrheim in 1895 on the Upper East Side to a family of German-Jewish immigrants, he was from his earliest days prone to fears and phobias, and there were long periods in his youth when he couldn't get to sleep unless his father stood beside him. Eventually he dealt with his insecurities by incorporating them into a stage act. He had a fear sound—*Gnong, gnong, gnong*—"a primitive, hilarious yawping," wrote his son and biographer John Lahr, "which seemed to sum up all his wide-eyed loss and confusion."[4] He was as original a buffoon as Bolger was a dancer, and rose to stardom in burlesque, in vaudeville, and on Broadway. But it wasn't until he worked with Harburg that he became a great comic actor. Harburg was the one who recognized the pathos in Lahr's slapstick and realized that if it was combined with pomposity, the result would be both hilarious and poignant. Toward that end, he and Arlen wrote a pseudo art song called "Things" that became one of Lahr's most memorable routines. He walked onstage in a tuxedo, stood beside a grand piano, and in his New York accent and with an out-of-control vibrato sang of his love for "things"—never saying what they were—while troubles developed with his toupee, his accompanist, members of the orchestra and, finally, a woman in the audience who threw a pie in his face. "I wanted to set sail into Broadway," Arlen recalled. "I wanted people in the profession to know that I could write things they didn't expect of me."[5] He certainly did that with this one.

Also in the show was Frances Williams, who sang the lone ballad, "Fun to Be Fooled." She and Harold were good friends now, nothing more, which was just as well since Anya was also in the cast. She had more to do this time than stand in the chorus. Not only was her name in the credits, she had a singing role—a small one, though. She supplemented Josephine Houston's performance of "It Was Long Ago" with a countermelody that Arlen wrote for her. Present on opening night were Samuel and Celia Arluck, who quickly figured out that this woman who appeared so skimpily dressed onstage was having a relationship with their son. The cantor didn't go to Harold for the facts but got them instead from Jerry, who told him that Harold and Anya were indeed a couple and that Anya belonged to the Russian Orthodox Church. Jerry didn't know if they were thinking of getting married, but they were certainly serious about each other. So as not to upset his wife, Samuel waited until they were back in Syracuse before telling her what he'd found out. From that point on, they were united in their aversion to Anya. They didn't want to know her, much less show her any goodwill.

On opening night Harold was so nervous he skipped the performance and walked around Times Square. The morning papers brought no relief. Critics liked the show's lyrics, actors, and sets (the stage could rotate like a giant lazy Susan) but had little to say about the music. Some songs became popular, particularly "Let's Take a Walk around the Block" and "You're a Builder-Upper," but none caused a stir. The show itself, however, did very well. A boost came from George Gershwin, who promoted it by having Arlen as his guest on his *Music by Gershwin* radio program. A few months later, to celebrate the two hundredth performance of *Life Begins at 8:40*, he walked onstage during the intermission to play Arlen tunes. But, in an unexpected way, Gershwin, too, became a problem.

Harold had been writing this lighthearted, superficial show as George worked on music that was, he ebulliently told a startled acquaintance, the greatest ever composed in America. At the end of each day they all got together—Harold, Ira, Yip, and George—to discuss what they'd come up with and when Gershwin played his *Porgy* music, a hush came over the room. Kay Swift described such moments with a baseball analogy: when a pitcher has a no-hitter going, you don't jinx it by mentioning it. But one day in the late summer of 1934, Arlen, unable to contain himself, leaned out of Ira's window and shouted, "Don't make it *too* good, George!"

He wasn't jealous, only impressed—and stimulated. Shortly after the successful launching of *Life Begins at 8:40*, he started a new composition, one with no show or lyricist in mind. He composed it as he had with Koehler, starting with a core idea and then going through the painstaking process of discovering where it ought to go. It seemed to him that this piece was an important one, and when it was finished he hurried to George's apartment to play it for him. To his astonishment, Gershwin dismissed it, saying it was too complicated, that people wouldn't understand it—this from a man who was writing three hours of music that people would still be grappling with fifty years later. Never before had Arlen received anything but encouragement from Gershwin, and he was hurt and puzzled.

In the end, *Life Begins at 8:40* wouldn't be remembered for Arlen's music or Ira's and Yip's lyrics, but for Bert Lahr and Ray Bolger. In sharp contrast was a musical that premiered a few weeks later at the 46th Street Theatre. It starred Ethel Merman and had a score by Cole Porter that included "I Get Kick Out of You," "All Through the Night," "You're the Top," "Blow, Gabriel Blow," and the title song, "Anything Goes." Porter had been allowed to be Porter, and his was the name that gained the most from the show.

CHAPTER 8

"Last Night When We Were Young"

After *Life Begins at 8:40*'s successful debut, Ira Gershwin joined his brother and DuBose Heyward to work on *Porgy and Bess*, Yip Harburg took an offer from Universal Studios to go to Hollywood and produce a movie musical, and Harold Arlen was asked to compose a work for orchestra.

The commission came from former bandleader Frank Black, who was NBC's musical director and had a radio program, *The General Motors Symphony Hour*, that featured popular and classical pieces. Arlen was pleased by the request but didn't know how to write for a symphony orchestra. It was only when Robert Russell Bennett was hired to do that part of the job that he became comfortable with the assignment and excited by the idea of composing such a work. He had a great love for symphonic music—Ravel and Stravinsky in particular. "'The only time I ever saw him angry was . . . many years ago," Jimmy Van Heusen said in 1947. "He threw his brother and myself out of his apartment with a shower of books after I had naïvely said, 'Who in the hell is Stravinsky?' while he was playing 'The Rite of Spring' on the phonograph."[1]

He called the new piece *Mood in Six Minutes*. According to Jablonski, who interviewed Robert Wachsman about those days, the composer could be seen after NBC Radio City rehearsals "dashing along Madison Avenue in a state of happy exhilaration."[2] He even spent some time thinking of the piece as a ballet for Anya, who had studied dance with the renowned Russian choreographer Michel Fokine. But it didn't become a showpiece for her or evolve into his *Rhapsody in Blue*. Like nearly all the songwriting greats of his era, he was having a go at this sort of thing, but only Gershwin and Ellington succeeded in writing and orchestrating their own large-scale pieces. It was an age when the two disciplines, classical and pop, were so different that to be brilliant at one all but guaranteed amateur status in the other. *Mood in Six Minutes* aired only once, on April 14, 1935, and hasn't been heard since—not in broadcasts, concerts, or recordings. Nor has it been published. Portions turned up in the *Hero Ballet* from the 1937 Broadway show *Hooray For What!* and then in the *Civil War Ballet* from 1944's *Bloomer Girl*. More of it was used in 1964 for a song, "Night After Night," written with Dory Langdon (Dory Previn). It was probably at around that time that Jablonski heard Arlen play the piece, because we have his description of it—melodically stark, gradually thickening harmonies, filled with agitated rhythms.

In the summer of 1935 Arlen's agent, A. L. "Abe" Berman, found him a job at the Samuel Goldwyn studios in Hollywood, where he was teamed with lyricist Lew Brown to do the film version of a Broadway show, *Strike Me Pink*. Songs for the stage version had been by Brown and composer Ray Henderson. Henderson was now working with Arlen's former partner, Ted Koehler, writing songs for Shirley Temple—including "Animal Crackers in My Soup." The Arlen–Brown movie songs would replace the Henderson–Brown stage songs. This was the way things went in Hollywood.

Upon arriving in Los Angeles, Harold and Anya found a temporary residence in a luxurious home on Rexford Drive in Beverly Hills that Yip Harburg was subleasing from Metropolitan Opera star Lawrence Tibbett. Yip, too, was trying to find his way in this world, and so far hadn't had much luck. His attempt to produce a movie at Universal Studios based on his and Vernon Duke's "April in Paris" hadn't gotten off the ground. His next stop was Warner Bros., where he was one of the scriptwriters for a movie called *Broadway Gondolier* (whose songs, by Warren and Dubin, included "Lulu's Back in Town"). Now he was living in this beautiful home, wondering what to do next. His two children were staying with him, taking advantage of the spacious grounds and the large backyard pool. Playing outside, they listened to music coming from the living room piano. It was mostly the same tune over and over again. Arlen played it as their father paced the room, trying to think of the right words. It was the melody Arlen had written in New York, the one Gershwin had dismissed.

Before playing it for Harburg he'd gone to Jerome Kern's suite at the Beverly Wilshire Hotel to try it out on him. Kern was fifty years old now and the dean of American songwriters. He'd had his first hit the year of Arlen's birth. Yet he wasn't a fogey; he'd kept up-to-date with and sometimes moved into the vanguard of songwriting trends. Recently, his works had developed a dazzling internal complexity. He would introduce exotic key changes and then somehow find his way back to the starting point just ahead of the thirty-two-bar deadline—while his audience sang happily along. A diminutive man who resembled an owl and could be as menacing as one when dealing with business associates, he was a softie among friends. And Arlen was a friend; Kern had taken to him just as Gershwin and Berlin had—in fact, a filial relationship developed between the two. In a 1964 interview, nearly twenty years after Kern's death, Arlen, when asked by CBS newsman Walter Cronkite about his friendship with Kern, choked up as he remembered the older man: "First it was Mr. Kern and it soon became Jerry and I'll never forget those days. He was one of the great big lovely giant talents of all time. In fact, I'm touched right now thinking about it."[3]

They weren't alike musically—Kern never had much use for jazz—but each admired the other's work. And they shared a similar sense of humor. Kern liked to startle strangers with impromptu temperance speeches—on sidewalks, from hotel balconies—and Arlen remembered how he'd kidded Kern:

> I'd . . . open the window and start tinkling away at the window shades and cock my head and play like he played and tinkle all over the place, and he'd get a big kick out of it. Tinkling music coming in through the window was a sign of a Kern show. He got a bang out of it and then sometimes he'd have some manuscript unfinished on the piano and be playing cards. It'd be maybe eight bars and I would develop it. And he'd look at me as if to say, "You devil, you." We had good days, wonderful days.[4]

On the golf course, Kern and Arlen tested the dress code with oddball outfits. "His specialty was impossible hats; Arlen's was freakish shoes," wrote Jablonski.[5] But affection did not keep the older man from delivering the same verdict on the new piece as Gershwin had. According to Harburg, who heard about it from Arlen, Kern said, "'Well, it's a hell of a tune, Harold, you know, for your colleagues, for your peers. But don't think the public's going to [like it]."[6]

As Kern and Gershwin saw it, the composition didn't lack merit; it lacked prospects. And they were right. It never caught on with the public. It had a Jewishness that was different from the cantorial manipulation of motifs that had worked so well in "Stormy Weather." That song was also blues- and jazz-based. This one was straight from the synagogue. Neither Kern nor Gershwin had ever attended shul, but Harburg had, and he "was awestruck by the tune."[7] That summer, as Arlen played it over and over, Yip struggled to get the words right, and it was during these days of clear skies and balmy air that this melody, with its weird, sighing "Kol Nidre" descents, became "Last Night When We Were Young." Harburg's lyric seems at first to be about the breakup of a relationship. But with successive hearings it becomes about the fleetingness of any happiness and the brevity of life. It was a song, he said, about the "whole pathos . . . of the human race."[8]

On September 4, 1935, Anya signed a contract with Samuel Goldwyn Inc., Ltd. that paid her $70 a week to be a Goldwyn Girl in *Strike Me Pink*. Harold bought a sixteen-millimeter movie camera to capture her as the wardrobe department fitted her in elaborate costumes. So began a series of home movies that would give later generations a glimpse of Hollywood in the mid-to-late 1930s. Harold's talent was what put Anya and himself in the center of that world during those years. She was not special in this land because of her blonde hair, apple-cheeked face, and alluring figure. She was exceptional because she was sweet, shy, and devoted to one man—qualities that were, if anything, damaging to an actress's career. Her role in *Strike Me Pink* was meager—all she did was stand with the other girls on risers as the headliners sang and danced. In one elaborate sequence, "The Lady Dances," venerable vaudevillian and popular radio star Eddie Cantor sang, Donna Drake (billed as Rita Rio) slithered around him, and a few Goldwyn Girls did some dance steps as Anya and other chorines remained in the background waving feathered fans back and forth across their knees. It wasn't a top-drawer Arlen song, and neither were the others he wrote for the film. He'd been uncomfortable working with Brown, who, being a composer himself as well as a lyricist, would arrive at the Tibbett house with words *and* music. Eventually, Arlen told him to just read him the lyrics over the phone. It was the opposite of how he liked to work. He needed a close collaboration, one that created what he always called a marriage of words and music. To him, a song was deficient if you could think of the melody without the words or vice versa. With the Arlen–Brown songs, no one would remember either.

Tibbett heard Arlen and Harburg working on "Last Night When We Were Young" and liked it so much he tried to get it into his new movie, *Metropolitan* (about the opera house). The result was the first of its many rejections by film producers. When he persisted and recorded it in New York for Victor Records, Gershwin and Kern's prophecies came true. It sold poorly and didn't impress anyone—except a girl who happened on it a few years later as she was thumbing through a remainder bin in a Hollywood record store. Opera singer Tibbett wasn't her style, but Arlen was. There was little she didn't know about popular songs, having sung them professionally since her stage debut at the age of two as Frances Ethel "Babe" Gumm, the youngest of the three Gumm Sisters. Their father was a singer, too, and their mother a pianist. When composer Burton Lane heard the sisters at the Paramount Theatre in Hollywood, he was so impressed with the youngest he hurried to MGM and told the head of their sheet music division, Jack Robbins, to arrange for an audition. Lane served as accompanist at that audition, where Robbins, too, became a believer. Dazzled by this thirteen-year-old, they took her to the top, to Louis B. Mayer, who, despite his belief that she was ugly, figured that these musicians were probably on to something. So on September 27, 1935, he signed her to a $100-a-week contract.

According to music critic Henry Pleasants, it was because she had sung so much as a child that she "learned to appreciate the appeal of her child's voice" and that, as she matured, she continued to sing with an "open-throated, almost birdlike vocal production, clear, pure, resonant, innocent." She was also skilled in her use of a natural vibrato that "contributed importantly to the heart-throb quality of her singing."[9] Just before signing with MGM she had, at comedian George Jessel's suggestion, changed her last name from Gumm to Garland, then taken a first name, Judy, from the title of a Hoagy Carmichael–Sammy Lerner song. The Tibbett recording of "Last Night When We Were Young" turned this young Episcopalian into the greatest champion of that song and of Arlen the composer.

CHAPTER 9

MARRIAGE

In the fall of 1935, Arlen and Harburg signed a three-picture deal with Warner Bros. They wouldn't be writing for Astaire and Rogers, whose films were the brass ring for songwriters. Rather, they would work on second-tier movies. The first was *The Singing Kid*, starring Al Jolson. Jolson had made his name with weepy ballads such as "My Mammy" and "Sonny Boy" and rhythm numbers with rudimentary lyrics like "Swanee" and "California Here I Come." Now his career was fading.

Oddly enough, Jolson—the most prominent purveyor of minstrel-style blackface—had been one of the first on Broadway to push for racial equality. And that's what he was doing in Hollywood. "Talk about integration," wrote Cab Calloway, who had been signed to appear in the film at Jolson's insistence, "hell, when the band and I got out to Hollywood, we were treated like pure royalty. Here were Jolson and I living in adjacent penthouses in a very plush hotel. We were costars in the film so we received equal treatment, no question about it."[1]

In *The Singing Kid*'s opening sequence, the camera pans from the bottom to the top of a skyscraper until it arrives at its highest ledge. Standing there is Jolson, facing a similar balcony atop an equally tall skyscraper where Calloway and his orchestra face him ("separate-but-equal-skyscrapers," wrote Professor Michael Rogin[2]). The song they sing—first Jolson and then Calloway—is "I Love to Sing-a," a jumpy Arlen tune with a Harburg lyric that makes fun of one of Jolson's vocal mannerisms—adding "a"s to the ends of words to make them more singable. Harburg throws in an extra "a" just about everywhere and in the process pokes fun not only at Jolson, but at all the songs that mindlessly glorified the South: "I love to wake up with the South-a in my mouth-a / And wave the flag-a / with a cheer for Uncle Sammy and another for my mammy / I love to sing!"

After Jolson and Calloway each take a turn with "I Love to Sing-a," the song is reprised by Jolson with extra lyrics not included in the published sheet music. This is where Harburg really lets loose: "We'd love to stuff the sunny South-a in your mouth-a" and "You'd suit your public finer / If you took your Carolina / and your mammy and your Dinah / and then hung them neck to neck-a / on the Mason-Dixon line-a." As Arthur Knight points out in his book *Disintegrating the Musical*, "Giving lines like 'We'd love to stuff the South-a in your mouth-a' to Calloway . . . would have been incendiary."[3] But with Jolson singing them, the joke is on him, not the old Confederacy. Harburg's point was lost anyway, because these additional lines are heard in a production number where Jolson stands on a crowded street trying to sing "My Mammy" as people around him counter with "I Love to Sing-a." Finally, a car drives by and splashes mud on his face, turning him into the blackface minstrel of old.

When *The Singing Kid* failed at the box office, Jolson's career as a Hollywood leading man was over. "I Love to Sing-a" might have been doomed, too, had it not become the title and basis of a cartoon released by the studio a few months later, in June 1936. In this film animator Ted Avery tells the story of a jazz-loving "Owl" Jolson, who is kicked out of his classical music–loving family only to score big on the radio with this song. It is one of the best-loved cartoons of the Warner Bros. Merrie Melodies series, often referenced in pop culture (in the television series *South Park*, for instance), and that has kept the song alive.

Another Arlen–Harburg creation for the film, "You're the Cure for What Ails Me," is sung by Jolson to child star Sybil Jason. There is some charm in the melody, but its real importance lies in the fact that it marked Harburg's first use, as a songwriter, of neologisms—newly minted words. Previously, he had used them only in his poetry. One of his poems from the 1920s, "Definition," calls a man with three women a "trigamist" and one with six a "pigamist."[4] In "You're the Cure for What Ails Me," the neologisms are derived from dropped final syllables—"you're the pink of my condish" / You're my Arrowhead Springs, and my Battle Creek, Mich." Ira had done the same thing earlier, beginning with "Sunny Disposish" in 1926, written with composer Philip Charig. The year after that, in his and George's "'S Wonderful," he'd dispensed with last syllables in the introductory verse, using "fash" for "fashion" and "pash" for "passion," and then sliced off first syllables in the refrain ("'S Wonderful, 's marvelous"). But Harburg would take this further, eventually venturing into the surreal in a way that wouldn't be matched in song until Bob Dylan and John Lennon came along.

The two other movies that Arlen and Harburg wrote to complete their Warner Bros. contract brought them face-to-face with the ennui that had come to be known as "Hollywooditis." The money was good and life was easy, but except for big-name actors—and not even all of them—everyone was subject to the mercurial and tyrannical temperaments of studio bosses. Some of their best songs for *Stage Struck*, which came out in October 1936, were inexplicably dropped. One was a lovely ballad, "Why Can't I Remember Your Name?" Another was a comedy song, "Four Fugitives from a Bolero Chain Gang." Among songwriters, Arlen and Harburg had become the undisputed masters of zaniness. The movie did use the beautiful ballad, "Fancy Meeting You," for which Harburg, in a series of introductory rhymes, gives his take on the theory of evolution.

The last of the three films, *Gold Diggers of 1937*, premiered in December. At the request of Busby Berkeley, who directed its musical sequences, the studio brought in the Warren–Dubin team to provide additional songs, which was a slap at Arlen and Harburg. Warren and Dubin assured their friends that they hadn't asked for the assignment and were agreeing to it because of contractual obligations. Harold and Yip understood this, and their anger—it was mostly Harburg's—was directed at Warner Bros. Yip had begun to view the Hollywood studio system in proletarian terms: movies were assembly-line products "like so many gloves or fur coats."[5] He, like Rodgers and Hart, longed for a return to Broadway. Harold, on the other hand enjoyed Southern California for the weather, the sports, and good times with his songwriter friends. The songs he'd been writing recently were a source of pride, even if there was a lull in his string of chart-toppers. "It was a great period," he remembered. "All of us writing pictures so well. We were all on the weekly radio Hit Parade. If we weren't first, we were second, if we weren't second, we were fourth. A sensational period. Lovely for me. I went to the studio when I damned well pleased, or when they called me. Got my check every week. And we were pouring it out!"[6] By this time he and Warren had begun kidding each other about their parallel careers—which of them had the most hits and who was more anonymous—and the Warner Bros. incident became fodder for their ribbing, especially when a Warren–Dubin song, "With Plenty of Money and You," became the standout song of *Gold Diggers of 1937* and went to the top of the Hit Parade.

More annoying to Arlen was increasing pressure from Leonore Gershwin for him and Anya to marry. "As the virtual leader of the Hollywood wives," wrote Jablonski, "she launched a campaign for the legal union of Anya Taranda and Harold Arlen, a source of uneasiness for both."[7] But Leonore did have a point. Arlen was allowing fear of his parents to dominate his life—and Anya's, too, because she seems to have had no say in the matter. Rather than make demands on him, she withdrew into herself, becoming increasingly quiet at social gatherings, where she was the only pretend wife, where Leonore harped at her, and where, among so many talented, accomplished, and witty people, she was the youngest and least sophisticated one in the room.

Irving and Ellin Berlin were her friends, but they didn't go to many of these parties; when Harold and Anya got together with them it was usually to go for Chinese food. Leonore's older sister Emily Paley was also a friend, but she and her husband, a schoolteacher, lived in New York. The only woman at these parties who made a point of befriending Anya was Edelaine Gorney. She was the sort everyone took their problems to, and was often on the phone with Anya as the younger woman unburdened herself. With little to do and in growing isolation, Anya took up painting and expressed her gratitude to Edelaine with a portrait that combined both their faces.

In the meantime, Jerry Arlen got married. His wedding to singer-songwriter Jeanne Burns took place in New York at the beginning of 1936. Harold wasn't there, not having learned about it until Jerry wrote him after the fact:

> I don't know how to start telling you and I hope you'll understand, as well as Ma and Pa did, don't let this shock you—but I'm married and very happy—to a lovely Jewish girl and above all clean and respectable like I always wanted. And Ma and Pa love her with all their heart . . . I've known her for three years and of course I'm not working, but she was willing as she is crazy about me and I know I'll get something and we'll be very happy. I hope we have your blessings, she is here with me and honestly Ma and Pa love her so, maybe my luck will change now.[8]

Harold sent a wedding gift of $500, and shortly after that received a letter from his father admonishing him for his generosity. "It's done," the cantor wrote to him about the marriage, "let them be happy. I think it was a foolish move on your part to send them a check for $500 at this time, to me there was plenty of time for that but it's done, let's hope he will connect somewhere and be able to support her. Money will never solve his problem, *he has to work.* She seems to be a nice respectful girl with a lot of common sense, more than he has at this time."[9] The cantor went on to say that he and Celia would go to the Jewish ceremony, from which we can infer that Jerry and Jean had initially said their vows in a civil proceeding, probably hastily arranged.

They now began their lives together as struggling musicians. He would get occasional gigs singing or playing the violin or sax. For a time he had his own band. She, a native New Yorker and, at twenty-two, a year younger, had more musical training. She'd studied at a local musical institute, was an accomplished pianist, and had sung professionally with bandleader Adrian Rollini. She was also the author of several successful songs, most notably "Everyone Eats Who Comes to My House," recorded by Cab Calloway. Now she and Jerry set out to make a living writing songs together.

While Arlen and Harburg were working on the last of their three Warner Bros. films, they were asked by Vincente Minnelli to write a song for his upcoming Broadway revue *The Show Is On*. He'd signed Bert Lahr and Beatrice Lillie as his stars, and Lahr wanted another operatic sendup like "Things." They gleefully accepted the assignment and wrote a goofy number, which they presented to Lahr via a demo record (Arlen doing a very good Lahr impression). It was called "Song of the Woodman," an idea that had come to Harburg as he toyed with the name of the Russian bass singer Feodor Chaliapin (sometimes spelled Shalyapin). It sounded to him like "chopping," which brought to mind the image of an opera singer chopping down a tree. Lahr performed this aria in jodhpurs and a plaid lumberjack shirt as he hacked away at a sapling and sang in his pompous and uncontrolled vibrato of all that would come from its wood: "A pipe for Dad, a bat for brother / An extra broom for dear old mother," "Cribbage boards for the Far West Indies / Toothpicks for the boys in Lindy's," "Handles for the Fuller brush / Plungers for the obstinate flush." As he sang he was pelted with wood chips hurled from backstage—a few at first, then a shower of them. It became one of his best routines.

When *The Show Is On* ran into difficulties during its Boston and Philadelphia tryouts, Harburg headed east. He was a good show doctor. Arlen went east, too. But he was thinking about more than the new revue. He and Anya boarded the *Super Chief* and, as Jablonski tells it, "by the time they reached Chicago to switch to the *Twentieth Century* for Manhattan, Harold Arlen had made up his mind about his Annie."[10] He didn't tell her his decision until they'd checked into a Manhattan hotel where, after taking separate rooms "for propriety's sake,"[11] he used the same method to propose to her as he'd used to separate from Koehler: a handwritten note. It read:

Dearest Anya—
We're getting married tomorrow—
'bout time, don't you think?
All my love.

H.

They were married on January 8, 1937, in Harrison, New York—a small town in Westchester County twenty-five miles north of Manhattan. The site was chosen by Arlen's lawyer, Abe Berman, who was one of the two witnesses; the other was Berman's wife, Patricia.[12] New York City had been rejected as a venue because Arlen's parents read the New York papers and he didn't want them to find out about the marriage. It isn't known how long he intended to keep this news from them, but Samuel and Celia were still unaware of it when, three months later, a reporter from the Syracuse *American* called Celia to ask if rumors of the marriage, as published in Sid Skolsky's Hollywood gossip column, were true. "If Sid is right," reads an article in the *American*'s April 18, 1937, edition, "then it's all news to Mr. and Mrs. Samuel Arluck, parents of Harold Arlen, Syracuse's most famous representative on Tin Pan Alley. Mrs. Arluck made it distinctly clear when questioned about the marriage report that she had heard nothing which would substantiate the report from her son."[13]

On the license, Harold gave his last name as Arluck. He never legally changed his surname; he used it on his driver's license and when he registered to vote. Officially, he and Anya were Mrs. and Mrs. Arluck, although they would always refer to themselves as the Arlens.

The elder Mr. and Mrs. Arluck didn't disown their son. But Celia told her best friend, Mrs. Sandler, that her husband had considered saying Kaddish for him—the prayer for the dead—and had also talked about jumping out of a window.[14]

CHAPTER 10

DEATH OF GERSHWIN

Harold and Anya returned to California in January 1937. They rented a two-story home on Lookout Mountain Avenue in Laurel Canyon, six miles from Beverly Hills, and went back to the lives they'd been leading, except now they were husband and wife. They made a handsome couple: he determinedly debonair, always fastidiously attired—a look that now included a pipe jutting assertively from his lips; she dressed primly, favoring belted skirts and high button blouses topped by lace collars. They liked to take their two dogs—a springer spaniel named Stormy and a Dalmatian named Pan—to the beach. In New York they'd had a mongrel, Shmutts, but he remained there with Jerry.

During the preceding year, Anya had been in a series of films following *Strike Me Pink*, including some estimable ones like *Top Hat*, *These Three*, and *Broadway Melody of 1936*. But her parts were minuscule, her characters were never given names, and her own name was never mentioned in the credits. In fact, studio head Samuel Goldwyn seems to have been dubious about her name. In a January 6, 1936, article in the Pittsburg *Press*, columnist Kaspar Monahan wrote that Goldwyn had hired "a numerologist for the purpose of changing Anya Taranda's name to something more in keeping with her 'rhythmic personality'—whatever that is." Above the text is a photo of Anya wearing black slacks slit to the hip and a leopard-print blouse parted to display her from the waist to the collarbone and with more than a hint of the rest. Her head is cocked back, her lips heavily painted and provocatively parted, her head topped by a broad-brimmed leopard hat. The caption reads, "Anya Taranda / What Will Her New Name Be?" Now, a year later, in early 1937, there'd been no name change and no further work for Anya except through the John Powers Modeling Agency, which found a place for her visage on bottles of Breck Shampoo.

Nor did Harold have work. He took the unusual step of recording demos of song ideas, which he gave to various lyricists, including his old partner, Ted Koehler. Koehler and Arlen had remained good friends and were often together at the Gershwin house. Although he was busy with other commitments, Koehler took time out to write a song with Harold, "Public Melody Number One." It was a jazzy up-tempo number that found its way into a 1937 Paramount movie, *Artists and Models*, performed by Martha Raye and Louis Armstrong and staged by Vincente Minnelli. Arlen also tried some tunes out on Ira Gershwin, but the Gershwins were hard at work on scores for two successive Astaire movies.

The first, *Shall We Dance*, was an unhappy experience for both brothers, especially George. The studio and Astaire rejected several songs outright. These as well as the ones that made it into the score were, the Gershwins felt, some of the best work they'd ever done. But they had no say about which would be accepted or how those that had been accepted would be arranged or performed. One of George's biggest disappointments was that Fred and Ginger didn't dance to "They Can't Take That Away from Me." Upon finishing that song in October 1936, he'd raced to Harold and Anya's house, entered without knocking,[1] and played it for them. Then they'd all sung it together.

But happy moments like that were becoming rare for George, who'd had doubts about coming to Hollywood and now regretted the decision. His and Ira's new songs were marvels of the art, but he was in a hurry to get back to the larger forms. He'd been working out a string quartet in his head and had received a request for an orchestral piece for an upcoming Italian music festival. In his letters and conversations he showed a sense of time ticking. One of his best friends, the conductor William Daly, had died suddenly of a heart attack at the age of forty-nine, and in the title song for *Shall We Dance*, written shortly afterward, Ira's lyrics for the first time addressed the subject of mortality. Dance while you still have time, he advises.

George, like Arlen, had spent 1936 thinking about marriage. Before leaving New York he'd broken off a ten-year relationship with Kay Swift in the belief that if Hollywood wasn't the best place to write music it was the ideal location to find his perfect woman: young, beautiful, talented, skilled as a hostess, career-minded, family-minded, *and* Jewish. Now he thought he'd met her—actress Paulette Goddard. But Arlen and other friends believed this was folly and tried to talk sense into him. For one thing, Goddard was already married, to Charlie Chaplin. For another, she wasn't serious about Gershwin. And he was conducting this romance in an adolescent manner with ruses and assignations. "We sat by the pool talking about it," Arlen remembered. "She was a great girl but George's life style was very free-wheeling. I knew that marriage would tie him down, so I told him that he would have to give up some of the freedom he had."[2] At that point the usually genial Gershwin became angry and ended the conversation. Something strange was going on with him, but Harold, like everyone else, believed it was nerves. Why wouldn't he be testy? He'd suffered the failure of *Porgy and Bess*, and two failed shows prior to that, as well as a string of unsuccessful concert works, including his ambitious *Second Rhapsody*. Now, in early 1937, box-office receipts for *Shall We Dance* were disappointing—the first of the Astaire–Rogers films to see such a dip. Irving Berlin said, "There's nothing wrong with George that a hit song won't cure."[3]

In the spring of 1937, Arlen had another, even more uncomfortable moment with Gershwin. "I felt that there was something wrong with him one day," he recalled, "when after a lot of us had played the piano, George said to me, 'No you don't. I'm not going to follow you.' I was shocked with surprise. Since we were always together in one bunch trying to help one another, there was little show of jealousy. When he acted that way, I felt uneasy. I knew something was wrong with him, and I thought it was Hollywooditis." This contrasted with how George usually treated Arlen. Dr. Rod Gorney, son of Jay and Edelaine, recalls being told that at a party "in happier times, George Gershwin invited each member to take the piano. For Arlen he announced, 'And now we'll hear from the best of us.'"[4]

Besides testiness, George was suffering from increasingly severe and sometimes debilitating headaches. There were also dizzy spells. While conducting a symphony rehearsal, he was saved from a fall off the podium by his valet, who rushed to catch him. A medical checkup concluded that he was most likely suffering from "hysteria," which prompted Leonore to say he was putting on an act. She became strict with him, ordering him from the table when he fumbled his utensils or couldn't get his fork into his mouth. One day he collapsed onto the sidewalk outside a restaurant and she ordered Ira not to help him up.[5] She disguised her hatred for him—its source remains a mystery—as a diagnosis,[6] one that his friends considered correct because sometimes the headaches and other symptoms subsided and he became his old self again.

As this was happening, Jerome Kern fell ill. He'd been vigilantly overseeing construction of his new house, attending to every detail. The wood paneling had to be just so, the flooring identical to what he'd seen in actress Irene Dunne's house, the bricks white with black trim. When it came to his most cherished possession, his Blüthner piano, he told the Steinway Company to be sure it was securely crated before they shipped it from New York. They glued, nailed, and screwed it into place, but when the crate arrived and was opened Kern saw that a screw had entered the soundboard. His face went chalky, his pulse raced, then came chest pains—it was a heart attack. Three weeks later, a stroke paralyzed his left side. As he lay bedridden, he asked his wife and daughter to spare him any bad news, so they didn't tell him of Gershwin's illness.

It was a terrible time for songwriters. In October of 1937 Cole Porter, while visiting friends on Long Island, decided to go riding. The horse he chose was, he was warned, skittish. But that made him all the more eager for the challenge. In a wooded area the animal became rattled, reared up, and fell on and shattered one of Porter's legs. It then tried to right itself and fell a second time, crushing his other leg. Porter would spend the remaining twenty-seven years of his life suffering through one surgery after another, always in pain.

Arlen's biggest problem in mid-1937—so far—was unemployment. Income from royalties and from payments made to him by the American Society of Composers, Authors and Publishers (ASCAP), which collected fees based on live performances of its members' works, kept him comfortable financially. But it was unnerving not to have work. Harburg was in the same situation. He'd returned to Beverly Hills and rented a small house near the Gershwin residence but had nothing to do. Rather than make the rounds looking for a film job, he decided to work on a project of his own, one he'd had in mind for several years. He wanted to write a Broadway musical about war. It would be a farce along the lines of the Gershwins' *Strike Up the Band*. But where that show's reference point was the Great War of 1914–18, his would be the war on the horizon. Fascists—Hitler, Mussolini, and the Imperial Japanese Army—were battle-testing their weapons in Spain, Ethiopia, and Manchuria. To forestall a general conflict, France and England adopted a forgiving attitude toward German resurgence, but this was an iffy policy at best, and should it fail, how long before the United States got involved? Although Harburg's plot took aim at fascism, his real goal was to portray war as everyone's folly. His protagonist was a tender-hearted gardener named Chuckles who invents an insecticide that will spare the worms in his apples (they provide silk, after all). But Chuckles inadvertently comes up with a death gas—a potential superweapon. Before long, every nation is after the secret, which he guards successfully until a temptress spy sees it in her hand mirror. Harburg's surprise twist—he loved O. Henry—is that the mirror has reversed the image, turning it into a formula for laughing gas.

This plot got Harburg the backing of the Shubert brothers, who'd been pleased with the success of *Life Begins at 8:40*, and they gave him the green light to assemble a formidable team: Howard Lindsay and Russel Crouse to help him write the script (they'd written Porter's *Anything Goes* in 1934 and would later write the Broadway scripts for *Life with Father* and *The Sound of Music*), Vincente Minnelli to direct, comedian Ed Wynn to play Chuckles, and Arlen to write the music.

It was to be the first major book musical for Arlen and Harburg, and they arranged to take the train to New York and get to work. In early July they and Anya went to the Gershwin house to say goodbye. There they saw George pale, listless, barely ambulatory, and suffering from headaches so bad he had to sit in the dark. Leonore asked Harburg for the keys to his house. She'd decided to move George out of the home he shared with Ira and herself and send him to Yip's now unoccupied cottage where, she said, he could find rest and solitude. There's no indication that Harold or Yip considered postponing their trip to remain with him, even though they heard him say, "All my friends are leaving me." On July Fourth—the day he was taken to the Harburg house—they and Anya boarded the train.

A few days later they were at work on the new show, *Hooray For What!*, at Howard Lindsay's vacation home in Bucks County, Pennsylvania, when the telephone rang. Arlen went upstairs to answer it. For a second he stood still. Then he vomited. Forty years later, Harburg spoke about that moment and the evening that followed:

> Harold . . . went up a whole bright ruddy-faced person and he came down he was gangrene. And he almost fell down the steps. And I said, "What is it? What is it? What's the trouble? He said, "Nothing. Nothing. Nothing." And evidently he'd gotten hold of Lindsay and Crouse and told them but they wouldn't tell me because I . . . had to drive them back home that day. And they were afraid if they told me I wouldn't be able to drive the car home. So those three guys suffered it out. I didn't know what happened, I thought some conspiracy against me, they wouldn't tell me what it was. In the car . . . it was like going to a funeral. It was a funeral. So I turned around and said, "What's happened to you guys? Where's all the humor gone? Is the show that bad? Are we really in trouble? I thought we all liked it." And finally out of Russel Crouse came something, he said, "Well, we're worried about something." I said, "Well, what are you worried about? Tell me. I think you've got a great show here." Well, the conversation was that way, then complete silence all the rest of the way until we got to New York. And finally I delivered Howard Lindsay and Russel Crouse to their respective homes. And Harold had rented Minnelli's apartment on 52nd Street, a lovely little apartment. He was living there, Minnelli was out on the coast. And Harold said, "Come on up with me for a while. Let's go over a couple of things." I went up and he was still morose. I knew that Harold when he took the call started to vomit and that they took him into the bathroom 'till he'd

vomited it all out. And then I said, "What happened? What did you eat?" And he said, "No. Yip, I have to tell you. I just got a call. George is dead." I said, "What are you talking about? What do you mean 'George is dead?'" He said, "George died on the operating table."[7]

It had been a brain tumor, not hysteria.

That evening, Vincent Youmans heard the news on the radio in Colorado Springs, where he was being treated for tuberculosis. Late that night he phoned the daughter of his doctor and asked her to join him and his wife. "He seemed so moved," wrote Youmans's biographer Gerald Bordman, "that she felt she could not refuse. When she arrived at his house, he was already well into a bottle of whiskey. After offering her a drink, he went directly to the piano, where he obviously had been before she came. Through the night he played nothing but Gershwin, stopping only to refill his glass. Early morning light seeped through the windows before Youmans and his vast repertoire of Gershwin songs were exhausted."[8]

CHAPTER 11

Hooray for What!

Songwriters preferred Broadway to Hollywood because they could be more in control of their work there and more involved in shaping a show. The other side of the coin was greater wear and tear on their psyches as they invested themselves in these shows. Having worked on Youmans's *Great Day!*, Arlen knew how badly things could go preparing a stage musical and how one might end up with something very different from what had been imagined.

Problems plagued *Hooray for What!* from the start, beginning with a period of inertia for its songwriters as they mourned Gershwin. Then came a health scare for Arlen: his own incapacitating headaches. People told him they were a psychological reaction to George's illness, but he now knew that George had been misdiagnosed as a hypochondriac, so he sought medical treatment. He went to a surgeon friend who'd been his neighbor in the Croydon Hotel in the early 1930s. This was Dr. Miguel Elias, whose occupation had so fascinated Arlen that he'd borrowed his medical texts, visited patients with him in their homes and at the hospital, and stood next to him in the operating room wearing a surgical gown. At one point he accompanied the doctor on a visit to a postoperative patient who needed but couldn't afford a full-time nurse, and Harold paid the bill.[1] Dr. Elias told him the headaches were due to a sinus cyst, which he removed, ending the problem.

Problems with the show were not so easily solved. They began with the need for a big-name star. Comedian Ed Wynn had been popular in vaudeville, on Broadway, and on radio, so he got the lead as Chuckles. Because his salary was high, there wasn't enough left in the budget for other big names, which meant that everyone else onstage was a newcomer. One of them was Kay Thompson, a tall, slinky pianist and singer who had the full-steam-ahead personality she would later give to her literary invention Eloise of the Plaza Hotel. She was known for devising quirky vocal arrangements in which she traded riffs with her backup singers—a group that presently included Hugh Martin and Ralph Blane, later to become a songwriting team and the authors of "Have Yourself a Merry Little Christmas."[2] Arlen, Harburg, and Minnelli were fans of Thompson and got the producer, Lee Shubert, to hire her as the femme fatale, Stephania Stephanovich. She was asked to bring her vocal group into the show, and they were billed as the Singing Spies. Other newcomers were choreographer Agnes de Mille, soon to be one of the great names of Broadway and in classical ballet, and twenty-eight-year-old Vivian Vance, whose fame would come on television in the 1950s as Lucille Ball's friend and foil, Ethel Mertz, on *I Love Lucy*.

The problems began with Vance. She hadn't actually gotten a role. She was Thompson's understudy, and chaffed at this because in her prior two jobs she'd been Ethel Merman's understudy. What she wanted was a real part—Thompson's—and she was determined to do what had to be done to get it. She started a romance with Russel Crouse, who then championed her as Thompson's replacement. When director Minnelli held out for Thompson, Vance bedded Harburg, and soon he was vying with Crouse to see who could do more to get her the role.

When Shubert saw things going awry he sent his domineering business manager, Harry Kaufman, to take charge of the production. Kaufman had constant run-ins with Minnelli, Thompson, and de Mille. In a memoir, de Mille wrote about what it was like to work for him and Shubert. Shubert she likened to an animal "who can sit unmoving . . . with unblinking eyes, apparently lost in thought, until something edible passes." Kaufman "smiled, or he thought he smiled. His lips twitched." He would send his girlfriends to replace de Mille's trained dancers, and if they couldn't dance that didn't matter to him. "I couldn't fire them," she wrote, "not if they fell down dead drunk at my feet, not if they were three hours late."[3]

To further complicate matters, de Mille had problems with Minnelli. Without consulting her, he, a former set designer, changed the layout of the stage so her dancers had just one exit route, not four as originally planned. Having also been a costume designer, he came up with outfits for de Mille's dancers that, for an orchestral number called *Hero Ballet*, included gas masks, barbed wire (made from rubber), and rifles with bayonets. Kaufman ordered de Mille to put the dancers back into traditional chorus girl attire, but she refused out of loyalty to Minnelli, so Kaufman fired her.

Then he tried to dismiss one of Thompson's backup singers, Ralph Blane, and when Thompson stood up for Blane, Kaufman fired her, too. Vance finally got the job. "To fire that marvelous woman was unforgivable," Hugh Martin said of Thompson. Her weeping "was the worst thing I have ever, *ever* heard. The screaming and sobbing were something you can't imagine out of Kay."[4]

Kaufman also tormented Arlen and Harburg. He kept asking them to write what he called "the jingle"—a signature song that would bring people into the theater. They brought a lot of songs to him, but he refused to designate any as "the jingle." Arlen, in dismay, took to his bed. Harburg was as upset with Wynn as with Kaufman, because the comedian had hired his own gag writers to supplement the script. In the meantime, Minnelli discovered uppers and downers.

Shortly after she was fired, de Mille received a phone call from Thompson, also fired, who gleefully told her that Kaufman, while yelling at the cast during a rehearsal, had stepped backward and fallen from the stage into the orchestra pit, breaking his back. They later learned he hadn't been injured that badly or broken anything except a few musical instruments—for which Shubert docked him.

Somehow, despite all this, the show was a success. Wynn had been wise to get jokes from outside comedy writers. His nonstop clowning gave audiences the vaudeville they expected of him and mitigated Harburg's satire. A year before, Kurt Weill and lyricist Paul Green had taken on the subject of war with a show, *Johnny Johnson*, that lasted only sixty-eight performances. It too had used the notion of laughing gas as an antidote to conflict. Yip must have been aware of that failure and suspected that his project's prospects were uncertain. Yet *Hooray For What!* succeeded, and Harburg lost none of his ambition to combine fantasy and satire.

But his and Arlen's score for the show was hardly noticed. One reason for this was Arlen's centerpiece, the *Hero Ballet*. Orchestrated by Don Walker, it was, as Harold said, "very Stravinsky."[5] It had the same opening as *Mood in Six Minutes*, and continued on with unmelodic harshness and alternating time signatures—disorienting qualities that were unlikely to please Broadway audiences. Unlike Stravinsky, Arlen didn't have devotees who followed his career from work to work. Nor could he expect any of his music, once overlooked, to eventually find an audience. Popular music has always been a now-or-never art form.

A year earlier, Richard Rodgers had written a ballet, *Slaughter on Tenth Avenue*, for his and Larry Hart's *On Your Toes*. It, like *The Hero Ballet*, dealt with weighty matters (it depicts two murders) but Rodgers gave it punchy tunes and a flowing central melody that guaranteed its popularity in and outside the theater. *On Your Toes* was the second of three great consecutive

Rodgers and Hart Broadway musicals of the mid-1930s. It was preceded by *Jumbo*, which introduced "Little Girl Blue" and "The Most Beautiful Girl in the World," and followed by *Babes in Arms*, which had "Where or When," "The Lady Is a Tramp," "I Wish I Were in Love Again," "Johnny One Note," and "My Funny Valentine." Having achieved fame a decade earlier, these two writers now became legendary. Each—but especially Rodgers—was astute in judging stories for their potential as musicals. Arlen didn't have that ability. Nor did he have Rodgers's capacity to strictly supervise his shows as they were put together. He had no ruthlessness in him—except when it came to his own music. According to Harburg, he was always throwing away good ideas in a search of better ones.[6]

The only song from *Hooray for What!* that became a standard was "Down with Love"—a rhythm number with a harmonically adventurous verse ("You, sons of Adam / You, daughters of Eve") and a catchy, breezy refrain ("Down with love / the flowers and rice and shoes") whose bridge ("Away, take it away") has the feel of a cowboy song—an inspired surprise. Other songs, if not hits, were hardly substandard. "God's Country" is a rousing syncopated march with lyrics that alternate between straightforward patriotism ("Hi there neighbor; going my way? / East or west on the Lincoln highway"), comic patriotism ("Where smiles are broader / Freedom greater / Ev'ry man is his own dictator"), and pop culture references ("Love its highways—love its alleys / Its Rocky Mountains and Rudy Vallees"). In May of 1938, while *Hooray for What!* was still on Broadway, fifteen-year-old Judy Garland sang "God's Country" on a radio variety program called *Good News of 1938*, and in that performance, which has been preserved, there are references to Harburg's hero, FDR ("There's one more thankee / Give thanks for a man called Frankie") and to Clark Gable and the Marx Brothers. He wrote lots of lyrics for this song, and a singer can take his or her pick. Decades later he updated it with references to "Jacqueline's hairdo" and cholesterol.

Another significant song in the score was the bluesy Cotton Club–style "Moanin' in the Mornin.'" Like many Arlen compositions, it has an unusual construction. The first eight measures ("I'm through with moanin'") are not repeated, as would ordinarily happen, but move directly into an eight-bar bridge ("I'm through with love, the thrill and the spell of it"). After that comes the eight-bar opening's return, followed by a pared-down four-bar version of the bridge ("Each time I found love"). Six measures of new material provide a coda ("If this is all love can do"). "Moanin' in the Mornin' is basically an ABAC song in its form—not unusual for pop songs of the time—but the irregular lengths of its sections show that Arlen was less interested in satisfying the expectations of his audience than in seeking—tenaciously—the right next note. Eventually he'd compose songs that were more than twice the customary length—"Blues in the Night," "That Old Black Magic," and "The Man That Got Away" among them. These "tapeworms," as he jokingly referred to them, were, despite their complexity, enormously successful.

Three songs written for *Hooray for What!* have a childlike quality. One, "Buds Won't Bud," is about all of nature going awry "when the one you love won't love you." Musically it sounds sweet and innocent yet proves complex. The refrain begins with a ninth chord whose most difficult note—the ninth—is given to the singer. Then comes a ten-bar bridge that transports us to Cantor Arluck's synagogue for a chromatic melody backed by mournful minor and diminished chords. Somehow, the song never loses its carefree quality. It's good enough to have become a standard, but it didn't even make it into the show, possibly because Harburg went overboard turning nouns into verbs ("my moods won't mood"). When Judy Garland tried to rescue it by singing it in the 1940 film *Andy Hardy Meets a Debutante*, her performance was cut. Finally, Ethel Waters introduced it in the 1942 film *Cairo*, but it never caught on.

The second of this trio of fanciful songs, "In the Shade of the New Apple Tree," did make it into the show. Its title is a play on "In the Shade of the Old Apple Tree," a 1905 song that was still popular in the 1930s. Harburg's lyric is about the old and the new ("Your dress is another's / But your smile is still your mother's"), and so is Arlen's music, which combines old-fashioned harmony and structure with loose jazz rhythms. It's an endearing song, but it failed to catch on, although it did charm one important person.

This was Arthur Freed, the MGM staff songwriter and co-discoverer of Judy Garland. A good-looking, inarticulate man—"Whenever Arthur talked, all you could do was guess at his meaning," said Harburg[7]—his all-consuming goal was to become the producer of great movie musicals. After the success of Disney's groundbreaking *Snow White and the Seven Dwarfs*, which premiered at the end of 1937, he decided that it and Disney's chief songwriter, Frank Churchill, had shown the way. He believed that MGM could make its own significant musical based on a classic children's story, one that would have songs like the heartfelt "Someday My Prince Will Come" and the childlike "Whistle While You Work." He talked Louis B. Mayer into buying the rights to L. Frank Baum's 1900 children's book *The Wonderful Wizard of Oz*[8] and made sure Judy Garland got the role of Dorothy. A prior film version had come out in 1925, but that was before sound and color. Freed imagined what could be done given the resources of a modern Hollywood studio. As he sat in the Winter Garden Theatre taking in *Hooray for What!* he listened to "In the Shade of the New Apple Tree" and liked its combination of the old and the new. Ostensibly, he'd taken this trip to New York to look for shows with potential as film musicals, but he already knew what movie he wanted to make. He was actually scouting Arlen and Harburg. And their "In the Shade of the New Apple Tree" was the deciding factor. It wasn't that the song itself was going anywhere, but it would lead to something that went everywhere.

The last of the three whimsical Arlen–Harburg numbers for the show, initially called "I'm Hanging On to You," was dropped before the opening, so Freed didn't hear it. But he'd get to know it later when Harold and Yip turned it into "If I Only Had a Brain/a Heart/the Nerve," to be sung and danced to by Arlen's former roommate Ray Bolger, Bolger's former co-star in *Life Begins at 8:40* Bert Lahr, and Lahr's old friend from burlesque and vaudeville, Jack Haley.

CHAPTER 12

THE WIZARD OF OZ

For a long time now, *The New Yorker*'s capsule review of *The Wizard of Oz* has been just one word: "Heavenly." But when the film debuted, their movie critic, Russell Maloney, wrote, "I sat cringing before MGM's Technicolor production of 'The Wizard of Oz,' which displays no trace of imagination, good taste, or ingenuity.'" More succinctly, he called the film a "stinkeroo."[1]

Had it not been for Arthur Freed, there's a good chance that "stinkeroo" would be the correct judgment. He wasn't the film's producer—he was still a staff songwriter—but he was lobbying Mayer to make him a producer and agreed to become an apprentice producer, a made-up title that brought a salary cut from $1,500 a week to $300. Producers were the ones with real power at MGM, and Freed's goal was to head a production unit that would make brilliant original musicals. And that's what he did. He started with *The Wizard of Oz* and eventually produced *Cabin in the Sky*, *Meet Me in St. Louis*, *An American in Paris*, *Singing in the Rain*, and *Gigi*.

Having coaxed Mayer into buying rights to the book, he became an indispensable arbiter among the many scriptwriters. One of the three principal writers was twenty-six-year-old novelist and playwright Noel Langley, who devised an opening scene in Kansas to ground the film in characters who would later have counterparts in Oz. One "cannot put fantastic people in strange places in front of an audience," he said, "unless they have seen them as human beings first."[2] Had it been up to the film's named producer, Mervyn LeRoy, there would have been no initial Kansas sequence and thus no "Over the Rainbow." The movie would have begun with Dorothy reading *The Wonderful Wizard of Oz*, which would later fall from a bookshelf and hit her on the head, launching her into the fantasy. But Freed sided with Langley.

Had Freed been an egoist of the conventional sort, he would have appointed himself lyricist and taken his pick of composers—Jerome Kern was being considered, as was Freed's old partner Nacio Herb Brown, with whom he'd written "You Are My Lucky Star" and "Singin' in the Rain." It would have been the sensible thing to do. He was still writing songs; in 1940 his and Roger Edens's "Our Love Affair" received an Academy Award nomination. But somehow he knew that Arlen and Harburg were the ones for the job, just as he knew that sixteen-year-old Judy Garland had to play Dorothy even though Baum's Dorothy was a six-year-old and despite Mayer's wish to sign ten-year-old Shirley Temple, which he would have done had Twentieth Century Fox been willing to loan her out.

Freed decided on Arlen and Harburg in New York but didn't tell them there. First he returned to MGM to discuss this and other matters with his boss. Mayer trusted his judgment about songs and was pleased that Arlen and Harburg would cost less than Kern. But Harold and Yip didn't know any of this when they returned to Southern California in February 1938. They came back for the weather and because they missed their friends.

Of course, things couldn't be the same after Gershwin's death. The pall of that tragedy lay on everyone—with more sorrow on the way. In the spring of 1938, nineteen-year-old Harry Warren Jr. came down with pneumonia and died within a day. His grief-stricken parents left their Beverly Hills home and moved with their daughter into a small rented apartment. But Warren's muse remained constant. Not long after the boy's death, he composed two merry songs: "Jeepers Creepers" and "You Must Have Been a Beautiful Baby," each with lyrics by Johnny Mercer, both charting at number one. Mercer, not yet thirty, had become one of the most sought-after lyric writers in Hollywood. Recently he'd had two big successes with composer Richard Whiting—"Hooray for Hollywood" and "Too Marvelous for Words"—and then, in February 1938, Whiting, a longstanding member of the songwriting fraternity and a particularly close friend of Warren and George Gershwin, died of a heart attack at age forty-six.

As these sad events were taking place, everyone kept a worried eye on Ira Gershwin. He had fallen into depression and ennui after George's death. Kern, recovered now from his own illness, tried to coax him back to work, and Ira provided words to some new Kern melodies, but they were half-hearted efforts. One, "Once There Were Two of Us," might seem to be a reference to George and himself, but it was only a recycled lyric from 1924 about a boy and girl who decide to end their independent lives and become one. When Arlen heard the song he tried to cheer Ira up by using it as the basis of what amounted to a comedy routine. In a homemade recording he declaimed the words backed by a recording of César Franck's solemn *Symphonic Variations*. We don't know if Ira found this funny, but gradually he emerged from the depths and was again socializing with his friends. Ed Jablonski has described recordings made at parties at the home of screenwriter Sonya Levien. On one, Arlen, accompanied by composer Milton Ager, sings two songs from *Porgy and Bess*—"Summertime" and "There's a Boat Dat's Leavin' Soon for New York"—and then Ira asks him to play "Hi-Ho!," a song by George and himself that had gone unused in *Shall We Dance*. As Arlen executes George's complicated piano arrangement, Ira joins in, giving this piece its unofficial premiere. At another Levien party Ira asks Harold to play "I Can't Get Started," which the lyricist had written with Vernon Duke in 1936. When Anya says she'd rather hear her husband sing his and Ted Koehler's new song, "You've Got Me Sitting on a Fence," Ira, amused, calls out, "Oh, Annie, you can sing an obbligato,"[3] which makes her laugh.

On May 19, 1938, Arlen and Harburg signed a contract to write the songs for *The Wizard of Oz*. They received $25,000 for fourteen weeks—far less than RKO had given Kern, the Gershwins, and Berlin for their work on the Astaire–Rogers musicals. But if they weren't getting top money, they were getting a great assignment, because Freed did what no one in Hollywood had ever done before. He brought the songwriters into the filmmaking process and asked for their input every step of the way.

More than a dozen writers worked on the script, but only a few made significant contributions. Langley, in addition to creating Kansas counterparts to the Oz characters, centered the plot around the contest between Dorothy and the Wicked Witch of the West over possession of the slippers. Baum's book had placed more emphasis on the struggle between the Witch and the Wizard for control of the Emerald City. The slippers were silver in the book. Langley made them ruby red. He also loaded the story with extraneous complications. His Witch wants to defeat the Wizard and replace him with her half-witted son, Bulbo, who will then marry the beautiful Sylvia once Sylvia's lover, Florizel, has been magically transformed into the Cowardly Lion. Nothing like that was in Baum's book. When the Langley script was handed to two longtime MGM staff writers, Florence Ryerson and Edgar Allan Woolf, they removed those digressions as well as a lot of extra adventures taken from Baum and came up with a simple storyline that focused on Dorothy's longing to return to Kansas. It was their idea to have her intone, "There's no place like home" as she clicked her heels—an idea Langley hated.

These three—Langley, Ryerson, and Woolf—were the only ones credited as authors of the script. But there was another significant contributor—Yip Harburg. He, like Langley, disliked the "no place like home" motif, preferring satire to sentimentality. Although Freed was far to his right politically, he allowed Harburg to make the Munchkins members in good standing of labor unions. Harburg also mocked the fatuousness of officialdom by writing the scene in which the Wizard—unmasked as a phony—hands out a diploma instead of a brain, a testimonial instead of a heart, and a medal in place of courage. In Baum's book it had been pins and needles for the Scarecrow, a red silk heart for the Tin Man, and a potion for the Lion. But Harburg wanted pointed humor. He was also responsible for casting Bert Lahr as the Cowardly Lion. Knowing Lahr's style and capabilities, he and Arlen wrote "If I Were King of the Forest" for him—the third and funniest of their mock arias. In it Harburg went to town slicing syllables off of words ("'f I, 'f I were king" and "Tho' my tail would lash / I would show compash"), creating lines that were laugh-out-loud funny ("Each rabbit would show respect to me / The chipmunks genuflect to me"), and becoming the first pop lyricist to venture into the absurd ("What makes the hottentot so hot? What put the ape in apricot?"). Matching these virtuoso lyrics was Arlen's clever and equally funny music.

In writing the score for *The Wizard of Oz*, Arlen and Harburg's great insight was that songs could do more than advance the plot. They could *be* the plot. As they saw it, Dorothy's arrival in Oz was not just the moment to go from black and white to Technicolor. It was also, they told Freed, the ideal spot for a ten-minute pop opera whose music and lyrics would introduce the Land of Oz. Freed gave his consent, and the result was a seamless flow of ingratiating words and music. "She's not only merely dead / She's really most sincerely dead," sings the Munchkin coroner.[4] In three weeks they had written this sequence, as well as all of what they called the "lemon-drop songs": "Ding-Dong! The Witch Is Dead," "We're Off to See the Wizard," "If I Only Had a brain/a Heart/the Nerve," "Optimistic Voices" ("You're Out of the woods / You're out of the dark"), and "The Merry Old Land of Oz." That they had a fine time doing it is obvious from their demo recording, which captured them singing raucously, putting the songs over with exuberance and skill.

In addition to the lemon-drop songs and "If I Were King of the Forest," they penned three pieces that didn't make it into the movie, at least not as written. "Lions and Tigers and Bears" was used only in part. "The Jitterbug" was cut entirely. It had been written for a scene devised by Harburg in which pink and blue mosquitos attack Dorothy and her friends on the way to Oz. After it was filmed, the footage, which includes a reel-like dance, was removed from the print and then lost. All that remains is a home movie made by Arlen during a rehearsal, as well as the studio recording and sheet music. Also deleted was music for Dorothy's triumphal return to Oz after the death of the witch.

Otherwise, these songs—so inseparable from the whole that the movie would be unthinkable without them—were used as written. And they'd been created in just a few weeks, leaving two full months to come up with the final composition, a ballad for Judy Garland. Given what they'd already accomplished, one would presume that Arlen and Harburg approached this part of their job with confidence. But they were apprehensive. They needed more than a good song; it had to be a hit—a blockbuster, if possible—to draw people into theaters, just as Churchill's "Some Day My Prince Will Come" had filled seats for *Snow White*. And it couldn't be about what other ballads were about—romantic love. Dorothy didn't have a crush on anyone. She had a vague restlessness, a desire for some indefinable thing that would make life better than it was.

In slow songs the music usually comes first, which is how Harburg and Arlen worked. So the task of beginning this job fell to the composer. And he, burdened by its unusual and nebulous demands, tensed up. In a 1964 interview he told Walter Cronkite what this was like: "Most people don't understand what you're worried about because they think you can do this [*he snaps his fingers*] and out it comes. But when you have to labor, most writers don't like this. It's nice to be gentle about getting at the piano and fooling around a little while and coming up with an idea. But when an idea doesn't come it becomes one of those things that bugs you."[5] Weeks passed, he still had nothing, and his agitation grew—a situation made all the worse by his belief in a capricious muse who might withhold inspiration from him, perhaps permanently. "I can't tell you the misery a composer goes through," Harburg said, "when the whole score is written, but he hasn't got that big theme song that Louis B. Mayer is waiting [for] . . . He surely sweated it out and he couldn't get a tune."[6]

The breakthrough finally came toward the end of their fourteen-week contract. "I said to Mrs. Arlen," he told Cronkite, "'Let's go to Grauman's Chinese . . . You drive the car, I don't feel too well right now.' I wasn't thinking of work. I wasn't consciously thinking of work, I just wanted to relax. And as we drove by Schwab's Drug Store on Sunset I said, 'Pull over! [*Arlen gives an exculpatory laugh*] please*! . . . And we stopped. I really don't know why—bless the muses—and I took out my little bit of manuscript and put down what you know now as 'Over the Rainbow.'"[7] "It was as if the Lord said, 'Well, here it is, now stop worrying about it.'"[8]

Anya turned the car around and they headed home, where Arlen spent the rest of the day working out the idea. He added the simple middle—the "Someday I'll wish upon a star" release that sounds like a child's piano exercise—as well as an eight-bar tag whose final five notes ("Why oh why can't I?") ascend up and up.[9] In the morning he phoned Harburg and asked him to come over.[10] Yip arrived at the Arlen residence and watched as Harold "approached the piano with his usual blue-eyes-to-heaven ritual and played the first eight bars of 'Over the Rainbow.' My heart fell. He played it with such symphonic sweep and bravura that my first reaction was: 'Oh, no, not for little Dorothy! That's for Nelson Eddy.' Harold, always sensitive, never aggressive or defensive, was shattered. His Hillcrest[11] suntan suddenly took flight. I was miserable. I confess with head bowed low: the song almost suffered extinction by me while it was aborning."[12] After that

he tried to get another tune . . . and he worked and worked but always kept coming back and [he said], "You know, this is a great tune, Yip, it's a great tune." And I said, "I know it's great but it's . . . for a big ballad. I love the tune . . . but I can't write it for a little girl" . . . Harold got real worried and anxiety-ridden, so did I . . . When Ira or George were working on a thing and they met an impasse, they'd always call me or they'd call Harold . . . so I called in Ira . . . being a third person, and more clear-headed and less involved, Ira said . . . "Harold, will you play that tune with a little more rhythm?" And Harold sat down, said, "What do you mean? This way?" . . . and then the thing cleared itself up for me. Ira said, "It's just the way Harold's playing." But . . . we were both too intense to have figured that thing out . . . I said . . . "Gee, you're right, Ira. That's fine."

I knew I wanted something with "rainbow" in it. Now, the original *Wizard of Oz* book had no reference to "rainbow" at all, nowhere in the book, but it did say that the soil of [Kansas] was arid . . . flowers didn't grow, it was a very arid place, cyclones always blew everything away. And so I said where would a little girl like that at twelve want to run to when she was in trouble and want to run away from her parents . . . Well, the only colorful thing in her life would have been . . . a rainbow . . . I would imagine [her thinking] . . . "There's a colorful place to run to. I wish I were somewhere away from here, some colorful place, maybe over that rainbow, beyond the rainbow." I didn't have "over" . . . I had "the other side of the rainbow" and it didn't fit.[13]

Harburg said, "I tried I'll go over the rainbow, Someday over the rainbow or on the other side of the rainbow . . . For a while I thought I would just leave those first two notes out."[14]

At that point Edelaine Gorney stepped in. By 1939 she'd left Jay Gorney and switched to Yip, although it would be a few years before they married. Yip "revered Eddie's opinion about writing," says her son, Dr. Rod Gorney,

> and often in lectures referred to her as his most important collaborator, "the woman with whom I share my bed, board, and thesaurus" . . . When he and Harold were working on "Over the Rainbow," Yip was agitated because he couldn't find the right words for the first two notes. So he sang her the song with the first two syllables, "Lah-lah." Wanting to quell his increasing distress, Eddie suddenly sang, "Some-where, over the rainbow." Yip exclaimed, "That's it!" and sang it himself. For years, Yip repeatedly begged Eddie's permission to put her name along with his on the sheet music, but she always refused, saying diffidently, "Don't be silly, it's your song."[15]

Somehow, Harburg had been able to put the meaning of Arlen's music into words.[16] And in an even less explicable way, Arlen had come up with a handful of notes that have meant more to people than those of any other song. It isn't known if he or his father ever considered it ironic that while the cantor toiled week in and week out at the synagogue, adhering to Sabbath and Kashrut law, improvising music as he davened on behalf of his congregation, it was to his wayward son, as he and his shiksa wife drove along Sunset Boulevard toward garish Grauman's Chinese Theatre, that the miracle had been granted.[17]

"Over the Rainbow" was in the movie's opening scene, which was the final one to be filmed. The principal director, Victor Fleming, had been re-assigned to MGM's other big movie in progress, *Gone with the Wind*, and replaced by veteran director King Vidor. It was Vidor who decided that Judy Garland should walk around the farmyard as she sang and not stand still, as was often the case with singers in movies. He staged the song perfectly. And Murray Cutter's orchestration was perfect, too. But Judy Garland's performance was more than that; it was so good that "Over the Rainbow" became associated with her and not with Arlen or Harburg. "When others sang," wrote Hugh Martin, "there was always an unspoken assumption that there had been a writer, or writers, who had created the song now being sung. When Judy sang a song, that assumption seemed to vanish. Something else was happening. The song seemed to be emerging for the first time, not by way of anyone's pen or piano but straight from the heart of the girl herself."[18]

After a sneak preview at a theater in Santa Barbara, studio executives concluded the film was too long and that's when "The Jitterbug" was removed. Arlen and Harburg hadn't been at that preview but were at the next one in the Los Angeles suburb of Pomona, and Anya squeezed Harold's hand when his name appeared in the opening credits. Then came the first scene with dialogue written by Harburg to set up the ballad. His words rhymed toward the end, smoothing the transition into music. "Help us out today," Aunt Em tells Dorothy, "and find yourself a place where you won't get into trouble." Dorothy, alone now, responds with words addressed to her dog: "Someplace where there isn't any trouble. Do you suppose there is such a place, Toto? There must be. It's not a place you can get to by a boat or a train / It's far, far away / Behind the moon / Beyond the rain." And then—no song. It had been cut. The Arlens and Harburg returned in shock to Beverly Hills. The following day, Freed, also shaken, got Mayer to agree to put the song back in. But at the next preview, it was still missing. Freed demanded another meeting and this time faced not just Mayer but Mayer's assistant, Sam Katz, executive producer Eddie Mannix, and MGM's sheet music publisher Jack Robbins. All four told him the song slowed the picture down, that it had been foolishly set in an ugly barnyard, and that it was too complex to be grasped by the public. Freed's response was, "Rainbow stays or I go."[19] He didn't have much leverage; he was still just a staff songwriter. But he was at work on the next Garland musical, *Babes in Arms*, which paired her with Mickey Rooney, and was looking like a moneymaker. Knowing it would be stupid to let him go, they allowed the song back in. And at the next screening, when the movie ended, the audience, after a moment of stunned silence, broke into applause and then cheers.

CHAPTER 13

AN ITINERANT SONGWRITER

The songs written for *The Wizard of Oz* marked the culmination of a decade in which the American popular song became an art form. It seems in retrospect that such an achievement ought to have ushered in the day when the careers of songwriters were taken as seriously as those of symphonic composers, novelists, and painters. But that didn't happen. Despite all the great popular songs of the 1930s, no songwriter was looked on as an artist whose body of work could be assessed as an oeuvre. No one was asking, "What will Arlen do next?"

Songwriters had limited and usually no control over stage or film productions. They were always hamstrung. Their imaginations might point to an interesting place, but they couldn't go there without the approval of those who controlled the money. That situation, however, was changing. In early 1940 Irving Berlin, as he wrote his first book musical, *Louisiana Purchase*, worked closely with the librettists and had final say about casting. Later that year, when John O'Hara suggested to Richard Rodgers that his *New Yorker* stories about a nightclub gigolo might make an interesting musical, the only thing needed to set the project in motion was a yes from Rodgers and Hart. Given their track record, there was no doubt they'd get the money to make *Pal Joey*. And during rehearsals Rodgers further asserted his authority when he had a disagreement with the show's producer, George Abbott, and fired him, at least temporarily. Songwriters picking their own plots, hiring their own casts, firing their producers—this was new, and it heralded the day when they would be the driving force in popular music.

Arlen and Harburg didn't have the clout of Rodgers and Hart. *The Wizard of Oz* had been well under way when Freed picked them to write its songs. And without Freed running interference for them, "Over the Rainbow" would have ended up on the cutting-room floor. Harburg understood this and craved the power that would bring artistic freedom. But Arlen didn't think in those terms. Riding herd on a bunch of touchy writers, directors, actors, and technicians was a horrifying prospect to him. He only wanted to write songs. He was an artist of the eighteenth-century type—an artisan who sent his work into the world knowing it would be enjoyed by people who had no idea who he was.

In the meantime, "Over the Rainbow" went to the top of the charts. A few days after *The Wizard of Oz*'s premiere in August 1939 it was number one and stayed there to become the biggest song of the year—the year of Berlin's "God Bless America" and Glenn Miller's "Moonlight Serenade." That summer, Arlen accompanied Garland in a live radio performance of what was now her signature song. A few months later, in February 1940, he and Harburg were at the Ambassador Hotel to accept an Oscar for the song. And a few months after that, at the Golden Gate International Exposition on Treasure Island in San Francisco Bay, he and Garland again performed it to a national radio audience—a memorable moment that has been preserved on records.

During the filming of *Wizard*, MGM transferred Arlen and Harburg to the Marx Brothers' *At the Circus*, where they turned out to be as good at writing for Groucho as they'd been for Lahr. In "Lydia, the Tattooed Lady," Marx brags about all the history and geography he's learned from his lady friend's tattoos. It's an infectious tune. When Arlen was demonstrating it for a producer, he heard a commotion as he sat at the piano and he stopped, swiveled, and saw the man dancing around the office. Groucho was particularly pleased with Harburg's leering rhymes. When the Motion Picture Code's enforcers balked at their lewdness, Harburg came up with a twist ending: "She once swept an Admiral clear off his feet / The ships on her hips made his heart skip a beat / And now the old boy's in command of the fleet / For he went and married Lydia"—"married" being the word that kept the song in the movie.

At this point, the Arlen–Harburg team might have reasonably expected another big Hollywood assignment. Yet none came. In fact, in 1940 they found themselves back at square one waiting for a job, any job, as they lived off their royalties and ASCAP distributions. Harburg hated being at loose ends and returned to New York, where he teamed with Burton Lane to write a musical, *Hold on to Your Hats*. It was an old-fashioned Broadway effort. They were subservient not only to the Shubert Brothers, who produced the show and owned the theater, but to Al Jolson, who as star and co-producer had the power to halt the performance midway every evening, step in front of the curtain, and sing a selection of his hits, going all the way back to

"Swanee" from 1919. Ira wrote a commiserating letter to Yip: "I have heard from many sources that the reason your score isn't selling as well as it might is because when Jolson goes into his medley one is apt to forget the earlier songs whether they are by Harburg–Lane or Beethoven–Goethe."[1]

Perhaps because he'd been a jazz musician, Arlen was more accustomed than Harburg to time off between gigs. Loving sunshine and golf, he remained in California and waited patiently for his next job. Nothing big turned up, but he got an offer from composer-conductor Meredith Willson, who hosted a national radio program, the *Maxwell House Good News Hour*. Willson had been asking pop composers to write song-length symphonic works for his show. Because war was now a fact in Europe and a threat to America, he wanted these compositions to have patriotic themes. After Duke Ellington contributed *American Lullaby*, Arlen decided to write one called *American Minuet*. The idea of studying the eighteenth-century dance form and adapting it to modern harmonic language intrigued him. He was also hoping that Anya might dance to it in a movie or onstage. Like *Mood in Six Minutes*, he wrote it for piano and left the orchestration to someone else—we don't know who, maybe Willson himself. It was broadcast in December of 1939, recorded by Willson, published, and then forgotten—which is a shame, because it's an endearing piece with old-time harmonies that are amusingly freshened now and then with modern chords.

American Minuet was one of a series of stand-alone compositions written by Arlen during the period following *The Wizard of Oz*. He wrote "I'll Supply the Title, You'll Supply the Tune" with Ira Gershwin for the same reason Kern had written with Gershwin—to lift him out of his depression and get him back to work. Although the lyric survived, the music was thought to have been lost until pianist Kevin Cole discovered it half a century later among Arlen's papers. It was published then and recorded, but it's not a major effort. The other works in this series of miscellanies were written with Ted Koehler. They had been collaborating again on and off since 1937, beginning with "Public Melody Number One," which was sung in the 1937 film *Artists and Models*. Then came "Love's a Necessary Thing," "Lonesome and Low," and "Like a Straw in the Wind." In these songs they wrote in their low-down Cotton Club manner—although one of their songs, "Sing My Heart," was a ballad in the style of Kern from his operetta days. And Kern loved it. It was introduced by Irene Dunne in the film *Love Affair* and has since become a minor standard.

After that came two Arlen–Koehler pieces that would be the culmination of their work together.

In the first, "When the Sun Comes Out," placid Koehler and easygoing Arlen created something urgent, even desperate. The melodic leap in "Stormy Weather" had been downward and sad, the one in "Over the Rainbow" upward and full of longing. In this song it's a scary ascent—a tritone that sounds like a howl. Arlen and Koehler wrote it without a venue in mind. They published it and hoped for the best. A few bands paid attention—there was a notable recording by Helen O'Connell singing with the Jimmy Dorsey Orchestra—but it failed to catch on and has only gradually gained favor as musicians recognize its power.

Next, they wrote a song cycle. It began in 1938 when Arlen composed what sounded to him like a Negro spiritual. He and Koehler turned it into a rouser, "Big Time Comin,'" but did nothing with it except, over the next three years, add five others, some up-tempo, some slow. They seemed in these songs to be remembering *Porgy and Bess* with *recitative* sections that were similar in style to Gershwin's. And, as with the Gershwin opera, a lullaby was at the heart of the work. But Koehler lacked the finesse of Gershwin's collaborator, South Carolina–born DuBose Heyward, when it came to this subject matter. Heyward had worked alongside southern blacks, attended their church services, studied their speech. Even with all that and with the best of intentions, he wrote some lines that, while not intentionally racist, became, with time, increasingly embarrassing. Koehler had an even tougher time of it. He called his and Arlen's lullaby "Little Ace o' Spades" and rhymed "kinky head" with "inky head." Moreover, the cycle was named *Americanegro Suite*—a phrase that had no negative connotations at the time but would work against the piece in later years. Arlen's contribution, however, was never less than beautiful. When he went to Kern's home to play the suite for him, Kern, visibly moved, made a gift to him of one of his treasures—a hand-carved cane that had belonged to operetta composer Jacques Offenbach, the son of a cantor. In a similar fashion and at around the same time, Ira gave Arlen George's final painting, a portrait of Kern.

Americanegro Suite was published in 1941 as a bound musical score with illustrations by Henry A. Botkin, the latter a cousin of the Gershwins. It received no public performances and remains all but unknown today. If it had an effect on Arlen's career, it was to further categorize him as a blues composer. In *The Wizard of Oz*, Herbert Stothart and his team of orchestrators had tipped their hats to him by making the first few notes of the overture, heard above the roar of MGM's lion, a bluesy riff. Not that Arlen was only or even primarily a blues writer or that he ever used a strict twelve-bar blues structure. But with roots in both black gospel and Jewish liturgical music, there was real melancholy in his music; his songs had the sincerity and authenticity of the blues. He'd always had a tendency toward gloom—Harburg recognized it when he first met him a decade earlier—and now, in the early 1940s, it reasserted itself and gained the upper hand.

He was having problems with Anya. Theirs weren't the usual marital troubles. They didn't cheat on each other or argue about money. They hadn't fallen out of love. If anything, there was too much love: she'd grown clingy. She wanted him with her all the time, and that meant with her in the house, because she no longer enjoyed going out. She had no interest in golf—his new passion. She was no longer comfortable at Beverly Hills parties. Some people, especially "Leonore Gershwin and her faction," as Jablonski put it,[2] made her especially uneasy. Harold still enjoyed going to the Gershwins', but with George gone and Leonore in power, Anya went only reluctantly. A few years earlier she'd enjoyed herself there and would, on occasion, even sing and dance for everyone. Now Harold usually went alone while she stayed home anxiously awaiting his return. She spent her days dabbling at watercolors, rearranging furniture, sitting at the mirror brushing her hair—sometimes for hours at a time. Sleeping pills kept her in bed until the late morning, sometimes into the afternoon. The few friends she had were people who'd taken pity on her. Edelaine Gorney provided empathy on the phone. Fanny Brice came over to help her redecorate. But something awful was happening to her, and no one could stop it.

Harold didn't discuss Anya's changed behavior with his friends, and they avoided the subject in his presence. Among themselves, however, they wondered if he was too proud to admit that his mother and father had been right, that she had been wrong for him. They attributed her moods to frustration over a career that had never gotten off the ground. Back in 1936, after *Strike Me Pink*, a trade paper, *The Film Daily*, reported that she, "one of the Goldwyn Girls, has been signed for a dramatic role for the forthcoming production *These Three* in support of Miriam Hopkins, Merle Oberon and Joel McCrea." But her role in that film was so small, only people who knew her personally could identify her onscreen. After that there were no parts for four years. Then, in 1941, something turned up. The June edition of *Film Fun* magazine devoted its cover to a photo of her with a caption that read, "Meet the Chorus in the *Ziegfeld Girl*." But her contribution to this film, which starred Judy Garland and James Stewart, was negligible, and it was her final screen appearance.

Another of her disturbing new moods was jealousy. It sometimes flared into rage even though Harold had shown no interest in other women. Tension at home had always been his bête noir, and he invariably responded to it by getting away. His principal refuge this time was the golf course at the Hillcrest Country Club. This was a Jewish preserve, as Jews were excluded from other Southern California clubs. He was captivated by golf in the way he'd once been fascinated by medicine. "I started playing golf out in California with Jack Benny and Groucho and all of the boys," he said in a 1955 interview in *The New Yorker*.

> I played it hard from 1945 to 1951. It's a game that gives you the feeling you're sure to be victorious over it someday, but, of course, you never are. I'd begin at seven-thirty in the morning. At nine I'd tee off for eighteen holes and play until twelve-thirty. After lunch, I'd have a lesson, then play another eighteen holes. Then I'd return home, eat dinner, and go for a ride, ending up at a driving range. After lining out balls for an hour or two, I'd go home, get into bed, and read a book about golf. The game consumed me but I never broke eighty. The lowest handicap I ever got was eighteen.[3]

This, of course, left little time for Anya. Yet they could still be happy together, as is apparent from a home recording made in the summer of 1941. On it, Koehler can be heard laughing and applauding as Arlen announces, "Introducing Anyushka Barabunchik Carumba singing Ted Koehlerovich und Harold Arlenovich's new bahl-lahde." This was a Russian-sounding melody that was never published or given lyrics. Anya sings it without words, and when she throws in a Russian phrase Harold responds with, "What all dot mean?" He concludes by apologizing for not playing it "for Anyushka Barabunchik Taranda in her right key." "You said it!" she laughs. "And she feels like a fool," he adds, "and has purrfect right. I ahm very sorreee! Dobre noche!"[4]

This recording, wrote Jablonski, captured "a happy, playful moment in the summer of 1941, when Anya and Harold Arlen, that 'ideal Hollywood couple,' were light-hearted with a happy future ahead." He follows this with the ominous words, "But that was then."[5] Harold could see he was losing her—not to someone else, but to something in her she couldn't control. And as she disappeared in plain sight, he became a drinker. He'd go off by himself and get drunk to escape.

CHAPTER 14

WRITING WITH JOHNNY MERCER

With no opportunity to follow up on his pioneering work for *The Wizard of Oz* or do an innovative stage show, Arlen continued to drift from assignment to assignment, accepting what came along, no matter how mundane. In mid-1941 Warner Bros. asked him to write the songs for a low-budget movie about a much-discussed topic of the time: how can you tell if you're hearing real jazz? Earlier that year Paramount had made a successful picture on this subject, *The Birth of the Blues*, starring Bing Crosby. Warner Bros. wanted to do one, too, so they hired Arlen for the music and paired him with lyricist Johnny Mercer, who'd been under contract to them since 1937. The two men had collaborated once before, on the 1932 song "Satan's Li'l Lamb," written with Harburg for the Broadway revue *Americana*. Now, nine years later, Mercer, at thirty-two, was a top-flight lyricist whose catalog included "Lazy Bones" (music by Hoagy Carmichael), "Goody Goody" (Matt Melneck), "I'm an Old Cowhand from the Rio Grande" (music by Mercer himself), "Hooray for Hollywood" and "Too Marvelous for Words" (Richard Whiting), "You Must Have Been a Beautiful Baby" and "Jeepers Creepers" (Harry Warren), "When the Angels Sing" (Ziggy Elman), "Day In, Day Out" (Rube Bloom), and "I Thought about You" (music by Jerry Arlen's onetime partner James Van Heusen).

Mercer and Arlen were like mirror images of each other. Each was from a midsize and out-of-the-way city. But Mercer's Savannah symbolized the laid-back South, while Arlen's Buffalo was the industrial North. Both grew up in comfortable circumstances. But Arlen's parents had been poor immigrants, while Mercer came from landed gentry who traced their lineage back to Hugh Mercer, a general under George Washington who'd died sword in hand at the Battle of Princeton. Mercer, unlike Arlen, had known poverty. When his father's business failed he couldn't afford to go to Princeton University—a family tradition—but went to work instead, and his low point came as a struggling actor and songwriter in New York when he lived in an apartment so tiny he had to put a board over his toilet to have a kitchen table.

They were similarly imbued with African American music. Both had grown up with black playmates, listened to music in African American churches, and searched for stores that sold "race" recordings, and each had a singing style that combined his own heritage with jazz and blues. Like Arlen, Mercer could write a good tune, although he refused to learn the piano or any other instrument and balked before the mysteries of music notation, which kept him, in the days before tape recorders, from converting the sounds in his head into musical notes. He did manage to come up with a few great melodies but mostly confined himself to lyric writing, which he'd been doing since boyhood.

Mercer's wife was a Broadway chorine of Jewish heritage, a fact that affected his devout Episcopalian parents much as Harold's marriage to a Russian Orthodox showgirl affected the Arlucks. Her stage name was Ginger Meehan, but she'd been born in Brooklyn as Elizabeth Meltzer and couldn't visit Mercer's family or Savannah in general without experiencing the undertow of anti-Semitism. Eventually, she stopped going. He continued to return home again and again throughout his life.

These similarities even extended to the lives of their siblings. Mercer's mother, whom people called Miss Lillian, talked her son-in-law, Henry Gilbert Keith, into settling in Savannah rather than in his hometown of Detroit. That way she could keep her daughter, Juliana, by her side. Johnny's father, George Mercer, employed Keith in his real estate business, but when he died, Miss Lillian took Keith off the payroll and harassed him so much he returned to Detroit minus his wife and daughter, leaving them with Lillian, which is what she'd intended. "There was something not exactly 'right' about my mother," Johnny Mercer wrote in an unfinished autobiography.[1] The Arlen side of this coin came when Samuel Arluck, after an initially favorable impression of Jerry's wife Jeanne, turned on her. In January 1939, three years into their marriage, he wrote Harold: "Your sister-in-law . . . is certainly trying to make the impression that she is the angel and your brother the devil. Well, I know different . . . if your brother is satisfied with her that's his business. I don't want any part of same because I despise her, she fits in on the East Side on Rivington or Hester Street . . . as long as my eyes will be open I will never have anything to do with her."[2] The problem, apparently, was that Jerry was having a hard time making a living, and Jeanne wasn't helping. In 1940 they moved from a small apartment in Lower Manhattan to a boardinghouse on West 88th Street, where, according to that year's census, Jerry was an unemployed "musical director, orchestral" and Jeanne, with no listed occupation, wasn't working or looking for work.

By 1941, when Warner Bros. teamed Arlen and Mercer, each was a heavy drinker. Arlen drank alone to deal with depression. Mercer drank in night-clubs and at parties where alcohol released his id, allowing him to lash out. Drunk, he could call his wife a kike, dump a drink on her head, make racist remarks to and about black people. At one party he walked up to Irving Berlin, his childhood idol, and told him he couldn't write a good lyric. At another he opened a closet door and urinated on his host's shoes. His apologies always came the next day and he was invariably forgiven, it being the universal consensus that the real Johnny was the sober one—a kind, generous, and broad-minded man. He was, in fact, one of the best-loved people in the music business, as was Arlen.

Both had troubled marriages, and neither divorced. But here, too, there was a significant difference. Anya was sick. In years to come she'd be insti-tutionalized for mental illness and eventually diagnosed with and die from a brain tumor. At this point Harold didn't know any of that; he only knew she'd become unlike herself: moody, fearful, prone to jealous rages. When others were present, he suffered in silence. When it was just the two of them he escaped—to his music, friends, golf, but not to other women. Anya was the one he wanted. And sometimes, miraculously, she was Anya once again as she used to be. With Johnny and Ginger it was different. They fought constantly. She, too, was an alcoholic, so it was rare for each to be in a good mood at the same time. Most devastating to their marriage was his belief that she was boring. Like Anya, she had few interests of her own. She wasn't a witty or even a passable conversationalist.[3] At parties, people gravitated toward him and away from her. Comedian and songwriter Steve Allen, who knew them both well, said, "Although I found it easy enough to talk to John I cannot recall a single comfortable conversational exchange with Ginger."[4] By 1941 they'd been married a decade, and Mercer, longing for another love, fell for eighteen-year-old Judy Garland. According to his biographer, Philip Furia, what he really wanted in a woman was the attribute "most truly at the center of Judy Garland—not the svelte sex goddess she wanted to be but the gifted artist that friends such as Phil Silvers, Mickey Rooney, and Gene Kelly, who could not bring themselves to love her romantically, adored in her."[5] Johnny's affair with her shocked and outraged Ginger. It also appalled two good friends of the Mercers: Jimmy Downey, who had been a childhood friend of Johnny's in Savannah, and his wife Betty. It was Betty Downey who took it upon herself to go to MGM, walk into Judy's dressing room, and tell her the affair had to end. Judy listened and agreed. She had, after all, just married composer-conductor David Rose. Moreover, if word got out that she was having an affair with a married man, the public, who still saw her as the girl who'd gone to Oz, and her studio, which was selling her now as the virginal girl next door, might have abandoned her. So she broke it off with Mercer, and it was probably the worst moment of his life. He never left Ginger, but Judy was the one he really loved, and it was torture for him not to have her.

These, then, were the men hired by Warner Bros. to write the songs for a picture tentatively titled *Hot Nocturne*. One of the numbers, it was hoped, would be a genuine blues song. Among the ongoing discussions about jazz at the time was a debate about whether white people could be true jazz or blues musicians. If Warner was trying to settle the question in the affirmative, they picked the right two white songwriters.

In the film, an impoverished combo plays real jazz while a commercial band hits the big time with inauthentic swing. Arlen and Mercer wrote a song for each group: "Hang On to Your Lids, Kids" for the true jazzmen and their vocalist, Priscilla Lane, and "Says Who? Says You, Says I!" for the ersatz players. But each song is so full of good riffs that no one would have been the wiser had the bands swapped them. Also in the score was a memorable ballad, "This Time the Dream's on Me," sung by Lane. In its lyric, as Furia has pointed out, Mercer takes the phrase "This time the drink's on me" and replaces "drink" with "dream," hinting at "the comforting but impossible dream of a future reunion" with Judy.[6] Arlen, as if to remind people of "Over the Rainbow," begins with an octave rise. But this time there's no poignancy or pain, only romance.

Arlen and Mercer saved writing the most important song for last, just as Arlen and Harburg had done in *The Wizard of Oz*. Although this movie didn't have the budget or prestige of the earlier one, both men wanted the song to be special. Arlen later recalled that the film's script

called for the jazz band to be in jail, and for a black man in the cell next to them to sing the blues. So I said to myself, any jazz musician can put his *foot* on a piano and write a blues song! I've got to write one that sounds authentic, that sounds as if it were born in New Orleans or St. Louis. So I did a little very minor research. I found out that the blues was always written in three stanzas, with twelve bars each. That was the first thing. Then I told my late wife—it was the only time I ever said such a thing to her, bless her—"Don't trouble me, don't bother me, until I knock or come into the house." I had a little studio off behind the place. It took me a day and a half. That's long for me . . . but I knew I could write a blues. Along the way, I got this little notion. You know how it is sometimes when you're writing—you get an idea and it works itself out. Sometimes it stumbles. Not this one . . . here I am with this notion, a musical idea, and, brother, the fires went up and the whole thing *poured* out . . . And I hollered, "Annie!" She came down and listened. She always listened . . . she was always there. And I played it and I knew in my guts, without even thinking of what John could write for a lyric, that this was strong, strong, *strong!*[7]

He took it to Mercer's house and played it for him, then went away and left the lyricist alone with it for a little while. He knew that Johnny liked to lie on a sofa and think about a lyric, sometimes for hour after hour. Because of this, Arlen had taken to using Harry Warren's nickname for him, "Cloud Boy."

"I came back later," Arlen said, "and he had written it down. He had everything as you know it today except the first twelve bars!"[8] Mercer's opening, "I'm heavy in my heart, I'm heavy in my heart," disappointed the composer, but as Arlen read on he came to "My mama done told me / When I was in knee pants" and knew that was it. Mercer agreed, and during the coming days he completed one of popular song's greatest lyrics. He wrote about a man who rides a nighttime train hoping it can outrace his despair. The man travels "From Natchez to Mobile / From Memphis to St. Joe," but the train can't take him past his problems: "A woman's a two-face / A worrisome thing who'll leave ya t' sing the Blues in the Night."

The only thing to do at that point was settle on a title. Arlen wanted "My Mama Done Told Me" but Mercer favored "Blues in the Night." They took the matter to Irving Berlin, who sided with Johnny. Thus "Blues in the Night" became the song's title as well as the title of the film, replacing *Hot Nocturne.*

In their excitement, Arlen and Mercer, anxious to try the piece out, dropped in on the family of Richard Whiting, Mercer's late songwriting partner. Whiting's widow, Eleanor, and her seventeen-year-old daughter, Margaret, had become like family to him, and he knew that Margaret was a talented singer. As it turned out, the Whitings were not alone that evening. Margaret later described the scene:

Mickey Rooney was there, and Judy Garland, Martha Raye, an old friend, and Mel Tormé. Around nine-thirty or ten Harold and Johnny came by, they'd just finished the song, and they went to our piano and did 'Blues' for the first time. Well, I want to tell you, it was like a Paramount Pictures finish—socko, boffo, *wham*! At one end of the room, Martha Raye almost passed out; for once, she didn't have a funny line. Tormé was so knocked out by the musicianship, he just sat there. Mickey Rooney kept saying, 'My God, this is unbelievable!' And Judy and I raced over to the piano to see which of us could learn the song first! You knew right away the song was so *important.*[9]

"Blues in the Night" is a traditional blues for its first twelve bars. Then come forty-six measures that dispense with every songwriting convention. It was, wrote Alec Wilder, "a landmark in the evolution of American popular music."[10] Although he had previously written songs that went beyond thirty-two bars—"Stormy Weather," for instance—Arlen had never written anything like this. It has two separate releases ("Now the rain's a fallin'" and "The evenin' breeze"), a section to be hummed, and another to be whistled. Like the train ride it describes, it offers one point of interest after another, and it does so in an audacious manner previously unknown in popular or blues songs.

It was nominated for an Academy Award but lost to Kern and Hammerstein's "The Last Time I Saw Paris." Kern had an odd reaction to his own win: anger. He felt that Arlen and Mercer should have taken the prize. His song had begun as a poem by Hammerstein in June 1940 after the Germans marched into Paris. Hammerstein then asked him to set it to music, and the result was published, recorded, and popular before it was inserted into the movie *Lady Be Good*. Kern felt it shouldn't have been in the running given those circumstances, that the honor ought to have gone to a song written expressly for the movies. He talked the Motion Picture Academy into changing its rules so that such interpolations would never win again. Actually, the Oscar could have plausibly gone to a couple of the other nominated songs: "Baby Mine" written for Disney's *Dumbo*, with lyrics by Ned Washington and music by Frank Churchill (who won for scoring that movie), and "Chattanooga Choo Choo" from *Sun Valley Serenade*, with lyrics by Mack Gordon and music by Harry Warren. That the prize went to "The Last Time I Saw Paris" was probably because of its connection to the war. Between the time it was written and the awards ceremony twenty months later, World War II had come to America with Japan's December 7, 1941, attack on Pearl Harbor.

CHAPTER 15

"One for My Baby"

The military draft went into effect in September 1940, more than a year before the United States entered the war. Men between the ages of twenty-one and thirty-five were required to register. Arlen, thirty-five at the time, wasn't called up and didn't volunteer. Jerry was drafted in 1942 when he was thirty, passed the physical, and joined the Army Air Forces. Of the approximately five million American Jews at the time, about half a million entered the military and eleven thousand would be killed in action. Samuel Arluck, afraid, "unleashed a torrent of letters from Syracuse demanding that Harold do something for his younger brother."[1]

Harold, as his father knew, had connections that would keep Jerry out of danger. One was composer-conductor David Rose, now a sergeant in the Army Air Forces, who was putting together a show, *Winged Victory*, for Army Emergency Relief. At Harold's request, Rose had Jerry transferred to this project. He became a saxophonist in the pit orchestra of the musical, whose long run on Broadway began in November 1943. For the rest of the war he was out of danger. Perhaps he'd wanted it this way, but it meant that once again he hadn't been his own man. For years he'd tried and failed to establish himself as a musician while envying his brother's success, and now he was dependent on Harold's connections. It wasn't an easy role. And to make things worse, he had to look on as his former songwriting partner, Jimmy Van Heusen, managed to do it all during the war years—spending his days in Burbank as a test pilot flying Lockheed's experimental military aircraft, and his nights writing one song hit after another with lyricist Johnny Burke: "Polka Dots and Moonbeams," "Swinging on a Star," "Moonlight Becomes You," "It Could Happen to You," "Aren't You Glad You're You?" Van Heusen had attached himself to Bing Crosby as he later would to Frank Sinatra—associations that were mutually beneficial and the closest thing a songwriter could have to guaranteed employment.

Arlen's output of great songs during the war years would be even more impressive than Van Heusen's, but unlike Van Heusen, he couldn't find a way to anchor his career. Like most songwriters of his era, he was an itinerant. This was true of even so august a figure as Kern, who was still going from lyricist to lyricist, studio to studio, assignment to assignment. Arlen, after writing *Blues in the Night* with Mercer for Warner Bros., spent nearly a year lurching from "Heave Ho! Let the Wind Blow!" with Harburg for MGM (a sea chantey for Burt Lahr, but unused) to "The Moment I Laid Eyes on You" and other songs with Koehler (unused by any studio), "Captains of the Clouds" with Mercer for a Warner Bros. film of that name, and "Long Before You Came Along" with Harburg for an MGM Abbott and Costello movie, *Rio Rita*. None of those songs caught on.

Van Heusen wasn't the only songwriter who figured out how to get job security. Harry Warren spent eight years at Warner Bros. and then had lengthy contracts with Twentieth Century Fox and MGM. Hoagy Carmichael became an actor and was in a series of movies that featured him as a pianist playing his own songs. Rodgers and Hart established themselves on Broadway with shows that were so innovative and surprising they became both eagerly anticipated and lucrative. But Johnny Mercer was the one who happened on an idea that would eventually solve the problem of how songwriters could have careers like other artists.

It began with his wish to find steady work for some of his favorite singers and musicians. Because of his own success singing on a weekly radio program, *Swing Time*, he came up with the idea of a new broadcast that would feature Jo Stafford, Martha Tilton, Margaret Whiting, Mel Tormé, and Nat King Cole. That notion took an unexpected turn when his wife hired a man to install a radio in his car. That man was Glenn Wallichs, an electronics wizard who subsequently opened Wallichs Music City at Sunset and Vine in Hollywood. It was an unusual store. Not only did it sell records and sheet music, it had rooms where customers could listen to recordings before buying them. It also had a recording booth in which people could make their own demos. Mercer dropped by one day, got into a conversation with Wallichs, and came up with an idea. Why not form their own record company? He'd be the talent scout, Wallichs the technician, and they could go for seed money to Mercer's songwriter friend B. G. "Buddy" DeSylva, now doing very well as head of production at Paramount Pictures.

The result was Capitol Records, the first major record company on the West Coast. It was also the first founded by and for artists. By the spring of 1942 it was a going concern and a place where musicians could work in a supportive, adventuresome, and joyous atmosphere. Had Mercer thought about where this idea might ultimately go—that, for instance, he and Arlen could now write a song or a collection of songs whose premiere would be on shellac (or, soon, vinyl) rather than on Broadway or in a movie—the history of popular music might have taken a different turn. But that idea was for the next generation—the one that ended Mercer and Arlen's Tin Pan Alley style of songwriting.

The coming demise of Arlen's era was also accelerated when, in 1940, ASCAP doubled the licensing fees it charged radio stations, causing many of them to turn instead to an upstart licensing group, Broadcast Music, Inc. (BMI). Radio stations needed licenses from ASCAP if they wanted to broadcast songs by ASCAP members. That organization monitored all such performances, gave its members ratings based on how often their songs were performed, and distributed the fees accordingly.[2] This was significant not just for Arlen and others who had high ratings and received big distributions, but also for writers who'd had fewer hit songs and who, because of ASCAP, were kept out of poverty. ASCAP also helped rescue nonmember musicians. When Hungarian composer Béla Bartók arrived in New York in 1940, a refugee from the Nazis, destitute and suffering from leukemia, money from ASCAP paid his expenses as he wrote his final great works. But by doubling their licensing fees, they overplayed their hand. The established writers of Broadway and Hollywood stayed with them, but BMI's membership came mostly from lesser-known and regional artists, including country and blues musicians who would become the forerunners of rock and roll—an era now just a decade away.

In 1942 James Petrillo, head of the American Federation of Musicians, took his union out on strike against the record companies, who were still mainly recording ASCAP songs. For two years his musicians were prohibited from making records, although some of the companies, including Capitol Records, settled with the union in 1943. Because Petrillo's prohibition applied to instrumentalists and not singers, vocalists who had been secondary attractions now became more prominent. Many of them issued records backed only by other singers, leading to the decline of the Big Band era and paving the way for the doo-wop groups of the 1950s. Also, the strike did not apply to recordings made before 1942, allowing Columbia Records to take advantage of Frank Sinatra's growing popularity by rereleasing his 1939 recording of "All or Nothing at All" (music by Arthur Altman, lyrics by Jack Lawrence), made with Harry James's band. It hadn't done much for Sinatra's career the first time around, but now it pushed him into mega-stardom as a solo artist and as the first teen idol. The Sinatra phenomenon, the rise of vocal groups, and the growing audience for small BMI-affiliated bands were changes that helped usher in the era of rock and roll.

And there was one more musical upheaval at this time—one that struck a blow *for* the musical style that had begun with Kern and Berlin. It came from a most unexpected and ironic source—the end of the Rodgers and Hart partnership. Although Hart's talent was intact, his alcoholism and depression had taken their toll and he was less able to work. After *Pal Joey* in 1940, which he and Rodgers considered their finest show, he went into a last downward spiral. That show's downbeat, noirish story had made it less than a smash hit, and when *New York Times* theater critic Brooks Atkinson summed it up with the line, "Can you draw sweet water from a foul well?" Hart, according to Gene Kelly, who played the title role, "broke down, cried, sobbed, because he wanted Atkinson . . . to say this show was a milestone."[3]

By that time, Rodgers was convinced that Hart was on the road to self-destruction and that sticking with him was going to mean the end of his own career. In 1940 he agreed to produce *Best Foot Forward*, a musical by Hugh Martin and Ralph Blane (formerly in the chorus of Arlen and Harburg's *Hooray for What!*). It was the first time he'd worked separately from Hart and the first time he'd taken on the job of producer. That year he also became convinced that Lynn Riggs's 1930 drama *Green Grow the Lilacs* could become a great musical. He believed that its elemental love triangle set in turn-of-the-century Oklahoma could, for a couple of hours, take audiences away from a world at war to a simpler and more hopeful time and place. Knowing that its western setting wouldn't appeal to Hart, he thought about who might like it, and Oscar Hammerstein came to mind. Hammerstein had a taste for distant locales: He'd written about Morocco with Sigmund Romberg in *The Desert Song*, the Canadian Rockies with Rudolf Friml in *Rose-Marie*, and the Mississippi River of the 1890s with Kern in *Show Boat*. Even more auspicious, he was a librettist as well as a lyricist and knew as much or more than anyone about how to construct a book musical. In June 1941, with *Pal Joey* still on Broadway, Rodgers visited the Hammerstein farm in Doylestown, Pennsylvania, where they discussed a partnership. As Rodgers remembered it, Hammerstein told him, "I think you ought to keep working with Larry just as long as he is able to keep working with you. It would kill him if you walked away while he was still able to function. But if the time ever comes when he cannot function, call me. I'll be there."[4] Hart was barely functioning during the writing of his next and final musical with Rodgers, *By Jupiter*, and when Rodgers spoke to him about *Green Grow the Lilacs*, he wasn't interested. So Rodgers and Hammerstein took the Riggs play and turned it into *Oklahoma!*, whose enormous success made the book musical an American art form and the aspiration of every Broadway composer and lyricist. Hart was in the theater the night of its premiere and later that evening told Rodgers at a party, "This is one of the greatest shows I've ever seen in my life, and it'll be playing twenty years from now."[5] He was right, and so was Hammerstein's prediction about him: a few months later, a drinking binge left him sitting in a rainstorm and he caught the pneumonia that killed him at age forty-eight.

Meanwhile, Arlen continued to ply his trade in Hollywood. During the final three years of the war, he went from studio to studio—Paramount to MGM to RKO, then back to MGM and back to Paramount—and from one lyricist to another, Mercer to Harburg to Mercer to Koehler to Harburg and back to Mercer again, as he wrote his songs. They were single songs, unrelated to plot or character or even to each other except that they were among the best ever written.

For *Star Spangled Rhythm*, a flag-waving extravaganza released by Paramount in December 1942, he and Mercer came up with "Hit the Road to Dreamland," whose swinging beat and hip slang make it a lullaby for lovers, not sleepy children. Its music is full of canny touches, like the major seventh given the singer on "Nod" in "Dig you in the land of Nod" that creates an ethereal moment; it's like a jazz dream. They also wrote "That Old Black Magic" for this film. It is even longer than "Blues in the Night" and more adult than "Hit the Road to Dreamland." A bass riff plays insistently as the melody snakes in and out of major and minor chords only to rear up and become one of Arlen's more startling releases ("I should stay away but what can I do"). One doesn't need the words to know it's about sex. But Mercer provides plenty of erotic imagery ("Those icy fingers up and down my spine" and "The same old tingle that I feel inside / And then that elevator starts its ride").

His next musical assignment was the film *Cabin in the Sky*, released by MGM in May 1943. It had been a successful 1940 Broadway musical with music by Vernon Duke, lyrics by John La Touche, choreography by George Balanchine, and an all-black cast that included Ethel Waters, Dooley Wilson, and Todd Duncan. The plot was about a womanizing gambler, Little Joe, who, after being shot, is granted six more months on earth to redeem himself. Russian-born Duke never had a problem writing in the American musical vernacular, but he wasn't confident about his ability to compose convincingly for black musicians. In his autobiography he recalled taking a trip south "to Virginia Beach to imbibe 'atmosphere,' although there wasn't much to imbibe in Virginia Beach except highballs." So he and La Touche "decided to stay away from pedantic authenticity and write our own kind of 'colored' songs."[6] Whatever his cultural limitations, he wrote a memorable score that included the songs "Cabin in the Sky" and "Taking a Chance on Love." When MGM bought the property they wanted additional songs, but Duke had enlisted in the Coast Guard and was unavailable, so Arlen and Harburg were hired. They reported to Arthur Freed, making this a reunion of sorts of the *Oz* team. Duke had wanted Harburg to write the lyrics for the Broadway version, but Yip turned him down because of, as Duke remembered it, the show's "lack of significance, social or otherwise."[7] But Yip never turned down a chance to work with Arlen. They were reunited, too, with Vincente Minnelli, who'd directed *Hooray for What!* and was now directing this, his first feature film. For Arlen, the homecoming went even further because many friends from the Cotton Club days were in the film: Ethel Waters, Lena Horne, Duke Ellington, Louis Armstrong.

To African American performers there was something refreshing about Arlen. He didn't care if the person he was with was white or black, Jewish or Christian. All he saw was another human being. This was and still is a rare quality, even among people of goodwill, and it was especially appreciated by Ethel Waters, who'd had difficulties with just about everyone—blacks, whites and Jews. At times during the filming she'd stop a rehearsal to vent anger at Lena Horne, who'd been given what Waters had always been denied—a long-term studio contract. Other times she railed against the studio bosses who'd refused to give her movie roles. Since they were Jewish, her tirades occasionally wandered into anti-Semitic territory. But she loved Arlen. He was, she said, "my son" and "the Negro-ist white man."[8] And now, in 1943, he wrote a truly great song for her, one that stands shoulder to shoulder with "Stormy Weather," her triumph from a decade earlier.

It was "Happiness Is a Thing Called Joe." According to Harburg, Arlen had long since composed the melody but hadn't used it because he didn't like it. "He thought it was too ordinary," Yip remembered, "and I'd always loved that tune."[9] If this story is true—and there is some doubt[10]—Arlen might have held off because the music begins in such an ordinary way. Anyone who has ever noodled at a piano has probably happened on the opening chords. They are the simplest that can be made on the successive notes of the C-major scale: C to D-minor to E-minor. Arlen's melody above these chords hovered around the note C. What could be good about something so obvious? But Harburg, in a process that reversed the way things had gone with "Over the Rainbow," championed this music. "Will you dig that tune out of the trunk?" he asked Arlen. "And he did," Harburg recalled. "And when I said, 'Happiness Is a Thing Called Joe' . . . he began liking the tune."[11] It had the catch-in-the-throat quality that Harburg loved in Arlen's music. As they worked on it, Yip provided memorable lines ("Sometimes the cabin's gloomy and the table bare / Then he'll kiss me an' it's Christmas everywhere"), and Arlen added one deft touch after another: exotic harmonies that enhanced but didn't intrude, a powerful but nonhistrionic climax with a downward octave leap at "Does he love me good, that's all I want to know," and an ending on the note D even though the key is C—something unique in popular song but satisfying and right.

Another Arlen–Harburg tour de force for *Cabin in the Sky* is a comedy duet for Lena Horne and Eddie "Rochester" Anderson called "Life's Full of Consequence." It's an appealing oompah tune that moves at a stately pace, allowing the lyric to be clearly heard, despite Anderson's trademark rasp. The back and forth between him (as Little Joe) and Horne (as temptress Georgia Brown) wittily sums up the theme of the movie and, as it happens, of Harburg's private life: whether to give in to impulsive desire or stay on the path of righteousness. Yip and Little Joe each had serious problems in this regard, but in the end, both were on the side of the angels.

Immediately after *Cabin in the Sky* came a return to Johnny Mercer for work on a Fred Astaire film, *The Sky's the Limit*, for RKO. It was always a plum assignment to write for Astaire, although his recent movies weren't guaranteed box-office successes, as had been the case when he worked with Ginger Rogers. In this one there was some incongruity as he, at forty-four, romanced eighteen-year-old Joan Leslie. And Astaire was even less convincing as an angry fighter pilot.

Mercer had already written for Astaire a year earlier when he and Kern contributed "I'm Old Fashioned" and "Dearly Beloved" to *You Were Never Lovelier*. But Arlen hadn't had the opportunity to write for the man who'd introduced more great songs than anyone else: "Lady Be Good" and "They Can't Take That Away from Me" by the Gershwins, "Dancing in the Dark" by Dietz and Schwartz, "Night and Day" by Cole Porter, "Cheek to Cheek" and "Let's Face the Music and Dance" by Irving Berlin, and "The Way You Look Tonight" by Kern and Fields. It's a list that could easily be doubled—or tripled—and now Arlen and Mercer increased it by two.

In "One for My Baby (And One More for the Road)" the music came first, which makes the lyric all the more impressive, as Mercer tells his story seamlessly, without strained syntax or shoehorned words. The opening line, one of the most memorable in popular song ("It's a quarter to three / There's no one in the place except you and me"), begins a tale that is never quite told, although by the end of the song we know what the singer has been going through and why he's in the bar ("This torch that I've found / Must be drowned or it soon might explode"). Arlen was in awe of this lyric and always believed it to be more responsible for the song's success than his music. But the music is equally great. As with "Happiness Is a Thing Called Joe," it begins simply, with a noodling-at-the-piano-idea. It is stated in E-flat and then in A-flat, as was the case in "Get Happy." But then comes an abrupt modulation into the key of G. The listener is hardly aware of this, except viscerally. Arlen himself didn't notice what he'd done until he realized he'd have to change the key signature.

It's music of quiet intensity, never rising to an arm-waving climax. In the movie, Astaire, who staged the scene, uses a montage to sing it in one bar after another until, really drunk, he goes into a wild and angry dance and eventually destroys a pyramid of stemware. He took this subdued song over the top, and it thus became one of the few great pieces written for him that didn't become associated with him. "One for My Baby" became Frank Sinatra's song instead—in fact, the leitmotif of his career. Whenever he sang it he kept his emotions in check, and the effect was all the more intense for being restrained and intimate. He understood that "One for My Baby" is *the* song of quiet desperation.

The other great Arlen–Mercer song in this film, "My Shining Hour," is in a class with "Over the Rainbow." In a few prayerful words and notes, it expresses the universal wish to see an absent loved one. That and the fact that its title echoed Winston Churchill's "Their Finest Hour" speech made it a keepsake during the war years.

As he approached the age of forty, Arlen's art deepened. His songs were more personal, deeply felt, and daring but always under the tight control of his craftsmanship. These were great works of art, but they weren't esoteric. Everyone knew them. Three were nominated for the 1943 Academy Award: "Happiness Is a Thing Called Joe," "That Old Black Magic" and "My Shining Hour" (the winner was "You'll Never Know" by Harry Warren and Mack Gordon). The public knew his work, but not him.

Perhaps this was just as well, given that his private life was going haywire. Anya was sullen, withdrawn, angry, and abusive. At one point she threatened Arlen with a knife. He would calm her down, sit with her, talk quietly to her, then let her take her sleeping pills. After that it was off to the golf course or the movie studio or a bar.

He didn't see the parallel between her and George Gershwin, who had also suffered sudden personality and mood changes. George, he knew, had been misdiagnosed as a hypochondriac. When he died from a brain tumor and Arlen began suffering headaches of his own he wasted no time going to Dr. Elias to find out if his illness was organic. But it didn't seem to occur to him that this could be true of Anya. Maybe this was because her sanity frequently returned, especially when he devoted his time to her or when they were with people she liked—or, more important, who liked her. How could something like that jibe with physical illness? After all, she was relaxed with Irving and Ellin Berlin and their daughters. She was pleasant around Harry Warren and Ted Koehler.

On the other hand, her worst times came when Celia visited California. During cold winters in Syracuse, the cantor wrote to Harold asking him to invite his mother to stay with him so she could enjoy the warm weather. Harold dutifully complied, and her presence filled Anya with dread, paranoia, anger. Celia had no sympathy for this behavior. She'd always believed their marriage was wrong and found nothing but vindication when she saw Anya acting this way.

And there was more trouble. One weekend in 1943, Harold and Anya went to Palm Springs, leaving their house to Anya's brother William, now twenty-one. He was on leave from the Army Air Forces, where he was part of a B-29 crew. Jablonski tells us most of the little we know about him. He was "a slender, tow-headed youngster they called Willy. He was also quite wild and had a drinking problem."[12] While in Palm Springs, Harold played golf and Anya sat by the pool. They returned Sunday night, found Willy asleep in the den, and went to bed. In the middle of the night Arlen was awakened by what he thought were his garden lights. He got up to investigate and found the floorboards hot against his feet. Then came the smell of smoke, and he realized the house was on fire. He woke Anya and told her they had to get out. His instinct was to exit via the bedroom door but she said no, this would only lead into the fire. Their escape, she told him, had to be through their bedroom window even though they were on the second story. "She lunged at me and cried, 'Don't open that door!' then pushed me toward the window and said, 'Follow me.' We were both barefooted; as luck would have it our next-door neighbor had run over and was directly beneath the window, and broke Annie's fall when she dropped. I fell into a rosebush—without a scratch."[13] After making sure that Willy was all right—he'd gotten out and came over to stand beside them—they went to the rear of the house and liberated their dogs. Later, there were rumors that Willy had caused the fire by falling asleep drunk while smoking or that an angry, jealous Anya had set it deliberately—something that hardly comports with the fact that she got her husband out safely. As they watched the place burn, Arlen suddenly rushed back inside. Anya screamed at him to stop, but he went into the living room and found his way through the flames and smoke to the painting above the mantel. It was George Gershwin's portrait of Jerome Kern. Harold rescued it and made it back outside just before the fire consumed the house.

Cantor Samuel Arluck—Arlen's father. Courtesy of Rita Arlen.

Celia Arluck—Arlen's mother.
Courtesy of Rita Arlen.

The Southbound Shufflers playing on an excursion boat, Arlen at the piano.

Arlen's first published song.

Young Harold Arlen in
tuxedo, photo inscribed to
bandmate Norman "Boots"
Booth. Courtesy of Norman P.
Booth (Booth's son).

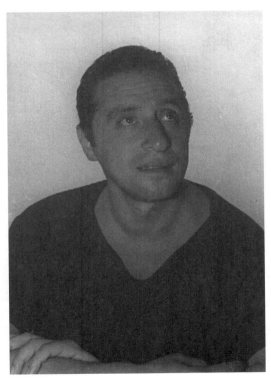

The young songwriter. Courtesy of Rita Arlen.

Anya Taranda glamour shot from 1938.

This photo was included in packs of cigarettes.

Studio photo of Jerry
Arlen. Courtesy of Rita
Arlen.

Jerry Arlen, Cantor Samuel Arluck, Harold Arlen. Courtesy of Rita Arlen.

Vincent Youmans

Ted Koehler

Good News radio program rehearsal, June 26, 1939. Standing from left: Ray Bolger, Bert Lahr, music publisher Harry Link, Meredith Wilson, Yip Harburg. Seated: Judy Garland and Harold Arlen. Credit: Yip Harburg Foundation.

Arlen and Harburg in Beverly Hills in 1935 as they worked on "Last Night When We Were Young." Credit: Yip Harburg Foundation.

Arlen, Jolson and Harburg in late 1935 or early 1936 during filming of *The Singing Kid*. Credit: Yip Harburg Foundation.

Bert Lahr in 1936 performing "Song of the Woodman" in *The Show Is On*. Credit: Shubert Archive.

Harold and Anya in 1930s Hollywood. Courtesy of Sam Arlen.

Left to right: Ray Bolger, Luella Gear, Frances Williams, and Bert Lahr in the 1934 revue *Life Begins at 8:40*.

Yip and Edelaine in the late
1930s or early 1940s. Credit:
Yip Harburg Foundation.

Harold Arlen and Johnny Mercer. Credit: Special Collections and Archives, Georgia
State University Library.

For Yipper –
One (if not the)
of my oldest and
most talented
friends,
With affection
and admiration –
Ira

Ira and George Gershwin, inscribed by Ira to Yip Harburg. Credit: Yip Harburg Foundation.

Jerome Kern. Credit: Library of Congress.

Irving Berlin in 1906, the year after Arlen's birth.

Dorothy Fields

Burton Lane. Courtesy of Lynn
Lane and Peggy Kaye.

Arlen in 1954. Courtesy of
Rita Arlen.

Jerry Arlen's wife Sherine and their son, Sam. Courtesy of Rita Arlen.

Martin Charnin. Courtesy of Martin Charnin.

Harold and Anya in the
1960s. Courtesy of Rita
Arlen.

Harold and Anya
Arlen at Burton and
Lynn Lane's home in
the 1960s. Courtesy of
Lynn Lane.

Pianist-singer Bobby Short, Harold Arlen, Edward Jablonski, and singer-comedian Lynn Lavner in 1973. Courtesy of Carla Jablonski.

Michael Feinstein and Harry Warren in 1980. Courtesy of Michael Feinstein.

Arlen and Harburg in 1977. Courtesy of Berthe Schuchat and Ken Bloom.

Arlen's lead sheet for "Over the Rainbow." Credit: Yip Harburg Foundation.

CHAPTER 16

"Ac-cent-tchu-ate the Positive"

In early 1943, a Hollywood costume designer named Lilith James was researching women's clothing styles and came upon a fashion item from the past called *bloomers*—puffy pantaloons designed in the 1850s by a women's-rights champion and antislavery activist named Elizabeth Smith Miller. Miller was closely associated with fellow activists Elizabeth Cady Stanton, Susan B. Anthony, and Amelia Bloomer. Bloomer took to wearing the apparel with the hope it would become a popular alternative to uncomfortable hoop skirts, which were petticoats made like harnesses, usually from whalebones. She gained nothing from these efforts except ridicule and her name in the dictionary. But her story fascinated Lilith James, who, with her husband, Dan James, made this story the basis of a script. They changed Amelia Bloomer's name to Dolly Bloomer and provided her with a suffragist niece, Evelina Applegate, who has enough beauty and charm to transform her slave-holding southern suitor, Jefferson Lightfoot Calhoun, into a women's-rights advocate, an abolitionist, and, finally, a Lincoln-loving Union soldier.

The Jameses had little writing experience but knew Yip Harburg from left-wing political circles. They brought him the script and asked if he'd turn it into a Broadway musical. He was dismissive. Its political themes were fine, he said, but the story was rudimentary. It lacked a subplot and secondary characters to act as foils for the principals. It needed a two-act structure so the second act could satisfactorily resolve a situation set up in the first. Most important, it lacked humor. Politics couldn't be effective without humor, Yip said. He also believed that such a period piece would look too much like an attempt to ride the coattails of *Oklahoma!*

When Arlen was shown the script, he felt differently. Dramatic structure didn't much concern him. Nor did he see anything wrong with riding those coattails if it meant taking advantage of the new form that Rodgers and Hammerstein had given to Broadway composers and lyricists. The American musical was no longer tied to the stand-alone song. Duets, soliloquies, ballets, and instrumental interludes would now go hand in hand with songs to integrate the score with the story. Sooner or later, every major songwriter was going to try to write in this new form. Arlen certainly wanted his chance. *Bloomer Girl* also appealed to him because he liked the challenge of writing unfamiliar types of music—*American Minuet* had been an example—and this task would require him to evoke the Civil War era without abandoning the musical sophistication of the 1940s.

To get Yip to say yes, Harold formed an alliance with Edelaine—who had just become Mrs. Harburg—and she was the one who got her husband to commit to *Bloomer Girl*, although he did so on the proviso that he be given carte blanche to write a proper script and oversee all aspects of the production. Arlen was amenable, so things proceeded swiftly.

For help with the script, Yip turned to two screenwriters. One, Sig Herzig, had written many movies but had little Broadway experience. The other was Fred Saidy, who'd worked on a few movies and had no Broadway experience. Their goal was to deliver feminist and antiracist themes in humorous situations. Toward that end they created a secondary character, Daisy, whose commitment to women's rights wavers whenever her boyfriend appears onstage and who at one point does a striptease; that is, she removes her hoop skirt and flashes her bloomers. Race was embodied in an amiable slave, Pompey, and his affable owner, Calhoun—a hoop-skirt salesman.

The solemnity in the play came from the work of choreographer Agnes de Mille, who was the only woman on the production staff. Seven years earlier, as a beginner, she'd been fired from *Hooray For What!*, which left her with a distaste for Harburg. Since then she'd made a name for herself on Broadway with *Oklahoma!* and in classical dance with Aaron Copland's *Rodeo*, and now she told Yip that her choreography was going to avoid his light-hearted approach and instead make a serious statement about the Civil War and war in general. In other words, she wasn't interested in anything comical like her *Hero Ballet* in *Hooray for What!* Harburg gave his assent, as did Arlen and the producer, John C. Wilson—the latter a Broadway veteran who'd worked with Noël Coward and Rodgers and Hart. So she went ahead and devised the *Civil War Ballet*, which portrays women as they wait to learn if their men have lived to return to them. De Mille's husband was in the army in Europe, and this was the summer of D-Day, so she knew what such waiting was like. The ballet would be the show's powerful conclusion. "I began rehearsals working under what I suppose could be called inspiration," she wrote in a memoir. "From the first rehearsal I seemed to be acting under a compulsion beyond myself."[1] The ballet's music consisted of songs from the show and other themes by Arlen that were turned into a coherent composition by a classically trained composer, Trude Rittmann,[2] who was the show's rehearsal pianist.

Arlen had written most of *Bloomer Girl*'s music in a single month while he and Harburg were still in Los Angeles. People who heard it were invariably impressed. Wilson was able to obtain financial backing for the show based on Arlen's demo recording of the score. One song, "The Eagle and Me," was so promising that Harold went out on a limb and told an interviewer he was sure it would be a hit. After he and Anya arrived in New York, he played and sang the music for de Mille, who later wrote, "The score contained one rhapsodic outburst, a colloquial Hymn to Freedom, 'The Eagle and Me' and eight or ten of the loveliest songs I'd ever heard."[3]

What happened next was round two in the Harburg–de Mille relationship. When Yip saw how de Mille's ballet ended—a dead soldier carried onstage and laid at his widow's feet—he said, "No. No. No. This is all wrong. Where is the wit? Where is the humor?"[4] De Mille replied sharply that there isn't a lot of wit and humor in war. Arlen suggested that all the soldiers return home to dance with their women. De Mille said war didn't work that way but reluctantly went along with this idea and redid the choreography. Her dancers, however, insisted she'd been right the first time, so she changed it again. Now all the men would return home except one, leaving a single woman without a partner. De Mille described the new ending this way: "As the circles of reunited men and women heeled softly in a gathering pulse, the bereft woman placed her hand on the earth and lifted her head in a gesture of ultimate remembering."[5] Arlen found this very moving, but Harburg still maintained that de Mille's work was too gloomy and would sink the show. On his instructions, Wilson told her it had to be cut. But Arlen took her aside and told her he'd thought up a way to keep it in. Let Yip think the ballet was out but perform it opening night during the Philadelphia tryout and let the audience decide. "I hope to God it stops the show," he told her. And it did. One woman in the audience was so moved she sought de Mille out after the performance and presented her with her son's navy wings. Later that evening at the cast party, Harburg was contrite. De Mille wrote that "Yipper put his arms around me. 'Goddamit! I've begun to like the dreary thing. To think that a lousy bit of movement can make people weep, and me among them! A lousy bit of movement!'"[6]

Bloomer Girl was a success. It ran on Broadway for 654 performances—more than a year and a half—and was one of the first shows to generate an original cast recording. When the performers assembled at Decca Records in New York, Arlen stepped in to sing "Man for Sale," a slave auctioneer's aria. This inventive, unconventional piece is typical of what can be found in *Bloomer Girl*, whose music is always interesting and often beautiful. Yet it is never unforgettable. "Right as the Rain" is almost another "My Shining Hour" but not quite. Something is missing—it's hard to say what—that would have made it timeless. "The Eagle and Me" is a rouser and the source of Stephen Sondheim's favorite line in any lyric: "ever since the day when the world was an onion." Lyricist Martin Charnin is also fascinated by that line. "It's an amazing metaphor," he says. "You keep peeling it. Sometimes it makes you cry, sometimes happy. It is a breathtaking word."[7] But Arlen's prediction that this song would be a hit turned out to be wrong. None of the songs caught on, although "Evelina" was briefly popular. Nothing in *Bloomer Girl* had the jaunty vitality of "It's Only a Paper Moon" or the goofy humor of "I Love to Sing-a" or the poignant beauty of "Over the Rainbow." Arlen, in trying to express the emotions and motivations of fictional characters, was less able to assert his own feelings and vitality.

While new productions of *Oklahoma!* appear regularly, *Bloomer Girl* has fallen into obscurity. Its advocacies of women's and civil rights have lost their novelty. Its characters, created to illustrate social issues, have no appeal as people. Arlen and Harburg couldn't bring them to life as Rodgers and Hammerstein did in *Oklahoma!* when they had Curly McLain walk onstage singing "Oh, What Beautiful Morning" or when his rival, Jud Fry, revealed his obsessions in "Lonely Room." Nor could the gimmicky plot of *Bloomer Girl* match *Oklahoma!*'s elemental story of two men courting the same woman—to the death. Harburg had agreed to do *Bloomer Girl* knowing it wasn't going to be easy to animate its stilted characters and their fabricated situations. That's why he turned to Saidy and Herzig for help. There was no point in turning to Arlen, because Arlen didn't know what it took for a story to work as a musical.

Two months after the October 1944 opening of *Bloomer Girl*, Paramount Pictures released *Here Come the Waves*, the last of Arlen's wartime film collaborations with Johnny Mercer. Like most Hollywood musicals of the time, it was short on plot and its characters were the ones its stars, Bing Crosby and Betty Hutton, had created for themselves and would play throughout their careers. Arlen and Mercer could relax and just write good songs. They quickly came up with several, including a sweet ballad, "I Promise You," and a leisurely rhythm song, "Let's Take the Long Way Home." They thought they'd completed their assignment when the studio asked for one more, something punchy for a big production number. So they returned to the piano in their office on the Paramount lot. Several unproductive hours later, they gave up and took a drive in the Los Angeles hills, each of them in an irritable mood. Mercer, trying to think of something cheerful, remembered an "offbeat little rhythm tune"[8] he'd heard Arlen humming a few days earlier, one that brought to mind a three-word phrase that had long intrigued him, "Accentuate the Positive." Later, he gave differing accounts of where he'd first heard that phrase. One was that he'd been in an African American church in Savannah when the preacher, Bishop Grace—called Daddy Grace by his congregation—used it in a sermon. The other was that he'd been told that Father Divine—a Harlem preacher who claimed to be God—had used it. Either way, it was perfect for a song, which he and Arlen created by singing to each other as they continued their drive. Given the source of its lyric and the music's gospel feel, it's ironic that it was used in a racially offensive way. In the movie, Bing Crosby and Sonny Tufts performed it in blackface. But "Ac-cent-tchu-ate the Positive" became a jukebox hit and an enduring pop classic.

CHAPTER 17

St. Louis Woman

By the summer of 1945, Arlen was ready to write his second big Broadway book musical. As always, he left the plot, script, and everything but the music to others. For him, music was the beginning and the end. Projects were always in progress when he joined them.

Rodgers and Hammerstein worked differently. In 1940 they had both seen a Broadway revival of the 1909 play *Liliom*, by Hungarian writer Ferenc Molnár. It is the story of a carnival barker who falls for a trusting young woman, marries her, and turns into an abusive husband. When she becomes pregnant, he—desperate for money to support her and the baby—attempts and botches a robbery. Rather than face justice, he kills himself. The next scene takes place sixteen years later in Purgatory, where he is told he can return to Earth for a day and if he can do a good deed for his daughter, now sixteen, he'll be allowed into Heaven. But he's still the same man. He argues with her, slaps her face as he'd hit her mother, and is condemned to Hell.

At the heart of this play is the theme of second chances as depicted in the lives of vivid, believable characters. Rodgers and Hammerstein felt they could make a great musical out of it—as long as audiences weren't too put off by its sadness. In *Oklahoma!* they'd dared let a man die onstage—but he was the villain. This time death would come to the hero and, after that, damnation.[1] Given that Broadway musicals were still thought of as musical comedies, it was hard to know how audiences would react. To find out, they attended nightly performances of a current hit, *Song of Norway*, which was about the life of composer Edvard Grieg and had some melancholy moments. They gauged the way audiences reacted to those moments, and when they saw not restlessness but tears, they decided to go ahead and turn *Liliom* into *Carousel*—which became a great success in 1945 and one of the most beautiful and affecting of all musicals.

Arlen's new show got underway when Broadway and Hollywood producer Edward Gross, having been impressed by the successful Broadway revival of *Porgy and Bess* in 1942—a pared-down production that was no longer an opera—remembered an all-black play from the 1930s that would, he thought, also do well as a Broadway musical. This was *God Sends Sunday*, a drama about African Americans in St. Louis in 1898 written by two black men, Arna Bontemps and Countee Cullen, each a well-known poet of the Harlem Renaissance. They'd based it on Bontemps's 1931 novel of the same name. It hadn't been a stage success—it never played on Broadway—but it was about horse racing and gambling, which meant colorful sets and costumes, and there were similarities between its plot and the Gershwin work. It, too, had a hero who was a long shot (in this case a jockey named Little Augie) who vies with an overbearing villain (a saloon owner named Biglow Brown) for the love of a less than faithful woman (Della Green). Unfortunately, many of its scenes verged on the ridiculous: Augie wins Della's love with a spectacular dance routine; Brown, shot by a former girlfriend, thinks Augie is the shooter and puts a curse on him; Augie defies the curse by winning his next horse race and, then, Della.

When Gross told Arthur Freed at MGM about this play, Freed became interested in it as a vehicle for Lena Horne, who, he hoped, would play Della onstage and later onscreen. He had assured her when she signed with MGM in 1942 that he wouldn't allow her to get stuck playing cooks and maids, and he kept his word, except that, in those days of Hollywood apartheid, she wasn't allowed to star in films that also featured white performers. The all-black *God Sends Sunday* was, he believed, just the vehicle for her. Her drawing power could make it a success on Broadway and then in Hollywood. He was so enthusiastic, he put his own money into it. Gross wanted Arlen and Mercer to write the score, and Freed was happy to place a call to Arlen, who quickly accepted—not because he was excited by the play, but because he liked working with Freed, who had rescued "Over the Rainbow," and with Horne, whom he'd known since their Cotton Club days.

Although Mercer enjoyed working with Arlen and wanted to try writing a Broadway musical, he was unimpressed with the script of *God Sends Sunday* and wanted to wait for something better to come along. He was doing well in Hollywood. He and Arlen had raised their fee to $60,000 per picture and got that much from Paramount for five days work on *Out of This World*, whose title song was another of their masterpieces: a forlorn, mysterious, sultry ballad.

Then Hollywood's vicissitudes separated them. Freed asked Mercer to write songs for a new movie, *The Harvey Girls*, with Harry Warren, who was under contract to MGM. It was an *Oklahoma!*-style musical about young women traveling west in the 1870s. Neither Warren nor Mercer had written a book musical before, and they weren't much good at it. Except for one big production number, "On the Atchison, Topeka, and the Santa Fe," their songs didn't advance the plot. And that one did so only because Freed's musical right-hand man, Roger Edens, and his vocal arranger, Kay Thompson, supplemented it with a section that introduced all the young women one by one. The song as written by Mercer and Warren became an enormous success, recorded by Bing Crosby, Judy Garland, and, most successfully, Mercer himself.

When Warren went into a Beverly Hills record store and saw Mercer's recording advertised as "Johnny Mercer's 'On the Atchison, Topeka and the Santa Fe'" he concluded—wrongly—that Mercer, as an owner of Capitol Records, was claiming credit as the song's sole author. This angered Warren, who was endlessly peeved about his continuing anonymity. Usually, he expressed this discontent with humor. Arlen liked to tell about the evening he and Warren and their wives were driving to the Palm Springs home of Arlen's publisher, Buddy Morris, and how when Warren heard on the radio that "Atchison" had brought him his third Academy Award, he hadn't reacted much; instead, he waited until they were walking up to Morris's front door and then he turned to Arlen and said, "Walk three Oscars behind"[2]—forgetting, apparently, that Harold had won one for "Over the Rainbow." But his anger at Mercer was no joke. It would be years before he spoke to him again.

It was at that point that Mercer agreed to rejoin Arlen to work on *God Sends Sunday*, now called *St. Louis Woman*—even though he'd known from the beginning that the play was badly flawed. Not only did it have a hackneyed plot, its characters were black stereotypes. Freed tried to forestall trouble over this by submitting the script—by two eminent African Americans, after all—to Walter White, head of the National Association for the Advancement of Colored People (NAACP). White's reply was that the play "pictured Negroes as pimps, prostitutes, and gamblers with no redeeming characteristics."[3] A similar reaction came from the Interracial Film and Radio Guild, who had also been sent an advance copy. They called it "atrocious" and "an insult to Negro womanhood."[4]

In her autobiography Horne wrote, "It was not until I had fallen in love with the music that I received the script to read. The role I was to play was a flashy whore who was in love with a jockey. There were all sorts of the usual cliché characters in it."[5] Some people told her to do the show because it would give a lot of black people a chance to work on Broadway. Instead, she followed White's advice and declined the role. One leading African American newspaper, *The Chicago Defender*, quoted her saying that *St. Louis Woman* "sets the Negro back a hundred years."[6]

Things got worse. After Horne was replaced by the inexperienced Ruby Hill, Rouben Mamoulian was brought in to replace director Lemuel Ayers, and he hired an experienced performer, Muriel Rahn, to replace Hill. Then Pearl Bailey, who was making her Broadway debut, led the cast in a successful effort to get Hill reinstated, and followed this victory by confronting Mamoulian over the show's clichéd characters. In 1935 he'd directed the original production of *Porgy and Bess*, whose cast had rebelled when they were booked into the segregated National Theatre in Washington, D.C. Because that situation ended with the theater's desegregation—if only temporarily—he had some credibility with the *St. Louis Woman* ensemble, and the roles remained as they were. As he saw it, the bigger problem was an overlong first act that led into an inadequate second act—a flaw he tried to fix by reconfiguring the play into three acts. He was still rearranging scenes as opening night approached. Then gloom descended on everyone when Countee Cullen died suddenly from a stroke at forty-two. Having spent his life fighting prejudice, he was, according to Mercer biographer Philip Furia, "broken by accusations that he had defamed his race."[7] Had he lived, he'd have had to cross an NAACP picket line to attend the premiere.

Show openings were usually scheduled for weeknights to give theater critics time to get their reviews in the Sunday papers. *St. Louis Woman*'s producers decided to open it on a Saturday so the reviews would come out on Monday and be read by fewer people. It got some positive notices, but most critics used the show as a punching bag. Arlen took his worst hit from novelist and literary critic Louis Kronenberger, who wrote in the New York City daily *PM*: "First-rate music might yet have turned the tide, but Harold Arlen's songs and orchestral tags and tid-bits are second-rate even for him. They are most of them romantic or atmospheric enough, but they lack distinction, they lack melodic urgency, they lack the excitement and cohesive power that folk drama demands."[8]

Kronenberger was writing about a score that, when Arlen and Mercer first played and sang it for the cast, received an impromptu standing ovation. "We sat in the room," Pearl Bailey said of that moment, "and this man[9] just sat there and sang the whole score . . . This man could sing his songs. He was one of the few people who could sing his songs better than anyone else could sing them. And every one was a masterpiece . . . He wrote his heart, and he sang his heart."[10] That was the key to Arlen and Mercer. It's difficult to imagine them creating a song like *Carousel*'s "When I Marry

Mr. Snow," in which a woman expresses bemused affection for her fisher-man fiancé—a feeling that Rodgers and Hammerstein could never have had themselves. Even when Arlen and Mercer put a character's name into a song, they didn't venture outside themselves. The opening number of *St. Louis Woman*, "Li'l Augie Is a Natural Man," isn't about Augie; it's another of their rousing gospel numbers like "Ac-cent-tchu-ate the Positive," a fact evident in Mercer's recording of the song.

The big hit of *St. Louis Woman*, "Come Rain or Come Shine," doesn't sound like it came from a Broadway show. Arlen and Mercer wrote it the way they wrote their movie songs, with no thought given to how it would be used in the production. They were in the den of Arlen's Beverly Hills home at his favorite piano, a Martha Washington Harpinette spinet, fooling around with a syncopated repeated-note idea. Suddenly, Arlen told Mercer he wanted to go off by himself to the living room and work at the Stein-way. Mercer stayed put until Harold returned with a three-bar melody. As soon as he heard it, Mercer said, "I'm gonna love you like nobody's loved you"—but then he stopped, stuck. "Come hell or high water," Arlen joked. "Of course," said Mercer, "why didn't I think of that? Come rain or come shine."[11] That evening, as they finished, Mercer was already thinking about getting it recorded.

By 1946, original cast albums made it possible for people away from Broadway to become familiar with show tunes as sung by casts chosen and supervised by composers and lyricists. Works like *Oklahoma!* and *Carousel* could now be heard exactly as their authors intended, which was how it had always been in classical music. Because cast albums included all the songs in a show, if the show was successful, the album would sell well and all the songs would become familiar. That's what made "The Surrey with the Fringe on Top" from *Oklahoma!* and the eight-minute "Soliloquy" from *Carousel* widely known. But when Mercer thought of recording "Come Rain or Come Shine," he wasn't thinking about the *St. Louis Woman* original cast recording. What he had in mind was a record made by a singer and a band unaffiliated with the original show. *St. Louis Woman* closed after just 113 performances and its cast album sold poorly, so nearly all its songs were consigned to obscurity. Mercer rescued "Come Rain or Come Shine" because he was determined to have it issued by Capitol Records as a single to be played on the radio and in jukeboxes.

He brought his protégé, Margaret Whiting, into a New York studio, and as he and Arlen sat in the control booth, she sang the song. "Something snapped in my mind," she wrote in her autobiography. "I started thinking about Harold, the cantor's son. On that last note, I just let it wail. Well,

Johnny burst through the door, mad as hell: 'What in God's name are you doing?' He was followed by Harold, who shouted, 'No, leave it, leave it in! That's the way I should have written it.'"[12] What she'd done was turn the composer's final note into a three-note phrase that had a cantorial sound. She, a Catholic, had created one of the most Hebraic moments in popular song.

With this recording, "Come Rain or Come Shine" became a success—one of just two songs from *St. Louis Woman* to become widely known. The other was "Any Place I Hang My Hat Is Home," whose boogie-woogie piano accompaniment is similar to but gentler than the one in "One for My Baby." It sways under the easygoing music and lyrics ("Sweetnin' water, cherry wine / Thank you kindly, suits me fine"). Two comedy songs performed by Pearl Bailey ("A Woman's Prerogative" and "Legalize My Name") went over well with theater audiences—in fact, some critics said they were the best part of the score—but never made it on their own. Another song was the gentle, bluesy "Lullaby," which also failed to catch on. And a similar fate lay in store for two great songs that, along with "Come Rain or Come Shine," are the heart of *St. Louis Woman*.

One of them, "I Had Myself a True Love," is an intricate sixty-four-bar composition whose four-bar kernel ("I had myself a true love") consistently undergoes melodic and harmonic changes, as does the four-bar release ("The first thing in the mornin'"). After a coda ("There may be a lot of things I know"), when the song, at thirty-two bars, might be expected to conclude, we get part two. It begins with a new four-note phrase that sounds like a forlorn birdcall ("In the evenin'"), followed by a recapitulation of material from the first half—some of it given to the singer, some to the piano. Throughout, the vocalist returns again and again to a blue note that stays the same as harmonies under it grow increasingly dissonant.

The other is "I Wonder What Became of Me." Because it was cut from the show before the New York opening, it never had a chance with audiences. Like "I Had Myself a True Love," it has an unusual structure—forty-eight bars—and it, too, is a sad song. But here the anguish is more overt. Melodic descents like those of "Last Night When We Were Young" combine with words of hesitation and puzzlement ("It's like, well maybe, like when a baby sees a bubble burst before its eyes") and regret ("But I can't be gay, for along the way something went astray") to express what Bob Dylan was referring to when he wrote of "the lonely intense world of Harold Arlen."[13]

CHAPTER 18

DESCENT INTO MISERY

Arlen returned to Beverly Hills in mid-1946 with no prospects for work. The studios were making fewer musicals in the postwar years, and those they did make tended to rely on songs that were already well known. It was the era of the songwriter biopic. Lesser-known writers like Arlen and Warren weren't in the running for such pictures, but Kern, Porter, Gershwin, and Rodgers and Hart were all portrayed in films that were inaccurate as biographies but filled with their music, often elegantly staged. This helped establish in the public mind a roster of those who'd made the songwriter pantheon. Irving Berlin had begun this trend in 1938 by working on a movie, *Alexander's Ragtime Band*, that drew from his extensive catalog and included a few—he insisted it be just a few—events from his own life.

Arlen was not waiting to have his life story filmed. He was waiting for his next job. And he waited alone, without a lyricist. He and Mercer hadn't exactly broken up, but with no project to keep them together they drifted apart. For a time Mercer busied himself with the affairs of Capitol Records, although he was hardly a typical company president. He wanted Capitol to remain small and intimate—a place where he could record a song whenever the mood struck him, even if he'd written it that day. He also wanted the freedom to record the singers and musicians he'd discovered or championed. After returning to California from months on the East Coast working on *St. Louis Woman*, he found that his company had blossomed. In 1946 it sold forty-two million records—one out of every six in the United States. It had also issued stock and added a children's wing whose Bozo the Clown series was doing well. Never one to spend much time at his desk, he now stopped coming to the office altogether and handed the presidency over to Glenn Wallichs. At thirty-four, he was falling into a pattern that would dominate the second half of his life: occasional attempts to create a Rodgers and Hammerstein–style Broadway classic alternating with what became his day job—writing lyrics for anyone in Hollywood who came to him with a good tune. When the instrumental theme for the movie *Laura* became popular, he put words to David Raksin's music. When a friend at Capitol Records told him that a French song recorded by Édith Piaf, "Les Feuilles Mortes," needed an English lyric, he wrote "Autumn Leaves."

Unlike Mercer, Arlen did get a chance to write a great Broadway show during these first postwar years—and he turned it down. Yip Harburg had come up with a dreamlike story that would become *Finian's Rainbow*, and he wanted to write the songs with Arlen. But Arlen thought the show too political. In *Bloomer Girl* Yip had targeted slavery and the subjugation of women. In *Finian* he went after racism and capitalism. Arlen had no problem attacking racism. But a broadside against capitalism—even in the whimsical Harburg manner—wasn't to his taste. After all, he was a Republican like his father. So the *Finian* job went instead to thirty-four-year-old Burton Lane, a tall, shy, and gifted man—friend to both Arlen and Harburg since the early 1930s—who now, with Yip, created a classic. Many of its songs went on to become favorites, including "How Are Things in Glocca Morra," "Old Devil Moon," and "Look to the Rainbow."

As had been the case with Mercer, there'd been no falling-out between Arlen and Harburg. In fact, Harold dropped by Yip's house to hear the *Finian* score in progress, and it was his enthusiasm for one of Lane's melodies that prompted Harburg and Lane to turn it into "Old Devil Moon." But he shrank from the stress that was always a part of working with Yip on Broadway—stress that now became Lane's. "Yip would do the damnedest things," said Lane's widow, Lynn:

> There was a revival of *Finian* at the City Center. There were going to be a couple of auditions. A well-known actor, Frank McHugh, was there. He was going to play the father role. When McHugh came in, Burton went over to say hello. They had known each other a little bit in L.A. He sat with Burton and me, and then when Yip came in, Burton said to me, "Watch this." There was something about the way Yip was walking over to us. He went to McHugh, and a minute and a half later McHugh was saying, "You can't talk to me that way. Who the hell do you think you are?" McHugh stormed out and never came back.[1]

The prospect of such moments was one reason Harold refused Yip's offer. The bigger problem was Harburg's political evangelizing. "Harold," Harburg explained, "thought I was too involved in politics all the time and that it was polluting the stage. The stage was not a pulpit, not a place for 'propaganda,' which he called it. I called it education; he called it propaganda . . . [He] forgave me the political exuberance which I exuded. [But] one of the reasons there was a little split when he started to work with Johnny Mercer was because he thought I was what Bert Lahr called 'too foivent.'"[2]

Arlen needed a lyricist not just to write the words, but to help him find work. He couldn't turn to Ted Koehler, who'd retired and was living the good life in Beverly Hills. Ira Gershwin had resumed work in 1941 and collaborated on Broadway and in Hollywood with a succession of notable composers: Kurt Weill, Aaron Copland, and Jerome Kern. But not with Arlen. If anyone was his brother's musical heir, Arlen was the one, but despite a close friendship the two hadn't worked together since 1934, when George was still alive. In any case, Ira was in New York working on a musical, *Park Avenue*, with composer Arthur Schwartz, and unavailable to Arlen as a lyricist or for socializing.

And there wouldn't be any more nights at Kern's home for poker, jokes, and fatherly advice and approbation. In November 1945, the sixty-year-old composer collapsed from a cerebral hemorrhage. He'd been in New York to work on a revival of *Show Boat* as well as a new musical, *Annie Get Your Gun*—the first to be produced by Rodgers and Hammerstein. The stroke came as he was out for a morning walk. The only identification he had with him was his ASCAP card, so they were called as an ambulance took him to City Hospital on Welfare Island—it was where Stephen Foster had died in 1864. ASCAP notified Oscar Hammerstein, who, with Rodgers, rushed to the hospital to find Kern in a room for indigent patients. It was usually a noisy place, but as people learned who'd joined them, they fell into a respectful silence. Kern died a few days later in Doctor's Hospital in Manhattan.

Misery was coming at Arlen from all directions: the loss of Kern, the end of his great years with Harburg and Mercer, lack of work, and family tensions. When Jerry was discharged from the army in 1946, Cantor Arluck told Harold to find him a job. Not as a songwriter—he had decided to leave that, he told a reporter, to his brother. What he wanted to do was conduct Broadway theater orchestras. It was the occupation he'd put on his 1940 Census form—and not without justification. In the late 1930s he had formed his own band and played Billy Rose's Music Hall on Broadway. In 1938 he'd successfully conducted the final performances of Harold and Yip's *Hooray for What!* So it made some sense when Harold gave him a job in the spring of 1946 conducting a Boston production of *Bloomer Girl*. But again things went badly for him. The cast and orchestra complained to producer John Wilson about Jerry's erratic tempos and inaccurate cues, and Wilson, in turn, wrote to Arlen in Los Angeles to ask that Jerry be let go. Harold's acquiescence unleashed the wrath of his brother and father. Why had he caved in? Wasn't *he* the composer, the one in charge?

So he tried to find Jerry another job. "It would mean a great deal to me, as well as my brother," he wrote to Irving Berlin on April 20, 1948, "if Jerry could direct your show . . . Dick Rodgers has promised me to give him a chance when he has an opening."[3] This was a futile request, and Arlen knew it. These men weren't going to entrust their shows to Jerry. And, given *St. Louis Woman*'s failure at the time of Rodgers's resounding successes with *Oklahoma!* and *Carousel*, it must have galled Arlen to have to make such a request of him. Nor could he have enjoyed writing a supplicating letter to Berlin, who was also having his greatest theatrical successes. His 1942 all-soldier revue, *This Is the Army*, after playing to standing-room audiences on Broadway, was taken by its fifty-five-year-old composer-lyricist to entertain troops on battlefronts in Europe, Africa, and the Pacific. Then, in 1946, Berlin wrote his hit-laden book musical *Annie Get Your Gun*—having replaced Kern on the project—which ran on Broadway for nearly three years. So when he answered Arlen's letter, it was to say he'd spoken to their mutual friend and lawyer Abe Berman "about your brother and will certainly keep him in mind."[4] But he never hired Jerry.

In the meantime, Arlen was becoming increasingly anxious about his own unemployment. His friend Bob Wachsman, who in 1933 had talked him into touring the Loew's vaudeville circuit, now came up with the idea of a radio program that would feature him singing at the piano backed by a studio orchestra. The show was to be called *Songs by Arlen, Stories by Skolsky*—it would feature columnist Sidney Skolsky's movie-land gossip. When CBS turned it down, Arlen and Wachsman revised the format and replaced Skolsky with guest jazz musicians. Again the show was rejected—and then again after yet another revision.

Dwarfing these tribulations was the tension brought on by Anya's increasingly erratic behavior. Some days she wouldn't leave the house or even her bed. She'd become dependent on sleeping pills. Other times she was up and about but apt to deliver furious tirades at her husband because he was spending so much time away from her, which made him stay away all the more. First thing in the morning, before she was up, he would head for the golf course, where he did more drinking than golfing. Evenings were spent in bars. If he went out with other women, he was a master of discretion. From all accounts the only woman he ever really wanted was Anya, as she used to be. And sometimes he got his wish. He'd find her relaxed, working on her paintings, tending the garden, planting flowerbeds. She was the one who planned, installed, and painted their brick walkway. She was even sociable at times, although it was strange how she'd refuse to see someone she'd once liked—composer Ann Ronell, for instance—yet go to a place she'd formerly avoided. Jonathan Schwartz, son of composer Arthur Schwartz, remembers being taken by his father to get-togethers at the Gershwin home in the mid-1940s and seeing Anya there with Harold. In his memoir, *All in Good Time*, he describes the scene: "Harold Arlen, dressed in tennis shorts, played George's songs on George's piano. We all sat around with gin and tonics, me with a Coke. A cantor's son from Buffalo, Arlen had a lovely singing voice, melancholy through and through, similar to Johnny Mercer's, even though Mercer, from Georgia, was touched by whimsy. Arlen's wife, Anya, seated on the carpet at Harold's feet and right next to me, put her arm around my shoulder, where it remained. Let it go on, let it go on, were my unspoken thoughts."[5] And she was, as always, happy to visit with Irving and Ellin Berlin. Mary Ellin Barrett, their eldest daughter, remembers seeing the Arlens at dinner parties given by her parents at their Santa Monica beach house during the summer of 1947 when her father was working on the movie *Easter Parade*. A music student herself, she liked to "hang over the piano" as Harold played. "He was a wonderful pianist," she remembers, with "a real sense of humor," and Anya "was just a very nice lady."[6]

Having once wrongly diagnosed George with "Hollywooditis," Harold now concluded that Anya had "Bored Hollywood Housewife Syndrome." She seemed too able to control her moods for them to be symptomatic of anything more serious. She could apparently throw off her lethargy and discontent at will. Yet she developed no friendships or interests that took her out of the house. And if she was suffering from this syndrome, it was certainly an exotic variety, because she didn't have affairs or even flirt, was indifferent to gossip, and didn't like to shop.

At the beginning of 1948, Arlen at last had some good news in his professional life. He'd been assigned to a Universal Pictures film, *Casbah*—a low-budget musical remake of the 1938 drama *Algiers*. Charles Boyer and Hedy Lamarr had starred in the original. In this version the principals were Tony Martin and Yvonne de Carlo. Martin was the film's only singer. Luckily for Arlen, he was a good one. And he was lucky, too, when he was teamed with lyricist Leo Robin.

The self-effacing Robin, five years older than Arlen, had a knack for writing lyrics that were both humorous and touching. The finest example of this was "Thanks for the Memory," written with composer Ralph Rainger and sung by Bob Hope and Shirley Ross in the film *The Big Broadcast of 1938*. It's one of the few songs that can make people laugh and cry at the same time. He was also good at devising memorable titles—"June in January," "Love in Bloom," and, when Arlen presented him with a slow, sighing melody, "What's Good about Goodbye?" It amazed him that no one had used that one before. The word "goodbye" fits this music. Its autumnal beauty unfolds for sixteen bars. Then, as the listener waits for—craves—a restatement, Arlen delivers a new section ("Your love could bring eternal spring") that concludes with a hint of the hoped-for restatement but, in a moment of real songwriting chutzpah, moves on to a third segment. Only after thirty-two bars does the initial melody return. This, in essence, was Arlen. He had a lovely opening, knew the listener would want a quick repetition, was well aware that he needed a hit song—after all, he hadn't had a job in two years—yet he still dared do this. What's more, the song has two endings: the first tranquil ("Say you're mine forever"), the second urgent ("We're in love, you and I / Darling don't say goodbye"). Somehow—as so often happened with him—the public accepted a complex and unpredictable song. *Casbah* flopped, but "What's Good about Goodbye?" became a standard. And the score had two other great songs. One was "Hooray for Love"—a lively, catchy rhythm song like "Ac-cent-tchu-ate the Positive." The other was "It Was Written in the Stars," a languorous minor-key ballad that, like all the songs in *Casbah*, takes one risk after another in form, harmony, and rhythmic complexity. When it came to songwriting, no one was bolder than Arlen.

CHAPTER 19

"She Was Sweet and Adorable and Then She Went Mad"

Casbah was the only collaboration between Arlen and Robin. After completing this job, the lyricist traveled east, where he and composer Jule Styne wrote the songs for *Gentlemen Prefer Blondes*. It was another in what had become a steady flow of classic Broadway book musicals: *On the Town* in 1944, with music by Leonard Bernstein and lyrics by Betty Comden and Adolph Green; *Annie Get Your Gun* in 1946, with music and lyrics by Irving Berlin; *Finian's Rainbow* in 1947, by Lane and Harburg; *Brigadoon* in 1947, by Lerner and Loewe; *Kiss Me Kate* in 1948, with music and lyrics by Cole Porter; *South Pacific* in 1949, by Rodgers and Hammerstein (It, like *Oklahoma!*, won the Pulitzer Prize); *Guys and Dolls* in 1950, with music and lyrics by Frank Loesser. But Arlen remained in Hollywood, where he went through another two-year drought with no lyricist and no work.

His personal life was in disarray. His father had retired in 1948 and moved with Celia to California and into the Arlen home. This was untenable for Anya. Although the Arlucks tried to be polite, she knew they didn't like or approve of her, and now she couldn't hide from them, not even in her own house. Harold rented a separate place for them to live in, but they were still nearby and liable to drop in at any time. The worst of it was that they—especially Samuel—harped at the Arlens about their childlessness. Anya was, according to Jablonski, "a barren woman,"[1] but Harold's parents couldn't have known this because they went on and on about not having grandchildren, and the cantor let Harold know that fathering children was more than a man's duty; it was a proof of manhood.

A distressing incident had occurred shortly after the failure of *St. Louis Woman* in 1946. On the way home to California, Harold and Anya, after calling on the Arlucks in Syracuse, went to Buffalo to visit his old neighborhood. At the Pine Street Synagogue they saw, sitting on its steps, an elderly man who'd been the *shames*—sexton—when Harold was a boy, and now the two men chatted in Yiddish as Anya went on into the temple.

"Shalom," said Harold.
"You Cantor Arluck's son?"
Arlen nodded.
"And the girl—your wife?"
"Yes."
"Got any children?"
"No."
"Then what good are you?"

In his first biography of Arlen, *Happy with the Blues*, written during the composer's lifetime, Jablonski says that Harold found this incident amusing. In a second biography, *Rhythm, Rainbows, and Blues*, written after Harold's death, he tells us that this was an unsettling moment for the composer because the *shames*'s cruel and oracular judgment "coincided with that of Cantor Arluck and his wife . . . The inflexible ideology of centuries, and of one autocratic, obstinate man, would have a lamentable effect on 'the girl' and on the marriage of Anya and Harold Arlen."[2]

Soon Jerry, too, turned up in California. He was on his own now—he and Jeanne had divorced—and he took an apartment at the beach in Malibu and made the rounds of movie studio music departments looking for work. When he couldn't find any he, like his parents, became dependent on Harold for financial support. In return, Jerry ran errands for his brother. Because Harold was determined to keep his personal troubles secret, his friends got only an inkling of what was going on and knew better than to ask questions. But Jerry knew, and because he did, he became Harold's only confidant.

One day the Beverly Hills police came to Samuel and Celia's house to ask if they were related to a Harold Arluck whose car had been sitting in the L.A. Airport parking lot for two days. Although the authorities were concerned about this, they weren't ready to start an official investigation, so Jerry set out to find his brother. He went to Harold's house, but no one answered the door. He phoned Harold's friends, but no one knew where he was. People at the Hillcrest Country Club hadn't seen him, either. Three days passed before the mystery was solved by a phone call from a hospital in Honolulu. Harold was there undergoing detox. He'd left a bar in L.A., driven to the airport to catch a flight to New York—with no particular reason to go there—and mistakenly boarded a plane to Hawaii. During the flight he became so ill from drink he had to be hospitalized.

Upon returning to Beverly Hills he got his first job in two years. Columbia Pictures wanted him and Mercer to write songs for *The Petty Girl*, based on the career of pinup-girl photographer George Petty. Although they agreed to write the score, neither of them was enthusiastic. Arlen was distracted by family and alcohol troubles, and Mercer was preoccupied with what had become a quest to write a great Broadway book musical. He'd failed the year before, in 1949, with *Texas, Li'l Darlin*,' a satire on Texas politics, with music by Robert Emmett Dolan. Now he was writing the words and music for *Top Banana*, about the life and times of comedian Milton Berle. Neither show was more than a modest success. As for *The Petty Girl*, only one of the five Arlen–Mercer songs was published—an agreeable if half-hearted waltz called "Fancy Free."

Then came another job. Producer Sol Siegel at Twentieth Century–Fox asked Harold to write songs for a picture called *My Blue Heaven*—its title taken from a 1927 song by Walter Donaldson and George A. Whiting. Because the studio had no lyricist in mind, he was told to find one. He couldn't ask Koehler, who'd retired. Robin and Mercer were in New York. Ira Gershwin was mired in legal disputes over what would eventually become the film *An American in Paris*. Harburg was unavailable because fears about political leftists had stopped his and hundreds of other movie careers; he'd been blacklisted. To get his name off the list he wrote to the MGM legal department to say he was "a firm, almost fanatical believer in democracy."[3] When that didn't work he returned to Broadway, where the blacklist was ignored, and wrote *Flahooley* with music by Sammy Fain—a fairy tale in which people dressed as puppets sing disparagingly about right-wingers. It wasn't a success.

Arlen found a lyricist for *My Blue Heaven* through Harry Warren, who recommended Ralph Blane. Blane, an ardent Arlen admirer, had appeared in *Hooray for What!* in 1937 as one of the Singing Spies, and now, when he heard from his agent that he was to become Arlen's partner, instead of being happy, he grew anxious. He lay awake wondering what he'd gotten himself into. What if he was handed another "Stormy Weather" or an "Over the Rainbow" or a "Blues in the Night"? What if he wrecked a great melody? Finally he asked his agent to turn the job down. Instead, the agent phoned Arlen about the situation, and Arlen called Blane to reassure him, saying he'd had similar qualms when he'd worked with Jack Yellen. It was a disingenuous analogy; he'd been intimidated by Yellen's bluster, not his talent. But it comforted Blane, especially when Arlen said they could work on the lyrics together and have some fun—which they did, for a while. They wrote a series of songs that parodied the styles of big-time Broadway composers. "The Friendly Islands" was a takeoff on Rodgers and Hammerstein's "Bali Ha'i"; "I Love a New Yorker" on Cole Porter's "I Happen to Like New

York"; "Halloween" on Irving Berlin, who, with "Easter Parade" and "White Christmas," seemed to be cornering the market on holiday songs.

Then the fun ended. "We were working on 'Halloween,' a song to be sung by the stars of the picture, Betty Grable and Dan Dailey," Blane recalled. "Suddenly, from the kitchen which adjoined the music room came Mrs. Arlen. She had a long butcher knife in her hand and began accusing me of coming between her husband and herself. She actually chased me out of the studio into the yard by the garage before Harold could catch and subdue her. Harold begged me not to tell anyone, that she didn't know what she was doing. We learned later that Harold slept in a separate bedroom and always kept his door locked. She roamed the house, slashing his valuable paintings."[4]

Blane now knew what he had really gotten himself into. When Twentieth Century–Fox offered him and Arlen a second film he accepted the job but warily, as did Harold. Their concerns weren't just about Anya. They knew the film was going to be second-rate. Its working title was *The Friendly Islands*, after the big production number they'd written for *My Blue Heaven*. But then the front office decided to once again use a non-Arlen song as the title—"Down Among the Sheltering Palms" from 1914. This was a slap in the face, especially since the older song wasn't even used in the film. Even worse, the movie, a poor imitation of *South Pacific*, was produced and directed by men who knew nothing about film musicals. It was a project that had "dud" written all over it, and the studio delayed its release for two years until 1953, when it arrived in theaters and quickly disappeared, taking the Arlen–Blane songs—the last they wrote together—with it.

But the assignments from Twentieth Century–Fox kept coming. The next was *Mr. Imperium*, another takeoff on *South Pacific*. This time Arlen's partner was Dorothy Fields, whose credits included "On the Sunny Side of the Street" and "I Can't Give You Anything but Love" with composer Jimmy McHugh in the 1920s, and "The Way You Look Tonight" and "Pick Yourself Up" with Jerome Kern in the 1930s. Like Mercer, she wrote in a natural, conversational style—a heightened form of everyday speech. She was one of the twentieth century's great lyricists.

She was also one of Arlen's favorite people. He'd known her for twenty years, since he and Koehler replaced her and McHugh as the Cotton Club's chief songwriters. They had nicknames for each other. She called him Schnitter, a made-up Yiddish-sounding word, and he called her the Red Arrow because of her reputation as a speedy writer. She wasn't a beauty—not like Anya—but she was alluring. In the 1930s, Harold and George Gershwin had each filmed her swimming gracefully in their respective pools. Anya knew how socially at ease Fields was and how she could always make Harold laugh. That she was married and the mother of two young children didn't bring any peace of mind, because she was in town on her own, living in a private bungalow at the Beverly Hills Hotel.

We don't know if Arlen and Fields had an affair. She did tell an interviewer he was "a man full of love,"[5] and he certainly needed a refuge from his suffering—physical now as well as mental because of persistent abdominal pain. Due to the disarray in his house, he worked at her place. He couldn't have gotten there without Jerry, who arrived in the morning, roused him out of a drunken stupor—sometimes he wasn't in bed but on a neighbor's lawn—and drove him to Fields's bungalow. Arlen and Fields wrote two films in quick succession. The first, *Mr. Imperium*, had just three songs, all forgettable. The second, *The Farmer Takes a Wife*, was a musical remake of a 1935 movie about life on the Erie Canal, and, as with *Down Among the Sheltering Palms*, the studio postponed its release for two years before finally sending it to movie theaters, where its run was brief and unsuccessful.

Anya became completely unhinged over the collaboration between her husband and Fields. According to Jablonski, "her doctor felt she had become a danger to herself and to Arlen"[6] and recommended that she be institutionalized. He doesn't tell us—and there is no other source—who the doctor was, what tests were performed, what the diagnosis was, or if the Taranda family expressed an opinion or even knew about the decision. In an undated and unaddressed letter titled "A brief, if not illuminating, lecture on Anya Arlen's illness," most likely prepared for his publisher as he wrote his second Arlen biography, Jablonski says he was never able to get the basic facts:

> This, I know, is frustrating, but in all the years I knew Harold and Anya—as well as friends and family—no one discussed her emotional problems. Even Yip Harburg who could be blunt . . . I doubt that Anya was placed in a real hospital, but rather in a rest home (Hollywood was full of them), but under medical supervision. I also doubt that she would have consented to seeing a psychiatrist. She was having emotional problems and she was sent to a place where they calmed her down (à la Judy Garland, many others) . . . I simply can't bring myself to conjecture on this when I have so little information.[7]

Harold couldn't bring himself to drive Anya to the facility. Instead, he asked Jerry to do it. It was Jerry who signed her in and handed her over to the doctors, which hardly endeared him to her. He had to do this a number of times, because it was easy for Harold to convince himself that she'd be better off at home. *He* was the one who drove to the institution to sign her out. On one of her furloughs he became convinced that the crisis had finally passed. This was early in 1952, when she had a sustained period of stability and good spirits. When Harry Warren suggested to him that they and publisher Buddy Morris take their wives to Europe, he agreed. And Anya had a good time. She enjoyed these people—Harry and Josephine Warren, Buddy and Carolyn Morris—and was delighted to be with Harold away from Hollywood. As they toured London, Paris, Rome, and Naples, Warren's stream of gruff, sarcastic asides kept her laughing. But then, when she came home, she unraveled. Many years later, when Michael Feinstein was working for Ira and Leonore Gershwin, he asked them to tell him about Anya in those days. "She was sweet and adorable and then she went mad," said Leonore."[8]

CHAPTER 20

A STAR IS BORN

Although Harold Arlen had been Judy Garland's favorite composer even before *The Wizard of Oz*, and even though his music in that movie did so much to launch her career, they didn't work together in the decade that followed—the 1940s—which was a period of great achievement for both of them. She was under contract to MGM, where Arthur Freed, himself an Arlen admirer, was in charge of musicals, but the studio didn't bring Arlen in to work with her again. No great Arlen song of the 1940s was written for her.

Disparate in age, temperament, and fame, they went their separate ways during that decade, but their problems were similar. Each was an addict—he to alcohol, she to barbiturates and amphetamines. Both dealt with mental illness—he out of the spotlight and through Anya's terrible descent, she with the whole world watching as drugs pulled her down. She'd been introduced to them by her bosses at MGM, who wanted to wring every working hour they could from her. They did this in collusion with her mother, who was intensely ambitious for her. Her resulting dependency and illnesses, along with a rebellious streak, made her a frequent no-show on movie sets. This put her films over budget, and even though they were still profitable, MGM began to think of her as more trouble than she was worth. By 1950, when she was twenty-eight years old and working on *Summer Stock*, she'd already been suspended numerous times, sent to sanitariums on both coasts, and given electric shock therapy. Having begun her working life while still a toddler, lost her doting father at thirteen, and struggled under her mother's thumb, she'd grown into a woman whose suicidal misery resided side by side with a tremendous joie de vivre. A great actress, she could sing "Over the Rainbow" at a party and have everyone in tears—herself included— and then suddenly stop to matter-of-factly ask that her drink be freshened. There were several headline-making suicide attempts—sometimes she cut her wrists, sometimes her throat—but the resulting injuries were invariably superficial nicks. She had an unending need for reassurance, and yet, when she began work on the 1948 film *Easter Parade* and found Irving Berlin giving her advice on how best to sing his songs, she "put her face two inches in front of his, poked a pugnacious finger into his stomach and said: 'Listen, buster, you write 'em, I sing 'em.'"[1] He took no offense. She was, after all, the best song-and-dance performer anyone had ever seen.

She arrived on the set of *Summer Stock* after a three-month stay at Peter Bent Brigham Hospital near Boston. Their regimen was good for her. She'd gone there a wasted-looking addict and come out healthy and plump—too plump, said the studio heads, who told her to slim down. So it was back to pill-popping, illness, and, for the first time, hallucinations. Yet the film somehow got made.

When *Summer Stock* was finished, she told a musical director at the cast party, "I'm a fat slob"[2] and headed for the seaside resort of Carmel, where, a few days later the studio called to ask if she would do one more song for the film. She surprised them by saying yes, and they surprised her by agreeing when she told them the song had to be "Get Happy." It had been Arlen's first hit—the first melody that had, it seemed, come to him from out of the sky. Back on the set and svelte—beautiful, in fact—she delivered a performance that made "Get Happy" one of the great standards. It was the movie's best moment and one of the best of her career, as well as a boost to Arlen, who'd been languishing in personal and professional troubles. She also tried to get "Last Night When We Were Young" into the film—she recorded it—but MGM said no. So she told her friend and sometime lover Frank Sinatra about the song, and he made the definitive recording for his 1955 *In the Wee Small Hours* album.

MGM fired Garland as she began work on her next film, *Royal Wedding*. So she embarked on a concert career. In April 1951 at the London Palladium, her set included "Get Happy"—associated with her now and not with Arlen and Koehler—and ended with her sitting on the lip of the stage, her legs dangling over the edge, doing a cathartic "Over the Rainbow." After the Palladium came an even longer run at the Palace Theatre in New York, where she put these songs over to bigger audiences.

In 1952 she married Sid Luft, who'd started life as a bullied Jewish kid in New York and grew up to be a broad-shouldered, good-looking man and something of a thug. He wasn't skilled at much except getting Judy what she wanted, and what she wanted now was a deal with Warner Bros. that would let her remake the 1937 film classic *A Star Is Born* as a musical. This tragic story about an actress on the rise who falls in love with an alcoholic star in decline had long appealed to her and many in Hollywood—every Christmas, Humphrey Bogart showed it to friends and ended up in tears. When Warner Bros. said yes, Garland asked Arlen and Harburg to write the score. The studio approved Arlen but wouldn't hire the blacklisted Harburg, so Ira Gershwin was brought in.

Harold and Ira hadn't worked on a project together since 1934, when they and Yip did the Broadway revue *Life Begins at 8:40*. That was twenty years earlier, when George had been alive and Anya was Harold's nineteen-year-old girlfriend. Now George was long gone, Anya institutionalized, Yip blacklisted, and Ira, after a series of Broadway and Hollywood failures, nearing retirement. He, too, had almost been blacklisted. Like Yip, he'd been a member of a suspect group, the Hollywood Independent Citizens' Committee of the Arts, Sciences, and Professions. Subpoenaed to testify before the California Senate's Subcommittee on Un-American Activities, his quiet laughter in response to the senators' questions made it clear to everyone, even them, that it would be absurd to try to link "Gershwin" with "un-American."

As Harold began work on the new film, he was suffering from alcoholism and stomach pain, and he'd just learned that his father was dying of liver cancer. A Beverly Hills physician, Dr. Morris Steinman, had told him that Anya's confinement would be long-term, maybe permanent. Not yet fifty, he'd aged visibly. His face was deeply lined, and he kept his red and watery eyes hidden behind dark glasses even when he was indoors. He'd stopped answering mail, paying bills, cashing checks. He would not, however, allow himself to become disheveled; he remained dapper, never without a boutonnière in his coat lapel.

He and Ira began their work in January 1953 at the Gershwin house at 1021 North Roxbury, a residence Ira and Leonore had purchased next door to the one they'd rented with George. Ira's secretary, Lawrence D. Stewart, wrote a description of the scene as this work began: "Harold Arlen arrives about two-thirty in the afternoon with his old tan briefcase under his arm . . . Gershwin moves to a cat-clawed green armchair nearer the piano, where he sits with Calliope, the Siamese, on his lap and pets her abstractedly as he smokes a cigar. He puts his glasses upon his forehead, leans back and closes his eyes, as he moves his hands in tempo with the music."[3]

The script called for an opening rhythm song to be sung by Judy's character, Esther Blodgett, onstage at the Shrine Auditorium in Los Angeles. When James Mason's character, Norman Maine, drunkenly interrupts her performance, she comes to his aid by nimbly incorporating him into her act. With this setting in mind, Harold came up with a lively musical phrase that, after he and Ira worked on it for two weeks, became "Gotta Have Me Go with You."

Next was what they and screenwriter Moss Hart called "the dive song." Judy was to sing it in a walk-down nightclub backed by a small jazz ensemble. As Arlen sat at George's piano and tried out a melody, Leonore called out from another part of the house, "Sounds like Gershwin to me."[4] It bothered Harold to be told he was imitating George or anyone else, so he switched to another tune, one written several years earlier. It had come to nothing then because Johnny Mercer, in a rare lapse, had failed to see its potential and gave it a lackluster lyric that began "I've seen Sequoia, it's really very pretty / The art of Goya and Rockefeller City."[5] Years later Arlen recalled that moment to an interviewer and, careful not to mention Mercer by name, said, "I wrote a song with a pretty goddam wonderful lyric-writer. He brought me a lyric that didn't have any strength. Sometimes a lyric depletes a melody, just as a poor melody can deplete a good lyric."[6]

But when Ira heard this music he was instantly on the alert. "Play it again," he said. Harold did. "Do you like 'The Man That Got Away'?" he asked.[7] "I like," Harold replied.[8] In a book about his songwriting career, Ira wrote that this "title hit me as a paraphrase of the angler's 'You should have seen the one that got away.'"[9] So there was poetic justice in the fact that it was hard work reeling the song in. Hours passed before Ira had its opening lines, "The night is bitter / The stars have lost their glitter / The winds grow colder / And suddenly you're older." Half a day was spent on "Good riddance, good-bye"—the first three words and five notes of the bridge. For Arlen, bridges were occasions to explore unusual musical territory, and this time he was particularly adventurous. At "fools will be fools," the melody and harmony seem to lose each other, making it necessary for the singer to thread her way through a sequence of unfriendly, almost atonal chords. At the end of the song, in the coda, Arlen returns—we don't know if it was intentionally—to Leonore's "It sounds like Gershwin" remark and goes ahead and writes like George, pitting the edgy "the night is bitter" music against a fresh and expansive setting of the title phrase—just as Gershwin had joined a nervous countermelody to the famous slow theme of the *Rhapsody in Blue*.

Arlen knew it was a powerhouse song and thought Ira's lyric "glorious."[10] But Ira wanted to wait a while before letting Judy hear it. It isn't clear why he felt this way. Maybe he was worried that her judgment would be clouded by their close friendship. He was godfather to her and Vincente Minnelli's daughter Liza, and it was to the Gershwin home that she repaired during the fights that led to the breakup of that marriage. But Harold had no doubt about the song and was eager to play it for her. He told Ira he was going to take a few days off and relax in Palm Springs—knowing that Judy was there with Sid Luft and scriptwriter Moss Hart. Ira knew this, too, and asked Harold not to go there to play them the song. Harold said he had no such intention, that he just needed rest, and drove the hundred miles to the Tamarisk Country Club, found Judy and Sid on the golf course, and walked it with them. "About the middle of the round," he recalled, "I started to whistle very softly. I don't know what tempted me. She was about twenty yards away—it was kind of a tease and I couldn't stand it. I love Ira and I love Judy, and well, I whistled the main phrase of 'The Man That Got Away.'" That was all it took. Judy asked him what he was whistling, he gave her a coy "I don't know," and she, certain it was a song for the movie, stopped the golf game and took him to the piano in the clubhouse, where he got what he'd come for: a happy moment. Judy loved the song, as did Sid Luft, Moss Hart, and Hart's wife Kitty Carlisle. They all went "went wild with joy," as Arlen later recalled.[11] Garland then insisted on phoning Ira to tell him how she felt about "The Man That Got Away" and "Gotta Have Me Go with You," which Harold had also played. At that point Harold was pretty sure Ira would forgive his duplicity, which he did.

A few months later, in the spring of 1953, Judy asked her old friend Hugh Martin—he'd written "Have Yourself a Merry Little Christmas" for her—to be her vocal coach and help with the film's instrumental and vocal arrangements. He agreed, and came to Los Angeles, took a suite at the Chateau Marmont Hotel on Sunset Boulevard, and had a piano delivered there. In his autobiography, he recalls Arlen coming over to play "the entire score for me, and I had been hypnotized. When he sang for me 'The Man That Got Away,' he dropped his volume to a smoky whisper that evoked the little after-hours joint where Esther Blodgett and her orchestra buddies congregated after their gig, to play and sing just for themselves. I remembered the way Arlen had sung it, and I could already hear, in my imagination, Judy singing it with moody, understated emotion."[12]

But everything went awry when Martin got to Judy's Sunset Boulevard home to rehearse the song. She'd been taking Dexedrine to lose weight and was jumpy. He played "The Man That Got Away" in Harold's understated way and she became irate—an anger made all the worse because Martin had chosen the key of B-flat. She insisted on singing it a whole tone higher in C. He warned her she'd have trouble in that key, that it would cause her to yell, especially during the demanding "fools will be fools" section. She replied, "There has to be a flash of something extraordinary at this moment. If I croon the damn song why would Norman Maine see the possibility that I might be a star?"[13] Arlen, Gershwin, and director George Cukor were on

Martin's side of this argument, but none of them weighed in. It was Martin and not they who attended the recording session in late August. And when he saw that she'd had the orchestration—which included his own haunting four-bar intro—written in C, he prepared himself for the worst. "She warmed up on takes one and two," he remembered. "Then, on take three she let us have it—all stops pulled out."[14]

Although Hugh Martin didn't like the way Judy Garland sang "The Man That Got Away," time has proven her correct. Her performance of this song was up to the standards of "Over the Rainbow" and "Get Happy," and her work in this movie was the best of her life. Yet *A Star Is Born* turned out to be her last great movie musical. And it was Arlen's final moment as a great movie songwriter. Each was dealing with forces they couldn't control. For Judy, there were her drug and emotional problems. During the shooting of the film, even though she and her husband were the producers and despite the fact that she wanted more than anything for this to be a significant movie and her big film comeback, she was always calling in sick, causing endless delays. "This is the behavior of someone unhinged," said Cukor.[15] At the same time she managed to turn in one memorable scene after another. Of her appearance at the end of the film as Norman Maine's widow, Cukor said, "It scared me. I had goose pimples, it was so extraordinary."[16]

Bigger troubles came with Sid Luft's suggestion that, to make sure there were lots of hit songs, they give up the idea of having an Arlen–Gershwin tune precede the intermission and instead let Judy do a version of her stage act, singing a series of proven standards. For Arlen and Gershwin, this was similar to what Harburg and Lane had gone through when Al Jolson interrupted *Hold on to Your Hats* to entertain audiences with a medley of his past hits, including "Swanee"—which was one of the songs Judy now chose for a fifteen-minute montage called "Born in a Trunk." It was an entertaining sequence, expertly arranged by Roger Edens and Leonard Gershe, that told the story of her real-life show-business career. But it had nothing to do with the rest of the film, which was now three and a half hours long. This worried studio head Jack Warner, because movie houses wouldn't be able to screen it more than a few times a day. So the chopping began, first by him and then by Cukor. *A Star Is Born* premiered successfully with a three-hour running time and did well in its first weeks, but then Jack Warner's estranged brother Harry ordered the removal of another half hour, which created a mangled version that got bad reviews. In the end, it barely broke even.

Several fine Arlen–Gershwin songs were cut, including "Lose That Long Face," which Judy performed tap dancing on a city street Gene Kelly–style.

Fortunately, a great love song, "It's a New World," was kept in. Its verse ("How wonderful that I'm beholding") has the elegant simplicity of the verses for "Over the Rainbow" ("When all the world is a hopeless jumble") and "My Shining Hour" ("This moment, this minute"), while the refrain that follows ("It's a new world I see") has a hymn-like feel. The fact that it never repeats except fleetingly at the end is extraordinary, given that popular music lives through repetition and that this was the big ballad of the movie. Arlen showed integrity and bravery in his refusal to cash in on an ear-catching premise but instead allow each note to grow into the next.

He and Ira received an Academy Award nomination for "The Man That Got Away," but the winner was "Three Coins in the Fountain." No one has ever called that a wise decision. Judy Garland was nominated for best actress but lost to Grace Kelly, who'd played a similar role as the wife of an alcoholic in *The Country Girl*. On the night of the ceremony, Judy was in the hospital, having just given birth to her third child, Joey Luft. Television crews were on hand to broadcast her thank-you speech, their cameras on scaffolding erected outside her hospital room because doctors wouldn't allow them inside. When the award went elsewhere, so did they.

It's a small irony that Arlen and Gershwin had also written songs for *The Country Girl*. "We didn't give it our best,"[17] Arlen admitted, and none of those songs—one with the unwieldy title of "Dissertation on the State of Bliss"—is well remembered. At that point Ira retired from songwriting. Judy returned to her concert career. And Harold, with Celia and Jerry, moved to New York to write a Broadway show, his first since *St. Louis Woman* eight years earlier. He didn't know how long he'd be on the East Coast, so he left everything behind: books, papers, clothing, furnishings in storage, and Anya in an institution. Upon his departure she gave him a gift, a wallet, with a note inside that read: "April 27, 1953. Inglewood Airport. Dear Hare, for you to joy and forget me not and I love—dats daf a big hug, a bigger kiss with all this you can't miss. Annie."[18]

CHAPTER 21

HOUSE OF FLOWERS

By 1954, Harburg hadn't worked with Arlen in ten years, not since *Bloomer Girl*. After asking Harold to write *Finian's Rainbow* with him in 1947, he invited him to work on *Flahooley* in 1951, but Arlen turned him down both times because the shows were too political and because he'd learned that working with Harburg on Broadway could be a nerve-wracking experience. When Yip was in charge of a production he tended to become confrontational and demanding, although never toward Arlen, whom he always treated with friendship and respect—even tenderness. In 1952 he brought Harold another idea, this one with no politics, just a love story based on a trio of plays by French writer Marcel Pagnol. He lined up producer David Merrick and then, on March 27, 1952, wrote to Harold to say the show would "give us an opportunity to express ourselves in more mature ways than we've ever done before."[1] When problems arose involving rights, he remained optimistic. "Merrick was here," he wrote Arlen on August 1, "and I am sure that the Pagnol situation can be straightened out! The show we dream of will rise like the Phoenix National Bank out of the ashes."[2] But it didn't—at least not for Harburg and Arlen. In 1954 it arrived successfully as *Fanny*, with music and lyrics by Harold Rome.

Actually, Yip's August 1 letter was more of a pep talk for Arlen than a discussion of the musical. In the summer of 1952, Harold was hospitalized for alcoholism and stomach ulcers. His old friend from the Croydon Hotel days, Dr. Miguel Elias, came to California to tend to him, and in this letter Harburg tried to do the same: "While my psyche is being torn apart and my ego scattered in six directions, here you are in a beautiful hospital where life is gentle . . . My thoughts fondly fly toward you. For never in all this land was there a sweeter minstrel. Yours is a throbbing note that occupies a special ventricle in the heart of America. Not to have written with you these past five years[3] was an irreparable waste. I am looking forward to our next collaboration as only a starved lyricist could to a gourmet cadenza."[4]

In February 1953, Yip tried again. As Harold and Ira were writing "The Man That Got Away," Harburg offered his old partner a bold proposal. "Over the weekend," he wrote on February 12, 1953, "I've done some deliberating over an idea which looms up as an exciting venture. I feel that *The Wizard of Oz* can be made into an American opera for children and grown-ups that would be to American music what *Porgy and Bess* is to Negro culture." Arthur Freed was interested in producing it on Broadway, he said, and he urged Harold to talk to Freed. "Close your eyes and give this a little thought and I'm sure you will see all the possibilities. Of course we would use the score we wrote for the screen play as a nucleus which would furnish about half the music."[5] It isn't known if this idea intrigued Arlen or if he contacted Freed. We do know that nothing came of it and that, instead of collaborating with Harburg, he turned to a writer who had no experience with songs or musicals.

This was Truman Capote, who at twenty-nine was already entering his second decade of fame. Born in New Orleans, sloughed off by his parents to a houseful of eccentric aunts and cousins in Monroeville, Alabama, he had, during a lonely childhood, charted a course toward literary greatness and celebrity—the two were inseparable to him. He arrived in New York at twenty with an impressive mastery of Southern Gothic writing, an impish but convivial personality, and startling looks: he was just over five feet tall, wore his blond hair in bangs, had a strange high-pitched baby's voice, and was openly and happily homosexual. He was also, as his friend and biographer Gerald Clarke put it, determined to "ruthlessly seize his glorious future the way a condor does its prey."[6] This he did with his first novel, *Other Voices, Other Rooms*, which got people talking not only about his writing, but about a dust jacket photo that showed him supine on a sofa giving the camera a come-hither look. When this picture became the centerpiece in a *Life* magazine photo essay on new writers, he got the fame he'd longed for.

At the urging of a young Broadway producer, Arnold Saint Subber, who'd come to prominence with Cole Porter's *Kiss Me, Kate* in 1948, Capote turned his second novel, *The Grass Harp*, into a play. After it flopped, Saint Subber (he later hyphenated his name) encouraged him to try again, this time by making a Broadway musical out of his 1950 short story "House of Flowers."

Capote had conceived the tale on a visit to Haiti in 1948 when he wandered into a red-light district on the outskirts of Port-au-Prince. There he befriended a madam and her prostitutes and spent several nights with them drinking and telling stories. Out of this came a bizarre fairy tale about a beautiful young prostitute, Ottilie, who marries a handsome young man, Royal, and returns with him to their native hill country, where they live in a house blanketed by wisteria—a house of flowers. Also residing there is Royal's intimidating grandmother, Old Bonaparte, who hates Ottilie and inflicts spells on her—a severed cat's head in her sewing basket, for one. But Ottilie knows how to deflect her magic, bringing on the old woman's demise. As punishment for killing his grandmother, Royal ties her to a tree, but she accepts this mistreatment as the price she must pay for his passionate lovemaking.

This little story would not at first seem to be prime Broadway musical material, and Capote, aware of this, spent the summer of 1953 in Rome making changes. The main impediment to Ottilie and Royal's happiness now became a formerly minor character, Monsieur Jamison, to whom Ottilie has been promised by the brothel's proprietress, the previously unnamed Madame Fleur. For a subplot, Capote made up a new character, Madame Tango, who runs a rival brothel and wants Ottilie to come work for her. Old Bonaparte was taken out of the story. In a concession to the prudish sensibilities of the 1950s, Ottilie became a virgin—who, for some unexplained reason, lives in a whorehouse.

When Arlen received this script in November 1953 he was dubious. He thought it more atmospheric than plot-driven and better suited to opera. He doesn't seem to have considered the fact that, like his failed *St. Louis Woman* eight years earlier, it asked an African American cast to portray a bunch of lowlifes. It was also like *St. Louis Woman* in having a weak second act. Still, he went ahead. It was by Truman Capote, after all, whose *Other Voices, Other Rooms* he'd read and admired and who, being an acclaimed young American author, presumably had a feel for current popular taste. It would also have the successful young Saint Subber as its producer, and choreography by the renowned George Balanchine. On top of all that, Capote had gotten Peter Brook, a wunderkind British director of Shakespeare and Puccini, to join the venture. Probably as important to Arlen as any of this was his desire to get out of Hollywood. He'd spent the better part of twenty years there and had only three good films to show for it: *The Wizard of Oz*, *Cabin in the Sky*, and *A Star Is Born*. The era of Hollywood musicals with original songs was ending, and prospects for future work were bleak. In vogue now were movies with just one new song—a theme sung over the credits, usually written by the composer who did the background music. For Arlen, New York was the only place left.

So he had his old friend and agent Abe Berman find an apartment big enough for him, his mother, and his brother. Anya would remain in California until her doctors pronounced her well enough to come home to him.

In November of 1953, as he made these plans, he started work on songs for the new show. In Capote's short story, Ottilie asks her prostitute friends how she'll know when she is truly in love. When they don't give her a satisfactory answer, she goes to a Vodou priest, a *Houngan*, who tells her to catch a wild bee, hold it in her hands, and think her lover's name. If the bee doesn't sting, then her love is real. Charmed by this, Arlen wrote the music[7] and most of the words for "A Sleepin' Bee." Capote was in Rome at the time, and Arlen was still in Beverly Hills, so he made an acetate recording of himself playing and singing the song and mailed it to Italy. "It was quite odd," Capote told an interviewer several years later, "listening to this disembodied voice and trying to derive from it some notion of what sort of man he might be, my collaborator. Obviously he was a gentle man, a modest one, but someone capable of immense intensity, and had I not known differently I would have assumed he was a Negro. His voice, especially his singing voice, had a warm, plaintive, muddy-colored tone and the diction also had a certain very pleasant Negro quality."[8]

Twenty years earlier, when Arlen had been a vocalist on commercial recordings, listeners often assumed he was black. This could even happen when people met him in person. Shortly after making his demo of "A Sleepin' Bee," he went to Las Vegas for the opening of Marlene Dietrich's one-woman show at the Sahara Hotel, and the fifty-two year old Dietrich, who loved Arlen's music—in the show she performed "One for My Baby" in a top hat and tails—phoned her daughter to tell her about meeting him for the first time. "I just stood there in awe in front of him. But you know he looks white! How can the man who wrote 'Stormy Weather' be white? He also wrote that Bluebird thing that Judy Garland insists on singing with all her blubbering"—Dietrich and Garland didn't get along—"but you know his hair is very kinky! I am going to ask Nat King Cole if Harold Arlen is black or white."[9]

He was white. But, in a way that African Americans had picked up on as early as his Cotton Club days, he was also black. Singer Paul Robeson was intrigued by the link between black and Jewish music and gave a lecture in Carnegie Hall that traced the two traditions to a common source in Eastern Europe. With "A Sleepin' Bee," Arlen created a sort of Russian-Jewish-Negro spiritual, and it was only the latest of his songs to provide Robeson's theory with supporting evidence. His musical language—the sound we associate with him—was far removed from the middle-of-the-road and sometimes corny fare that reigned on Broadway at the time. This quality was just as apparent in the next two songs he and Capote wrote for the show. In January of 1954, while he was still in Beverly Hills and Truman in Paris, they collaborated by phone on "I Never Has Seen Snow." It, like "I Had Myself a True Love" from *St. Louis Woman*, backs a lonesome melody with alternating major and minor chords. The music sways and drones; it's like a union of African American and synagogue choirs. The first time we hear the word "beautiful" ("Snow ain't so beautiful, can't be so beautiful like my love is"), the melody clashes with the harmony, yet the resulting sound is peaceful, not harsh. When "beautiful" is heard again, a minor alteration in the harmony results in a consonance that has elegance and depth. There are similar moments in the title song, "House of Flowers," whose simple melody is supported by adventurous chords. At the bridge ("I never had money") they turn into bright harmonic colors. Nothing else on Broadway in 1954 was like this. Nothing had been like it there since *St. Louis Woman* eight years earlier.

"Eventually, when I did meet Arlen," Capote recalled,

> and we began to work together, I found all my long distance impressions confirmed. The sadness, the echo of loneliness that wails through [his] music seemed to me the foundation of his sensibility for he is a man obsessed with the tragic view of life. At the same time, amid the sighs, the long sad looks, laughter was always ready to run rampant. He had one of the most distinctive laughs I've ever heard—a wild, high-pitched chuckling that reddens his face and fills his eyes with tears. I had no true understanding of songwriting (and Lord knows still do not). But Arlen, who I suppose had never worked with an amateur before, was tolerant and infinitely encouraging and, well, just a gent about the whole thing. A brave gent, too.[10]

In February 1954, as Arlen and Capote were writing songs in the spacious apartment Arlen had rented at Park Avenue and East 52nd Street, Capote decided to throw a party for Harold's forty-ninth birthday. One of the celebrities who came was Dietrich. According to her daughter and biographer, Maria Rivas, she had begun an affair with Arlen the previous November in Las Vegas. Rivas wrote: "The night Arlen came to see my mother's show, he fell madly in love with her and remained so 'til the day he died."[11] They undoubtedly became sexually involved and were later good friends, but there is no evidence for Riva's contention that Dietrich inspired great jealousy in Arlen or that he became her "ever devoted victim"[12] It was a relationship that reached its greatest intensity when he became seriously ill and she, seeing how alone he was, stepped in to take care of him.

Shortly after this party, the abdominal pain he'd been suffering for years because of ulcers became so severe he was admitted to Doctor's Hospital, where exploratory surgery by Dr. Elias found a bleeding liver. Blood trans-fusions were administered, but they were just a stopgap. Unless the liver regenerated itself—a slim hope—the condition was fatal. Upon hearing this, Arlen didn't appear particularly concerned. In fact, he seemed strangely indifferent. That's what Capote was referring to when he talked about his bravery—that and the fact that he continued composing, even in his hospital room. He worked out the complex rhythms of "Two Ladies in de Shade of de Banana Tree" by tapping them with a spoon on his dinner tray, an IV in his arm. Despite his illness, an atmosphere of levity spread through the room. Capote made a game of reading his mail without permission. When Harold tried to hide the letters and telegrams, Truman said, "Dads, where are they?" At one point the young author was surprised to find an envelope addressed to himself. He opened it and read: "T—Aren't you ashamed of yourself, you little bastard?—H."[13]

In the meantime, Dietrich was commandeering police cars to take her, sirens wailing, to the hospital. She insisted on participating in consulta-tions between Dr. Elias and the other physicians and thought nothing of undressing and getting into bed with the patient. In his first biography of Arlen, written when Anya was still alive, Jablonski doesn't mention Dietrich except to say she had appeared in the 1944 film *Kismet*, for which Arlen and Harburg had written three obscure songs. In the second, written after Harold and Anya had died, he discusses Dietrich's relationship with Arlen during this period but refers to her disparagingly as "The professional angel of mercy."[14] In fact, she nursed and catered to Arlen when no one else could or would, and her decency was genuine. In the 1930s, when the German Reich demanded that she return and make her films in Berlin, she took on American citizenship. During the war she accompanied Allied troops in Africa and Europe and was with General Patton (sometimes in his bed) as the Third Army crossed the Rhine.

Defying all expectations, Arlen rallied and was able to return to his apart-ment, where he stuck to a bland diet, refrained from alcohol, and kept work-ing. He had insisted that Jerry be the show's conductor, and now, for the first time, they were musical colleagues, discussing how to use steel drums and other South American and Caribbean instruments in the orchestration. Capote was in the apartment all the time, laboring over the songs with Arlen, who pitched in on the lyrics. The young writer made himself so much at home that he got his hand slapped by Celia as he helped himself to a snack from the refrigerator.

Then Arlen's illness returned. It was another bout of internal bleeding, this time in his esophagus. Back at Doctor's Hospital, Dr. Elias staunched the flow with a drug, vasopressin, that constricted his blood vessels. A tube was threaded through his throat to withdraw blood from his stomach. Additional transfusions were given—he had more than thirty in all. Once again the prognosis was poor and again Dietrich was at his bedside, although now she had competition. Singer Lisa Kirk, who'd been introduced to Arlen by Saint Subber, had fallen in love with him. This made for some madcap moments—Kirk hurriedly escorted by nurses from the sickroom as Dietrich drew near, Dietrich hustled away as Kirk approached. Perhaps, in addition to his sturdy constitution, it was the pleasure of having these women fuss over him that caused Arlen, to his doctors' amazement, to rally once again. By late May he and Capote had completed the *House of Flowers* score.

Then came troubles with the show. Director Brook, like Capote, had no experience with Broadway musicals. Or with African Americans. Early on he posed a strange question to the stage manager, Lucia Victor: "Tell me," he asked her, "how do you handle them?" "Who do you men by 'them'?" she replied. "The blacks. I just don't know how to handle them."[15] As rehearsals got underway he assembled the cast and said: "I should like all of you to know, first of all, that I am not prejudiced."[16] A little later, he told them: "Before I left London somebody told me that all you blacks were a lazy, shiftless lot and that it was going to be a lot of trouble working with you. If you don't all snap to it . . . I think you should just all be sent back to the islands, or wherever you come from."[17]

Pearl Bailey, who'd starred in *St. Louis Woman* and led a protest against its stereotyped characters, was in this show too, playing Madam Fleur. Upon hearing Brook say these things she left the theater—only to return and demand that *he* leave instead, which he did. Eventually he quit and was replaced by Herbert Ross, who also became Balanchine's replacement after the choreographer saw how badly things were going and walked out. Problems also developed between Pearl Bailey and Diahann Carroll, who portrayed Ottilie. Bailey was expropriating the nineteen-year-old Carroll's best songs. This angered Jerry Arlen, who got them back for Carroll, although he earned Bailey's enmity for doing so. When Capote heard a rumor—untrue—that Johnny Mercer would be rewriting some of his lyrics, he told everyone he had to take his sick dog to a Palm Springs veterinarian and dropped out of sight until opening night. Even Arlen had an angry moment. Saint Subber gave one of his tunes to lyricist Michael Brown, who wrote it up as "Indoor Girl," a song Harold considered too suggestive. It was an odd complaint, given that the show was about prostitutes, featured a wild Vodou dance by Geoffrey Holder, and had a heroine who got an erotic thrill when her lover tied her to a tree. But Arlen, hearkening back to his Cotton Club days, disliked having his name associated with any song he considered smutty. In typical fashion, he didn't confront Brown or Saint Subber or demand that the song be taken out of the show. Instead, he expressed his frustration by writing the word "shit" next to it in the conductor's score.

Throughout all these troubles, Dietrich was there with encouraging words, coffee and pastries for the cast and crew, and foot massages for Pearl Bailey, who'd collapsed from exhaustion during the Philadelphia tryout. For a while it seemed that Bailey would have to be written out of the show, which guaranteed a disaster because she'd come to dominate it—*House of Flowers* had devolved into "an extended vaudeville act for Miss Bailey," grumbled Capote.[18] But she regained her health in time for the New York opening, which took place at the Alvin Theatre on Thursday, December 30, 1954. Arlen and Dietrich sat together near newspaper columnist Walter Winchell, who told them after the first act that he liked what he was seeing. Arlen turned to Dietrich and said, "I hope he doesn't come back for the second act."[19]

Everyone knew it was a mess, and no one was surprised when the reviews were negative. Capote received most of the blame. In fact, *House of Flowers* was usually referred to as a Capote show. Brooks Atkinson's *New York Times* review was titled "Truman Capote's Musical," and he didn't mention Arlen until he'd first criticized Capote's decision to write a musical about a bordello, approved of British designer Oliver Messel's costumes and scenery, and taken another swipe at Capote. Then he finally got around to the music. "It begins," he wrote, "with an uninteresting overture and continues through the familiar set pieces of business-like musicals . . . Mr. Arlen's big numbers are second-rate Broadway or Hollywood." In conclusion, he discussed the cast: "Tall and short Negroes, adults and youngsters, torrid maidens in flashy costumes and bare-chested bucks break out into a number of wild, grotesque, animalistic dances."[20]

Nearly twenty years later, eminent Broadway composer and conductor Lehman Engel summed up *House of Flowers* this way: "All motivations are deep secrets. Romance is a muddle. There is no subplot. There are songs. There is no show."[21] But by then his dismissal of Arlen's music—"There are songs"—was a minority opinion. People had gradually come to realize that this was a great score. Walter Kerr of the New York *Herald Tribune* was one of the few critics who felt that way at the time of the premiere. Unlike Atkinson, he loved the overture and wrote that he wished they'd played it twice. It's a dynamic piece that begins with a police whistle and then delivers the rhythms Arlen had tapped out on his hospital dinner tray—only now they were played by steel drums, steel pans, gourds, and bongos. Jerry Arlen conducted the orchestra with assurance and was at the helm for the original cast recording in January of 1955. Harold was there, too, and can be heard scat singing on "Mardi Gras" and delivering the high note in "I Never Has Seen Snow"—Diahann Carroll couldn't reach it because of a cold. Like the *St. Louis Woman* cast recording, this one sold poorly. The sinking show took its songs down with it and most of them remain unfamiliar to this day. Only "A Sleepin' Bee" was immediately popular—but with performers, not the public. Richard Rodgers remarked that for a time he couldn't go to an audition without hearing it. "I Never Has Seen Snow" and "Don't Like Goodbyes" were two others that, in time, became favored by musicians, although neither has ever achieved widespread popularity.

In 1968 Capote and Arlen tried to revive *House of Flowers*. This time Capote returned to his original story about the contest between Ottilie and Old Bonaparte. But it didn't work. It disappeared after a brief run in Greenwich Village. By 1968 Broadway had long since seen its final Arlen show.

CHAPTER 22

IN SEARCH OF FAME

Just after *House of Flowers'* 165th and final performance on May 21, 1955, Pearl Bailey stepped in front of the curtain and addressed the audience. She spoke about the musical's failure and about rumors of discord among its cast and crew. Whatever troubles there'd been, she said, had been family squabbles, all of them resolved. Then she surprised Arlen by asking him to join her onstage, and he stood diffidently beside her as she extolled his talent, recited a list of his best-known songs, and led the audience in a sing-along that filled the house with the emotion and energy he'd captured in his music.

This tribute had a valedictory feel, given the show's demise and Arlen's uncertain future. Truman Capote was able to quickly bounce back from this failure by giving up playwriting and returning to fiction, nonfiction, and then, with *In Cold Blood*, a combination of the two. But it was different for Arlen. He was tied to a single form—the popular song—whose only outlets, as he saw it, were Broadway and Hollywood shows. With Hollywood no longer in need of his services and Broadway leery of another failure, his future was problematic. Making things worse was the arrival of a new generation of songwriters with a new way of writing songs.

In his youth, Arlen sought and received encouragement from songwriting elders who were able to continue their careers as he embarked on his. This new generation was different. They weren't looking for his approval and were oblivious to the fact that their success meant his eclipse. Instead of intricate melodies, evocative harmonies, and subtle rhythms, they designed rudimentary tunes that could ride bumpily on an all-important backbeat. In 1950, two seventeen-year-old transplants from the East Coast, Jerry Leiber and Mike Stoller, met in Los Angeles and discovered a shared love of rhythm and blues. This was music that had become known outside the African American community in the early 1940s when radio stations balked at ASCAP's rising licensing fees and turned to less costly BMI artists, many of them black. Had Leiber and Stoller, who were Jewish, been born a generation earlier, they would have been a team like Arlen and Koehler, writing for Ethel Waters and Cab Calloway. Instead, in 1952, they wrote "Hound Dog" for rhythm-and-blues singer Big Mama Thornton, and it sold a million records. Four years later, Elvis Presley's recording of the song sold more than ten million. Just ten years had passed since everyone, young and old, was singing "Ac-cent-tchu-ate the Positive." Now juveniles willfully separated themselves from the music of their parents. They wanted rock and roll.

The new generation of songwriters didn't need Broadway or Hollywood. Everything they required was in the recording studio, where they worked alongside singers and bands—sometimes they *were* the singers and bands. Arlen's finished products were the notated piano-vocal arrangements he gave to his publishers, who printed them as sheet music to be played by amateurs or used by orchestrators as a guide when making arrangements for performers. Leiber and Stoller didn't bother with a piano–vocal arrangement—let someone at the publishing company do that—and they eliminated the orchestrator. In 1960 they were in a studio with singer Ben E. King, who, after singing several of their tunes, showed them one of his, which he hadn't yet finished. They completed the lyric and added a bass line that became an essential part of "Stand by Me." Other young writers, such as Carole King, Burt Bacharach, and Neil Sedaka, began their work at pianos in Tin Pan Alley–style cubicles in Midtown New York's Brill Building, but they, too, brought their ideas to life in recording studios. That is where they invented the vocal harmonies and instrumental solos that became inseparable from their songs. Their generation, which had at first seemed poised to make a lesser art of songwriting, turned out to be the one that finally crossed the line to become composers, responsible for every note. Given Arlen's talents as a singer, pianist, and arranger and his great songwriting gift, it's easy to believe he would have flourished had he come of age in the 1950s and that he would have loved the music of Little Richard, Carl Perkins, and Buddy Holly as he'd loved Louis Armstrong and Bix Beiderbecke.

But he wasn't young in the 1950s, and the only musical homes he had—Hollywood and Broadway—had shut their doors to him. So, without work and without Anya, he returned to the nightclubbing days of his youth. He was seen around town with Marlene Dietrich, Lisa Kirk, Gloria Vanderbilt, and Margaret Truman. His name made the gossip columns. At one club he danced with Marilyn Monroe and was overheard telling her, "People are watching us." "They must know who you are," came her witty reply.[1]

If he was looking for a new love, it seems unlikely he'd have gone about it in this public manner. It's more likely that he was trying to become famous. With his best-known songs identified not with him but with those who sang them, and with his health still precarious—he'd contacted hepatitis B from the transfusions—if he was ever going to become known for what he'd accomplished, the time to do it was now.

In November 1953 he appeared on television. The show was NBC's *Colgate Comedy Hour*, where, before a national audience, he sat at a baby grand wearing a dark suit and black bow tie and sporting a split mustache. The cameras watched him raise his fingers over the keys, pause, and then launch into a boogie-woogie lead-in to "It's Only a Paper Moon," which he sang breezily, taking liberties with the notes—his notes. It was a riveting moment in the sun for him but a short one because one by one, a parade of other singers joined in. The first was Connie Russell, who sang "Over the Rainbow." Then came the show's host, Eddie Cantor, who did "Accent-tchu-ate the Positive." After that Frank Sinatra walked onstage and the heliotropic cameras focused on him as he sang "Come Rain or Come Shine." A similar thing happened during a June 1954 appearance on *The Ed Sullivan Show*—called *Toast of the Town* at the time. Arlen sang and played a few of his songs, and then opera star Risë Stevens took over to do *her* version of "Come Rain or Come Shine." This time, however, the spotlight returned to Arlen as he gave the first public performance of "The Man That Got Away."

After that he recorded his own versions of his songs at Walden Records, which had been founded in 1952 by Edward Jablonski and Jablonski's friend Leon Seidel. A decade earlier, at the beginning of the war, Jablonski had been a nineteen-year-old Catholic kid in Bay City, Michigan, who loved airplanes and music, particularly the music of George Gershwin. Tall and gangly, he'd been rejected for military service because he was underweight but bulked up and got in. By 1942 he was in New Guinea with the U.S. Army Field Artillery, where, from his barracks, he wrote a fan letter to Ira Gershwin. Ira answered, and their correspondence turned into a close friendship. Several years after Jablonski returned from the war—with a Silver Star—Ira introduced him to Arlen, and Jablonski became Harold's best friend and his chronicler. He didn't have much money—Walden Records was more a labor of love than a business—but he did have good connections. One was pianist David Hancock, who served as recording engineer (having learned that art from Peter Bartók, son of the composer). Another was *New York Times* illustrator Al Hirschfeld who drew the album covers for free. And there was Ira, who, unbeknownst to Harold, helped foot the bill for these sessions.

Walden issued two Arlen records in 1955. On the first, *The Music of Harold Arlen, Volume 1*, he accompanied himself on twelve of his lesser-known pieces, including the *American Minuet* piano solo. He also recorded "It's a New World," "Buds Won't Bud," "I Never Has Seen Snow," "Last Night When We Were Young," and "Hooray for Love." *Volume 2* featured twelve other little-known songs, this time with various singers. Arlen did one, "Can I Leave Off Wearin' My Shoes?" from *House of Flowers*. Louise Carlyle and Warren Galjour were among the singers who did "I Love a New Yorker," "I Had Myself a True Love," and "Halloween." The arrangements were by Peter Matz, who'd been a rehearsal pianist for *House of Flowers* as well as one of its orchestrators. Because of budgetary constraints, Matz had to write for small ensembles, sometimes a trio and never more than an octet. The low budget also meant limited publicity and a very small distribution. It was a whimsical project. Given the company's scanty resources and the obscurity of the material, there was no chance that these recordings would make Arlen widely known. But they did bring Jablonski into his life. The young music aficionado and writer—he'd published a book on aviation in 1946—who was the same age as Capote and, like Capote, called Harold "Dads," became as much a son as a friend.

In another recording venture in 1955, Arlen performed better-known songs and worked at a much larger studio—Capitol Records. This time he had some hope of making his name known and getting it associated with his work. That he was working for Capitol had nothing to do with the fact that Johnny Mercer had founded the company. By that time Capitol was owned by the British conglomerate EMI, a transaction that had made Mercer a very rich man and allowed him to make good on his father's debts from the 1920s. Dick Jones, a producer at Capitol, was the one who initiated the Arlen project. He provided a substantial budget that allowed for a full orchestra, and Harold brought in Peter Matz to again do the orchestrations, which this time were a lush backdrop to his singing. He recorded twelve of his classic songs, including "Blues in the Night," "Over the Rainbow," "I've Got the World on a String," "Stormy Weather," and "The Gal That Got Away."

But none of these recordings, Capitol or Walden, sold well. He had reached for public fame and it eluded his grasp. Among musicians, however, he was legendary. During one Walden session, soprano Miriam Burton had just finished recording "I Wonder What Became of Me" and was about to begin "I Had Myself a True Love" when Arlen walked into the control booth. His presence made her so nervous, she couldn't continue. The song had to be sung by June Ericson instead. He was not an intimidating or a famous man, but musicians were liable to go weak in the knees in his presence.

CHAPTER 23

AN OPERA

Robert S. Breen was a theatrical producer who in association with million-aire philanthropist and producer Blevins Davis formed Everyman Opera in 1952. Its sole purpose was to mount the first operatic presentation of *Porgy and Bess* since the original 1935–36 production. With the backing of the State Department, they took the show to London, Paris, Vienna, and Berlin. Breen was eager to follow this success with another opera, and he came up with the idea of finding a composer to write a piece that could alternate with *Porgy* in performances by a repertory troupe. At first he was inclined to go to an experienced opera composer but figured that he wasn't likely to get any good melodies that way, and he needed a melodic piece if it was to be featured side by side with *Porgy and Bess*. The story goes that he made a list of songs that were examples of what he wanted and asked Cab Calloway to tell him who had composed them. Calloway said they were all by Arlen. Whether or not this is true, Breen, like so many others, knew the songs but not who'd written them.

In 1953, when Breen proposed this project to him, Arlen hesitated. He knew what he'd be in for. He'd watched Gershwin prepare himself for op-era by making his Broadway musical comedies proving grounds for choral and recitative writing and by creating concert works that made him an increasingly sophisticated orchestrator. Moreover, *Porgy and Bess* had an overarching musical structure. Arlen's inclination was to write one song at a time and not worry about how one related to the other. Certainly he was in Gershwin's class as a songwriter—in fact, George had called him "the most original of us all" and Irving Berlin had said, "Harold's best *is* the best."[1] But aside from the *Americanegro Suite* and the Munchkinland sequence in *The Wizard of Oz*, he'd stuck to individual, unrelated songs and had never written for full orchestra. We don't know why he said yes to Breen, given that he was already overextended with work on *A Star Is Born* and *House of Flowers*, but it's a good bet he saw this as his last and maybe best chance to became a famous composer. To write an opera and have it linked to and playing in tandem with *Porgy and Bess* would all but guarantee public recognition.

When he and Breen discussed story ideas, they were at first drawn to American folk tales—the John Henry legend, for one. Then they considered established plays such as *The Madwoman of Chaillot* by French writer Jean Giraudoux. Finally, they took lyricist Betty Comden's advice and decided to make an opera out of *St. Louis Woman*. Some of its songs, like "Come Rain or Come Shine" and "I Wonder What Became of Me," had a blues feel and harmonic complexity that made them fit companions for *Porgy and Bess*. Songs from *St. Louis Woman* that wouldn't work as opera could be dropped and replaced by new songs. The big problems were leitmotivs, recitative, orchestration, and, most daunting of all, plot. *St. Louis Woman*'s story of a jockey who gets his woman by winning a horse race hadn't worked on Broadway and was silly even for opera. Breen assured Arlen that he and his wife, Wilva, could successfully overhaul the script, although neither had any writing experience. Conductor Samuel Matlowsky was hired to do the orchestrations. The piece would be called *Blues Opera*.

As with all his projects, Arlen quickly got to work. He did so as he lay in his hospital bed working simultaneously on *House of Flowers*. He composed the recitatives in his head and, too weak to write them down, hummed them to Matlowsky, who did the notation. He also wrote new songs, including one, "Dis Little While," of which he said: "although not having hit potential [it] moves me more than anything I've written."[2] But as time went on, the rigors of this work became a drain on his limited strength, and he started to pad the score with some of his and Mercer's older songs, including "Blues in the Night" and "That Old Black Magic." Then he included songs he'd written with Koehler: "I Gotta Right to Sing the Blues," "Ill Wind," and two from *Americanegro Suite*.

By the summer of 1954, *Blues Opera* was complete enough for Breen to announce a Paris premiere that December. It was then that he and Arlen discovered that MGM owned the rights to *St. Louis Woman* and was contemplating a film version. Even after the studio abandoned that project they continued to hold the rights, prompting a legal confrontation that didn't end until November 1956, when they at last gave Arlen and Breen the go-ahead for their show. By that time, however, *Blues Opera*'s big chance had come and gone. A new Breen and Davis production of *Porgy and Bess* had already taken place, and with spectacular success. After a long run on Broadway, it toured cities in the United States, Canada, South America, the Middle East, and Europe before arriving in the Soviet Union during the height of the Cold War.

Arlen was at the Moscow performance. Breen had asked him to talk Ira into going—not an easy task given Gershwin's sedentary nature and increasing lethargy—which Arlen did by agreeing to accompany him. Leonore had traveled ahead with the troupe, so for a time it was a Harold and Ira adventure. They flew to Sweden, where, at dinner in Stockholm, they heard the orchestra playing Cole Porter songs and wired the composer-lyricist with the news. Porter's reply read, "Have fun, boys."[3] Visa problems temporarily stranded Arlen in Finland while Gershwin went on ahead. At the gala Moscow performance, attended by Premier Nikita Khrushchev and other high-ranking Soviet leaders, Breen brought Ira and his wife onstage, and the last surviving co-author of the opera received a standing ovation. Then Breen pointed to Arlen, who was sitting in the audience, and asked him to stand. Weak and exhausted from travel, he'd fallen asleep and had to be awakened by a tap on the back from Truman Capote (who was present because of Arlen's suggestion that he write about the *Porgy and Bess* tour, which he was doing for *The New Yorker*). Harold got up and looked around dazed as he was applauded by people who had no idea who he was.

The most important moment for him during his time in Russia came when he phoned Anya from Moscow. It was 6:00 A.M. California time, and she had to be awakened by the staff, but she was instantly alert and, as Jablonski writes in his second Arlen biography, "rational, composed, and laughing," which Harold found "thrilling."[4] There is a question about how Jablonski got this information given his statement in "A brief, if not illuminating, lecture on Anya Arlen's illness" that no one ever discussed her confinement with him. But there's no doubt that Arlen became convinced at this time that Anya was improving and grew determined to have her back with him.

He moved from his spacious Park Avenue apartment to a cramped duplex above an antiques shop on East 55th Street. It had two small upstairs bedrooms and a downstairs living room that could barely accommodate his Steinway. Celia got the hint and moved into a place of her own a couple of blocks away. Jerry left, too. He'd married a young woman, Sherine (Sherry) Altman, and they rented their own place on East 57th Street. Now, with a setup more conducive to Anya's return, Harold traveled to California to see her, ask her doctors if she could be released, and tell them that if she needed further treatment he'd like to transfer her to a facility nearer to him. He was thinking about one in Boston—most likely the Peter Bent Brigham Hospital, where Judy Garland had spent time in the late 1940s. Among Jablonski's papers is a note from Dr. Morris Steinman to Arlen. It is dated September 10, 1956, nine months after the call from Moscow. It states: "Enclosed are prescriptions for Mrs. Arlen. Spoke to her on the phone last week and she sounded fine at that time." Attached is a page from his prescription pad that tells us his office was on North Bedford Drive in Beverly Hills but gives Anya's location only as "Pacific Coast Highway, Malibu."[5] There are two prescriptions. One is for a small dosage of Sparine, the trade name for Promazine, an antipsychotic of the 1950s used for people suffering from hallucinations. The other was for a medium dose of Noctec, which is the sleeping aid chloral hydrate.[6] According to Jablonski, the doctor agreed with Harold that Anya ought to come back to him, "but advised waiting longer—even a year."[7] Arlen reluctantly accepted this advice, so Anya remained in Malibu. As it turned out, she wouldn't come back for another three years.

The reunion he did get was with Harburg. Although they hadn't worked together in twelve years, they'd been in frequent touch—by mail and phone when one was on the East Coast and the other out West. When both were in New York, Yip joined Harold on his walks, opining as they made their way across town. He was knowledgeable about a wide range of subjects, not just words, music, and the theater, but science, inventions, sports. His son Ernie recalls his father teaching him to pitch a curve ball by explaining the applicability of Bernoulli's Principle of moving liquids and gases to a sphere's velocity and direction.[8] Ideas and information flowed from him endlessly, which Arlen found diverting except when Yip got around to politics, which he always did. His great concern in the mid-1950s was the nuclear standoff between the United States and the Soviet Union and the fact that the two nations could, in an instant, blow each other up and take the world with them. Arlen contended that they needed to sit down together and work out a sensible solution. Harburg thought the United States was at fault—that the problem was collusion between capitalist corporations and the military. These discussions agitated Arlen and he tried to avoid them.

In January 1956, when he was visiting Anya in Los Angeles and speaking to her doctors about when she might be released, Yip was in town, too. Arthur Freed had asked him to come to MGM to discuss a new movie musical. It would be about Elizabeth Jane Cochrane—better known as Nelly Bly—a nineteenth-century journalist who'd taken her pen name from the title of a Stephen Foster song. While working for Joseph Pulitzer's *New York World*, she made a name for herself by fooling a team of doctors into thinking she was insane, getting herself admitted to New York's Bellevue Hospital, and publishing a series of articles that unmasked the horrors of treatment there.

In 1887 these articles were collected into a successful book, *Ten Days in a Madhouse*, which led to a criminal investigation of the asylum. Bly achieved even greater renown when she traveled around the world in fewer than the eighty days it had taken Jules Verne's fictional Phileas Fogg.

Because Yip had written a successful Broadway musical about Amelia Bloomer, Freed felt that this was his kind of project. Harburg agreed and proposed that Arlen compose the music. The prospect of reuniting the *Wizard of Oz* team at last for a high-budget musical made sense to Freed. But there was a stumbling block: the blacklist. Yip's name would have to be okayed by communist hunter Roy Brewer. He was the Hollywood representative of the International Alliance of Theatrical Stage Employees and Motion Picture Machine Operators and had the final say about who could work on a movie. As soon as he saw Harburg's name, he said no. Freed told Yip to have a talk with him and allay his concerns.

Harburg was not unsympathetic to Brewer. A one-time projectionist who'd risen to prominence as a labor leader, he'd been beaten up while striking for higher wages and decent working conditions. Not only that, he'd figured out how to get out from under the thumbs of Louis B. Mayer and Jack Warner and make them come to him. Yip told Brewer they were alike in their concern for the downtrodden and said he'd never been a communist, just an FDR liberal—the FDR who'd done so much to make labor unions legal. Brewer listened attentively and then brought another man into the room. This was a self-confessed former communist named Mr. Cardigan who had a dossier on Harburg that was, in Yip's words, "thicker than all my works."[9] At that point the meeting turned into an interrogation by Cardigan, whose questions included, "Did you write a song called 'Happiness Is a Thing Called Joe?'" Harburg said yes. Cardigan asked, "Which Joe were you talking about? Was it Joe Stalin?" It was such an absurd question that Yip, taken aback, could only think to say, "Don't you want a little happiness? Another 'Over the Rainbow' maybe?" Brewer replied that Harburg would do no more movie writing until he'd penned an article titled "I Was a Dupe for the Communists" to be published in the American Legion's *Legionnaire* magazine. After replying that he didn't write for fourth-rate publications, Yip left the meeting, the project, and MGM. Arlen supported him by bowing out, too. The Nelly Bly movie was never made.

Back in New York, Harold found himself alone in his little apartment. Anya wouldn't rejoin him anytime soon and there were no prospects for work—not, that is, until Harburg came to him with an idea for a new Broadway musical. It would be about—atomic bombs. If that wasn't enough to set Harold on edge, it had a Caribbean setting that would require calypso songs.

Given that he'd just written a calypso-saturated show—the ill-fated *House of Flowers*—he wasn't anxious to do it again. He never had liked calypso much, although he recognized Harry Belafonte's talent and had a fondness for "Jamaica Farewell" and "Marianne." As it turned out, Belafonte was a fan of his. The singer remembered that Harold had treated him graciously at the start of his career. Moreover, he'd loved "Over the Rainbow" since childhood. When Harburg asked if he would consider appearing in a show with a new Arlen–Harburg score he received a quick yes, which all but assured the musical of success.

Its story, which Harburg wrote with his longtime writing partner Fred Saidy, was, he told Arlen, not overtly political. The setting was a mythical place called Pigeon Island. Koli, a handsome fisherman, wants to marry a beautiful young woman named Savannah and live happily in their island paradise. But she longs to see the wonders of modern civilization and insists that he take her to New York. Into this situation walks the sophisticated Joe Nashua from Harlem, who woos Savannah and is able to talk all the island's fishermen except Koli into becoming pearl divers. Pearls are not particularly useful, but they're worth more money than fish. Joe is about to take Savannah with him to New York when mushroom clouds appear across the sea over the United States. That's enough to cure Savannah of her longing for civilization. She returns to Koli, the fishermen go back to fishing, and Joe sets off for New York and the dubious rewards of civilization. Luckily, the clouds weren't a nuclear holocaust, just a big storm.

Arlen was unimpressed—even when producer David Merrick joined the project. A former lawyer, Merrick was a hard-driving promoter and public relations man, fresh from successes with *Fanny*—the musical that had fallen through for Arlen and Harburg in 1952—and Thornton Wilder's comedy *The Matchmaker* (later the basis of *Hello, Dolly!* which he also produced). The arrival of a go-getter like Merrick meant the show would receive publicity, but it all but guaranteed the sort of tension that was always, it seemed, part of any Harburg musical.

Arlen signed on to the project out of boredom. Consequently, he was off his game. In their writing sessions he and Harburg tended to stall after completing a few bars of a song, then move on to another and get stuck again. In a radio interview Arlen called it a "devilish job."[10] One day, playing some of the music for Jablonski, he stopped and exclaimed, "God, how I hate calypsos!"[11]

Then Belafonte developed a throat problem that took him out of the show. Everyone agreed this was a major crisis and that another big star was needed. For a time actor Sidney Poitier was considered. Although he'd

never sung professionally he was said to have a passable baritone—hardly
encouraging to the songwriters. At a meeting to discuss the situation, Arlen
came up with the idea of asking Lena Horne to step in. Merrick and Harburg
immediately saw this as the ideal solution. She was certainly a big star. Her
recent cabaret act at the Waldorf Astoria had led to a best-selling album.
She and Arlen had admired each other since their Cotton Club days. True,
she'd refused to appear in *St. Louis Woman* and had also turned down the
role of Ottilie in *House of Flowers*. That show, she wrote, "had Harold
Arlen's beautiful, beautiful score . . . but I told him I hadn't felt like an
ingénue since I was sixteen, so I regretfully declined."[12] But when she was
contacted about this new show, called *Pigeon Island* at first and renamed
Jamaica, she was definitely interested. She was anxious to leave cabaret for
Broadway and to at last appear in an Arlen musical. His songs, she said,
were "difficult but soul-rewarding."[13] She was also enthusiastic about the
role of Savannah. Harburg had told her, "We have a show for you which
will show you as you really are—not the sleek, sophisticated lady of the
cabarets, but a really basic, earthy, human being."[14] But when she saw the
script she felt that he'd reneged on that promise. Savannah was, she concluded, "a stupid broad who has somewhere gotten hold of a TV set and
believes that the only place where things are really happening is New York
. . . We had agreed that the real me was earthy and basic, and that certainly
did not describe Savannah."[15]

    She took this complaint to Merrick and director Robert Lewis, who took
the script away from Harburg and Saidy and rewrote it for her, throwing
the storyline out of whack. "They're changing the goddam thing," Harburg
said to Arlen."[16] During the Philadelphia tryout, Yip confronted Merrick
while Arlen, as was his custom, stayed out of the fray. In fact, he feigned
illness and checked himself into a hospital, leaving Harburg to battle Merrick on his own, which he continued to do as *Jamaica* moved to Boston
for another pre-Broadway run. He said that Merrick's rewrite made him
and Saidy look like amateurs. Merrick responded by locking Yip and Saidy
out of the theater. For Arlen the worst moment came when Merrick—at
Horne's request—fired Jerry as the show's conductor. Harold had gotten
his brother the job, and Jerry, perhaps anticipating problems, had asked
for a run-of-the-show contract, which served him well because he received
paychecks throughout *Jamaica*'s year and a half on Broadway. The show
was a solid success, but all the glory went to Horne and Merrick, not Arlen
or Harburg. Their score, while enjoyable, produced no standards. In an interview, Horne said she was disappointed that there'd been nothing as good
as "Come Rain or Come Shine" or "A Sleepin' Bee."[17] Not that she didn't

have a good time singing "Cocoanut Sweet," "Push de Button" (not about the bomb but about the conveniences of modern society), and "Napoleon." The latter was a leftover from 1937's *Hooray for What!* In rewriting it for this show, Harburg created a funny statement about the fleetingness of fame: Napoleon had ended up as a pastry, Bismarck a herring, Lincoln a tunnel, and Hoover a vacuum cleaner. Of course, the song wouldn't have worked if people didn't still know those names. As for Arlen and Harburg's names, despite all they'd accomplished, hardly anyone outside the music business knew who they were.

At the end of November 1958, Celia died. She'd lived to see her first and only grandchild, named Sam for her late husband, born to Jerry and Sherine earlier that year. "It was probably sheer coincidence," Jablonski wrote, "but quite soon after the death of Celia Arluck, Anya joined her husband in the little duplex on East Fifty-fifth Street sometime in early 1959."[18] This conjunction of Celia's death and Anya's release was probably more than a coincidence. When Harold traveled to Los Angeles to be present as his mother was buried alongside his father, he told Anya's doctors that Celia, who'd been a source of agony to his wife, was gone. Also, Anya's distaste for Jerry would no longer be a problem, because he now had a place of his own and a wife and a child. It was time for Anya to come home.

"Now in her early forties," Jablonski wrote about meeting her for the first time, "she was still strikingly beautiful, svelte and charming. Anyone not knowing her recent history would not have imagined that this quiet, often subdued but frequently effervescent and amusing woman had been institutionalized for several years."[19] She seemed well. And they resumed the life they'd led in years past, going to shows, parties, visiting friends. But when he wanted to see Jerry and his sister-in-law and his nephew, Harold went alone.

CHAPTER 24

Two Debacles

Soon after Anya's return, she and Harold went to Los Angeles, where they checked into the Beverly Wilshire Hotel. Harold had two exciting job prospects.

One was an animated musical version of Dickens's *A Christmas Carol*. The idea had originated with two Londoners: graphic artist Ronald Searle and playwright Christopher Fry. When Fry said he wanted to give lyric writing a try, Harold explained that this was a specialized art and suggested they call Ira Gershwin. But Ira said no. He was annotating his brother's papers for the Library of Congress and simultaneously writing humorous backstories and glosses for a hundred of his lyrics, to be published as a book in 1959. That was enough work for him. Consequently, the Dickens project fizzled out.

The other prospect involved Pulitzer Prize–winning novelist Edna Ferber. For a long time she'd wanted her 1941 novel *Saratoga Trunk* to become a Broadway musical. She was sure it could be the basis of something as great as what Kern and Hammerstein had made of her 1926 novel *Show Boat*. *Saratoga Trunk* is the story of a Creole woman, Clio, who has a grudge against the family who mistreated her mother and is in love with a Texas gambler, Clint, who has a grudge against the railroad men who swindled his father. Shortly after the book's publication, Ferber suggested to Richard Rodgers that he and Larry Hart ask Oscar Hammerstein to help them turn it into a musical. Rodgers and Hart proposed the idea to Hammerstein, who declined, so it was dropped. But Ferber continued to have Broadway aspirations for *Saratoga Trunk*, even after the novel succeeded as a movie drama in 1945. In the 1950s she sounded out Rodgers and Hammerstein, Lerner and Loewe, and Meredith Willson, who all said no. Two prominent Broadway people did express interest. One was Moss Hart, the director of *My Fair Lady*, who worked with Ferber on a *Saratoga Trunk* scenario until they had a falling-out. The other was Morton Da Costa, who'd just directed Willson's *The Music Man*. He told Ferber he would commit to the project if she allowed him to write the script. He'd never written one before and wanted to prove he could do it. She wasn't pleased by this request but went along with it. She also gave in to Moss Hart's suggestion that Arlen be asked to do the music, although her initial reaction was "Who? What's he done? What are his credits? Never heard of him."[1]

This was the first time in a long while that Harold was enthusiastic about a project from the start. Although Ferber had never heard of him, he'd certainly heard of her. *Show Boat* was the finest and most lasting of Jerome Kern's musicals. Ferber—who, according to Oscar Levant, was America's greatest writer[2]—would attract good people to the show, which was now called, simply, *Saratoga*. Carol Lawrence, who'd portrayed Maria in *West Side Story*, became Clio. Rock Hudson, fresh from acclaim for his performance in the movie *Giant* (also from a Ferber novel) agreed to play Clint—and take singing lessons. Cecil Beaton had recently designed the costumes for *My Fair Lady* and would now do them and the sets for *Saratoga*. The venerable actress Jane Darwell, who had portrayed Ma Joad in the film version of Steinbeck's *The Grapes of Wrath*, would be a Saratoga Springs socialite. Given such stellar talent, financing was no problem. NBC and RCA pooled $400,000—a huge amount at the time. And Arlen was granted his request that his brother be hired as the show's conductor.

Harold also wanted Johnny Mercer to write the lyrics. Mercer's most recent attempt to write a classic Broadway musical was *Li'l Abner*, based on Al Capp's cartoon strip, with music by Gene de Paul. Like *Jamaica*, it was successful but quickly forgotten. He was forty-seven years old now, energetic, and at the height of his powers. Once or twice a year he'd be asked to provide lyrics for a movie theme song but otherwise he was unemployed. That he was now offered *Saratoga*—with its big names and big budget—would seem to have been a godsend. But he didn't look at it that way. It was too late, he said—thirty years too late—to write a *Show Boat* sequel. He was convinced it would flop and, given the size of the production—thirty-two speaking roles—this would be a belly flop. Still, he couldn't say no. "The reason," wrote one of his biographers, "is quite simple: his immense respect and love for Arlen. I think that John would have done anything Harold wanted him to do, and if Harold wanted to do *Saratoga*, then so be it."[3]

Mercer never changed his mind about the show—"No amount of style nor gloss could cover the humorless and out-of-date book," he wrote in his unfinished autobiography.[4] Nevertheless, he worked hard on the score. During the first half of 1959, he and Arlen spent five months writing more than twenty songs. They worked in a Beverly Hills house that Harold and Anya had rented. Mercer, who lived in Newport Beach, drove there several times a week—two hours each way—and continued writing when he returned home. In a series of letters, Arlen kept Jablonski apprised of his progress. On June 16 he wrote: "What does amaze me about the work is the difference in style from Jamaica—Blues—Flowers, etc.—When I ponder about it & rest assured I do—often—it makes me stop in my tracks and wonder how long this can go on—I don't think an audience nor the critics realize (alas why should they) how much is taken from a writer every time he goes to bat."[5] He was finding it difficult to compose music appropriate for *Saratoga* and still be Harold Arlen—although sometimes he did it, as in the beautiful ballad "Love Held Lightly."

When rehearsals began late in the summer of 1959, things quickly fell apart. Jane Darwell, at eighty, could no longer memorize lines and had to leave the show. Rock Hudson dropped out, too, citing movie commitments. He was replaced by veteran baritone Howard Keel, who was better suited to musicals but not as intriguing an attraction. Da Costa, having given in to Ferber's demand that his script include all her novel's many plot threads, wrote a badly bloated play. Mercer complained that Da Costa's directorial style and Beaton's costumes were giving the show a patina of homosexuality that undercut the romance between Clio and Clyde. Under the stress, Da Costa checked himself into a hospital.

Suddenly, Arlen and Mercer were in charge of the show—which meant that Mercer was in charge, since Harold was not the sort to wield power. The play was in such bad shape that Arlen couldn't bear to attend rehearsals for the Philadelphia tryout but returned to New York, where he, too, entered a hospital. Responsibility for *Saratoga* then passed into the hands of the one person who'd disliked it from the start: Johnny Mercer. Like Arlen, he lacked a director's temperament. He didn't enjoy staging scenes or telling actors what to do. Still, he tried. When cuts had to be made, he revised the script. When new songs were needed, he wrote them—words and music. But he had always known that this show couldn't come alive. New York theater critics put it out of its misery shortly after it premiered on December 7, 1959.

Harold skipped that premiere, but Jerry had to be there to conduct the orchestra. Of all the people connected with *Saratoga*, he was the least known and least catered to. Howard Keel constantly berated him for miscues, erratic tempos, and excessive volume. During one performance, the actor let the audience in on his discontent by halting during an exit to glare pointedly at Jerry in the pit. If that wasn't enough, Jerry's thirty-year-old wife Sherry was dying of breast cancer.

In the meantime, *Blues Opera* was reaching its own sad denouement. In the spring of 1959, Robert Breen had asked Stanley Chase, the producer of a successful revival of Kurt Weill and Bertolt Brecht's *Threepenny Opera*, to become his co-producer on the Arlen opera. The two men traveled to Beverly Hills, where Harold was writing *Saratoga*, to talk to him about the project, and they were all optimistic about its prospects. Breen and Chase announced a tryout in Brussels and a formal premiere in Amsterdam on December 7. After that would come performances in Paris, a European tour, and a Broadway opening.

Then Breen and Chase had a falling-out, which was followed by a power struggle, and Chase won. He changed the name of the show from *Blues Opera* to *Free and Easy* and omitted Robert Breen's name from the program notes. Arlen's phone rang with calls from one man and then the other, each presenting his side of the dispute. This was bad enough, but then came an angry letter from Mercer, who'd learned that some songs in *Free and Easy* had lyrics by other writers.

The show itself was a shambles. At its Amsterdam opening the musicians were directed to come onstage and mill about as they played, which made it difficult for the actors to find their places and remember their lines. Ted Royal's highly regarded orchestrations from the original 1946 production of *St. Louis Woman* had been lost (forty years later they would be reconstructed from the original cast album), and the new arrangements by Quincy Jones were not to Arlen's taste. Then, when Breen announced he would rejoin the company in Paris, Chase told a reporter that the cast wouldn't welcome him, adding that the man was deranged and on drugs. So Breen skipped the January 15, 1960, Paris premiere and thus missed the opening of the last Arlen show ever to reach the stage. A week later, it shut down. Quincy Jones took his musicians on tour in Europe, and the cast and crew borrowed money to go home.

Arlen's opera has never been recorded or revived. In 1957, two years before the stage production, he and orchestrator Samuel Matlowsky created *Blues Opera Suite*, a twenty-five-minute piece that conductor André Kostelanetz premiered with the Minneapolis Symphony. On November 2, 1957, Kostelanetz conducted it again in Carnegie Hall, Arlen in attendance, and the composer was visibly delighted when he saw his name in the printed program alongside the names of Berlioz, Prokofieff, Villa-Lobos, and Rachmaninoff. Kostelanetz's recording of the *Suite* for Columbia Records has long been the only remnant of what, for a time, Arlen thought of as his magnum opus. He wrote some seventy vocal, choral, and instrumental pieces for this project—a 336-page manuscript housed at the Library of Congress and waiting to be rediscovered.

CHAPTER 25

THE 1960S

Work assignments were now so sporadic that Arlen was unwillingly becoming a composer emeritus. His 1960 output consisted of two piano pieces, *Ode* and *Bon-Bon*, each improvisational in style, neither written for any particular occasion or premiered or recorded. In 1961 there was a lone composition, a song written to mark the publication of Jablonski's *Happy with the Blues*, bearing that title with lyrics by Peggy Lee. This was also the title of an episode of NBC Television's *The DuPont Show of the Week*, which aired in September and featured Arlen, Peggy Lee, Vic Damone, and Bing Crosby.

That program was one of the first in a series of tributes to Arlen. It was as if his admirers were determined that he not disappear, at least not until he'd been properly acknowledged. Earlier that year, Ella Fitzgerald had released a two-disc collection of twenty-eight of his songs. She'd already engaged in similar projects for the works of Cole Porter, Rodgers and Hart, Duke Ellington, Irving Berlin, and the Gershwins. Her Gershwin recordings featured arrangements by Nelson Riddle, and Harold looked forward to hearing his songs given the lush Riddle treatment. He was disappointed when producer Norman Granz engaged Billy May, who was jazzier and thus, Granz thought, more suitable to Arlen. Still, he appreciated the honor.

On April 23, 1961, at Carnegie Hall, Judy Garland gave the performance of her life. It became the basis of what is still considered the finest of all live concert recordings. She sang four Arlen songs that night, including a spine-tingling version of "Stormy Weather." As the evening drew to a close, she was speaking to the audience, joking and reminiscing, when she suddenly stopped. She'd spotted Arlen in the first row. Microphones caught the sound of her quickening footsteps as she went to him. "Harold," she said, softly. And then: "Harold Arlen! Stand up!" And the Garland audience, who knew who he was, erupted into a roar of approval. *Judy at Carnegie Hall* was released in July 1961, charted at number one for thirteen weeks, won five Grammy awards, and became one of the best-selling albums of all time. Some of Garland's patter was included on the record, but not her introduction of Arlen. Had that moment made its way into millions of homes, he might at last have become famous.

Later that year she got him his first job in two years. United Productions of America had signed her to sing and voice a feature-length cartoon, *Gay Purr-ee*, playing the role of a French cat who leaves her country home for Paris. The producers granted her request that Arlen and Harburg be hired to write the score. Eight years earlier, when she'd wanted them to write *A Star Is Born*, the blacklist made Harburg's inclusion impossible. That era ended in 1960 when actor-producer Kirk Douglas hired blacklisted screenwriter Dalton Trumbo to work on the film *Spartacus*. So Arlen and Harburg were together writing songs in Hollywood for the first time since 1944. Harold and Anya rented a house on North Crescent Drive in May of 1961. They were there five months as Harold and Yip wrote some fine, if not well-remembered, songs—"Paris Is a Lonely Town" "The Money Cat," "Little Drops of Rain," among them. It would have been a happy time for them had Anya not taken ill again.

Not only did she become, in Jablonski's words, "withdrawn, strained, nervous,"[1] she developed physical symptoms, too. "Even before they had left for California in May," he wrote, "she had shown signs of what might have been a nervous affliction. At times her face contorted, her smile was a grimace. The fingers of her left hand appeared to be arthritic."[2] During this period they were visited by Rod Gorney, the son of Jay and Edelaine Gorney. He'd first met the Arlens in the mid-1930s when Anya was a starlet and he a dazzled adolescent. "She was no longer a young woman," he recalls, "but she was beautiful-looking in her middle age. When I first walked in I saw her in the garden in this wheelchair and I walked over to her and I said, 'Anya, you're as beautiful as ever.' And she looked down, grinned as if to say, 'Yeah, I know what a wreck I am.'"[3] Gorney, a practicing psychiatrist, observed none of the neurological symptoms mentioned by Jablonski. And no one else has recalled seeing her in a wheelchair.

There were other friends who saw no symptoms at all—physical or emotional. One of them was the young composer-conductor-pianist André Previn, a musician Arlen greatly admired. He also admired the talent of Previn's wife, lyricist Dory Langdon. When he asked Langdon to work with him she readily agreed, and in early 1962 they began their collaboration at the Arlens' elegant and spacious new residence, a sixth-floor apartment in the San Remo building at 146 Central Park West. While Dory and Harold worked, André and Anya chatted and became friends. He wrote a song for her, "Anya," which he recorded on an album of Arlen songs. There was nothing physically or emotionally amiss with her as far as he could tell. She was, he recalls, "an absolutely adorable woman, very friendly and hospitable."[4]

Others had a different experience. Lynn Lane found Anya to be an "an exceedingly difficult and strange woman."[5] One day she and her mother asked Anya to lunch, an invitation Anya happily accepted. But when they arrived in a taxi to pick her up, she wouldn't get in. She demanded they hire a limousine instead—which they did. Then, at the restaurant, just as they were seated, Anya said she had to go home. The limo was summoned and off she went. This wasn't an isolated incident. The same thing happened one night when she and Harold arrived at Jerry's apartment for a Friday-night dinner. Sherry had died from her cancer in 1960, and in 1962 Jerry met a young woman, Rita Wegrzynowicz, who became his third wife. Rita Arlen devoted herself to Sam, became a good friend of Harold's, and wanted to be close to Anya, too, but Anya's antipathy to Jerry made that difficult. Although she wasn't Jewish, Rita had learned to cook a Sabbath meal and repeatedly invited Harold and Anya over on Friday nights. Anya usually begged off, but this night she agreed to come. Then, just after she and Harold stepped into the apartment, she said, "When can we go?'"[6]

It's possible that these moments were caused as much by her fear of illness as by the illness itself. She knew that the twitches and grimaces could come on at any time, which made her panicky and always looking for escape. "At times her nervous spasms were too severe to go unnoticed," wrote Jablonski. "When an attack flared up, Anya, embarrassed, preferred staying home."[7] Others blamed pharmaceuticals—a suspicion reinforced by another incident witnessed by Lynn Lane. She and Burton were with Harold and Anya in a theater lobby. When Anya said she was going to the ladies' room, Harold said, "Just a minute—let me have your pocket book," and went through it looking for pills.[8]

He tried to get her to see a specialist, but she wouldn't go to any doctor except Maurice Schachtel, who'd become their physician after Dr. Elias retired. Harold and Dr. Schachtel went back a long way. They'd grown up together in Buffalo, each was the son of a cantor, and the two families had known and vacationed with one another. When Dr. Schachtel opened an office at the Lombardy Hotel on East 56th Street, Harold reconnected with him and often went there for a chat—they both loved to talk sports—and a vitamin B-12 shot. After his bouts with liver illness, he'd forsworn alcohol except an occasional glass of wine, but he hadn't ruled out chemical supplements, especially sleeping pills and tranquilizers. He and the doctor both urged Anya to see a specialist about her worsening condition, but she wouldn't hear of it. She hated doctors—to the point where she wouldn't take her broken eyeglasses to an optometrist but repaired them herself using tape—but she did like Dr. Schachtel, who was as accommodating in prescribing for her as for Harold.

Shortly after moving into the San Remo, she and Harold began a tradition of hosting what they called Christmas–Chanukah breakfasts on Christmas mornings. The Jablonskis' three children and Jerry and Rita's Sam were the centers of attention. Carla, the Jablonskis' eldest, remembers these as happy occasions, at least in the beginning, in the early 1960s, when Harold was "incredibly dapper," charming, and solicitous of the children. He'd tape-record them as they sang and told stories. Then, as the decade wore on, the celebrations became "sad, oppressive, gloomy. He was distracted. He was glad we were there but at the same time I could tell it was an effort for him."[9]

The problem was Anya's worsening condition. She was closing herself off from nearly everyone. She would occasionally see her mother—who lived in a small apartment downtown—and the Jablonskis. She often phoned Ed's wife Edith Jablonski to unburden herself as she'd once done with Edelaine. She continued to feel close to Irving and Ellin Berlin. The elderly composer phoned every day to see how things were with her and Harold. His solicitousness took a more tangible form when he gave Anya a painting—by the mid-1960s he was producing more canvases than songs—of a vase of flowers, the loveliest bearing her photo. She expressed her gratitude in a handwritten letter to him that reads:

> Dear Dear Irving,
>   I'm a stinker—I don't often write letters, I usually call local or long distance. I have never called or written about your visit to our abode. I was so happy to see you. I cried afterwards—I was touched and warmed spiritually by your presence. Then when you said 'I love you Anya Kalanya and "sealed it with a kiss" that was a lola palooza of a first act finish. You made Cary Grant look like a "shlump." It was a rare experience for me and I loved you for it. Since you almost give no one your [indecipherable] leaves me with inadequate phrases of my stunning experience of your gracious thought and act. Also including my photograph. My ["My" is crossed out] dear Irving again I thank you deeply and respectfully and with love.
>
>   Anya[10]

Meanwhile, the tributes to Arlen continued. On the evening of February 9, 1964, CBS's half-hour Sunday television program *The Twentieth Century*, hosted by Walter Cronkite and usually devoted to world events and history, was expanded to an hour to feature "The Songs of Harold Arlen." Cronkite said in his opening remarks: "Harold Arlen is a shy, retiring man which perhaps explains the paradox of his fame. People know and love his music but they do not know his name. They do not connect Harold Arlen with 'Over the Rainbow' as quickly as they connect Irving Berlin with 'White Christmas" and Richard Rodgers with '*Oklahoma!*' But to the men who make the nation's popular music, the musicians, the recording artists, and his fellow composers, Arlen's name is well-known indeed. And it is generally agreed that no one writes better or more lasting songs."

In the interview, which took place in Arlen's living room, Cronkite asked him about his moment of inspiration for "Over the Rainbow," and Arlen recalled how the melody had arrived from out of the blue as he and his wife were driving in Hollywood. He made the point that without Harburg's words there is no "Over the Rainbow."[11] As they spoke, the camera looked past him to a plate on the mantel laminated with a still from an Arlen home movie. It showed George Gershwin at the moment he'd plopped himself onto Anya's lap as she sat in a lounge chair by his pool. There they were, still healthy and happy, still laughing. Not shown by the CBS crew was a full-length portrait of Anya by renowned American artist Abram Poole. It showed her at seventeen, when Harold first met her. There was also a recent painting of her by Harold that revealed, in Jablonski's words, an ""anguished face."[12] And "in pride of place"[13] was George Gershwin's painting of Jerome Kern, for which Harold had risked his life during the house fire of 1943.

Cronkite went to the homes of four of Arlen's lyricists to interview them. Koehler, Harburg, Ira Gershwin, and Mercer all spoke of him as a friend and as a composer. In another segment, Harold was shown in a recording studio conducting the orchestra as Tony Bennett sang his and Dory Langdon's "So Long, Big Time!"—a jazzy song with the musical and lyrical verve of an Arlen–Koehler number from the Cotton Club days. Lacking, though, was the euphoria of inspiration that had once been such a hallmark of his music. The muse to whom he jokingly paid obeisance each time he approached the piano was, he knew, fickle. It had arrived unsummoned in 1930 as he played the piano for dancers rehearsing Vincent Youmans's *Great Day!* Since then, when it gave him "Get Happy," he had known it could just as easily fly away. He wasn't sure if that had happened, but ten years had passed since the last of his standards, "A Sleepin' Bee" from *House of Flowers.*

The foreboding that had long since settled over his personal life now affected work. *Gay-Purr-ee* came and went with no impact. The only other job from Hollywood was another from Judy Garland, who asked him and Yip to write the title song for her upcoming film *I Could Go on Singing*. The movie, released in 1963, sank quickly along with the song. It was the last song Arlen would write for the movies, and the film was Garland's final screen appearance.

By the mid-1960s, career troubles were hardly unique to him. They afflicted nearly every songwriter of his generation, all of whom, like Arlen, were nearing the age of sixty or well past it. For Harry Warren, who turned sixty-seven at the end of 1960, Hollywood work, long plentiful, dried up. He still had lots of music in him[14] but no outlets, a situation that had been going on since the 1950s, which were fallow except for "That's Amore," written with lyricist Jack Brooks for the 1953 Martin and Lewis film *The Caddy*, "An Affair to Remember" for the 1957 Cary Grant-Deborah Kerr film of that title (lyrics by Harold Adamson and Leo McCarey), a few songs for Jerry Lewis movies, and some television theme songs—"The Life and Legend of Wyatt Earp," for instance.

Tough times also arrived for Warren and Arlen's better-known colleagues. Oscar Hammerstein died shortly after he and Richard Rodgers wrote *The Sound of Music* in 1959, leaving Rodgers adrift. For the final twenty years of his life this once surefooted man searched in vain for a compatible lyricist and another great Broadway musical. Irving Berlin, too, encountered the unthinkable when he developed a crisis of confidence in the mid-1950s and was unable to finish any project until he finally wrote a Broadway show, *Mr. President*, that flopped in 1962. After that he quit. Cole Porter reached the end at about the same time. For twenty years he'd refused to let doctors amputate his injured legs and, by doing so, spare him ceaseless pain and nonstop surgeries. When he finally relented in 1958, the physical pain subsided but he felt disfigured and withdrew to his Waldorf Towers apartment and retirement.

A few of Arlen's contemporaries managed to keep their heads above water. Johnny Mercer never did write a great Broadway musical, but his willingness to put words to movie themes brought a collaboration with composer Henry Mancini that resulted in "Moon River" for the 1961 film *Breakfast at Tiffany's*, based on Truman Capote's novella. It was one of his most evocative lyrics and probably his best known. He and Mancini followed that up with "The Days of Wine and Roses" for the 1962 film of that title. Both songs won Academy Awards. Another lyricist who kept going was Dorothy Fields. In 1959 she and composer Albert Hague wrote a Tony Award–winning musical, *Redhead*, and in 1966 she and Cy Coleman wrote *Sweet Charity*, a show that yielded "Big Spender" and "If My Friends

Could See Me Now." Jimmy Van Heusen and lyricist Sammy Cahn gave Frank Sinatra "Love and Marriage" in 1955, "All the Way" and "Come Fly with Me" in 1957, "High Hopes" in 1959, and "Call Me Irresponsible" in 1962.

Yip Harburg, on the other hand, had a tough time. During his ten-year banishment from Hollywood he wrote just two Broadway musicals: *Flahooley*, which failed in 1951, and *Jamaica*, a success in 1957 but as producer David Merrick's conception, not his own. As the 1960s dawned, he turned Aristophanes' two-thousand-year-old antiwar play, *Lysistrata*, into *The Happiest Girl in the World*, using music by nineteenth-century operetta composer Jacques Offenbach. It folded after a brief run. Undeterred, he moved on to another look at history, this time the thirteenth-century Children's Crusade, when the youth of Europe went to the Holy Land to convert Muslims to Christianity. He wanted Arlen to work with him on it, but Harold took a pass, as did Burton Lane, and the idea ended there. Lane turned instead to lyricist and librettist Alan Jay Lerner, and in 1965 they created *On a Clear Day You Can See Forever*, a successful musical about reincarnation.

Meanwhile, the new generation of songwriters was hard at work. Burt Bacharach and lyricist Hal David were in the studio with Dionne Warwick; Phil Spector with the Crystals and the Ronettes; Brian Holland, Lamont Dozier and Eddie Holland with the Supremes and the Four Tops. Bob Dylan, Paul Simon, and Brian Wilson came up with remarkable performances and arrangements of their own material.

Then the Beatles upped the ante. With their producer, George Martin, they turned the studio into an experimental lab that saw the creation of one astonishing song after another, each superbly written for their own voices, solo and in two- and three-part harmony, and for their instruments and other instrumental combinations—sometimes creating sounds never heard before. They, like Arlen, had an affinity for unusual song construction. "A Day in the Life" matched "Blues in the Night" as a multisectional experiment that managed to catch on with the public (as did Wilson's "Good Vibrations"). Unlike Arlen, they preferred not to hand their ideas over to arrangers. Instead they created just about every sung and played note.[15] In 1967's "Hello, Goodbye" they gave the lead guitar a countermelody and then turned it into a vocal line. In "Hey Bulldog" from 1968, one of their instrumental ideas was a catchy two-bar riff, first for piano and then guitar, which, at the song's conclusion, was given a surprising and satisfying new ending. Great songwriting, singing, and instrumental lines, not to mention a worldwide influence on style and attitude—it was all theirs. The only thing they couldn't do was last. Their center wouldn't hold. But while they were together, it was difficult for musicians of any generation to compete with them.

With all this, Arlen's career seemed finished. But then, in the early spring of 1964, during a visit to the 54th Street office of his publisher, Buddy Morris, he was chatting with a group of songwriters when one of them, twenty-nine-year-old Martin Charnin, slipped a note into his pocket that read: "I can be good for you." Charnin had written words as well as music for off-Broadway revues, and lyrics for a show, *Hot Spot*, that ran briefly on Broadway, music by Mary Rodgers (Richard Rodgers's daughter). Amused by the young man's inventive and cheeky approach, Arlen accepted him as a new partner and in the process found a new friend. Later that year when Charnin's daughter Sasha was born, Harold composed a melody for her and called it "Welcome to the World."

One of their first songs, appropriately enough, was "I Could Be Good for You."[16] Then came two for the New York mayoralty campaign of Congressman John V. Lindsay. Lindsay had been Arlen's representative on the Upper East Side, and they'd gotten to know each other. Although Harold shied away from partisanship, as he did from all confrontation, he preferred Lindsay to his opponent, the archconservative William F. Buckley Jr., and pitched in on Lindsay's successful run.

In April 1965 Broadway and Hollywood producer Hillard Elkins put on a concert called "Broadway Answers Selma" at the Majestic Theatre on West 44th Street. Its purpose was to raise funds for the families of the Reverend James J. Reeb and Jimmie Lee Jackson, both of whom had been murdered while working for black voter registration in Alabama. Martin Luther King Jr. was present, as were some fifty Broadway and Hollywood stars, including Barbra Streisand, who, when asked by Elkins to close the show, said she would do so if Arlen and Charnin wrote her a new song for the occasion. She had always called Arlen her favorite songwriter; she'd sung "A Sleepin' Bee" at her first audition. Now, having achieved superstardom with her Grammy Award–winning *The Barbra Streisand Album* in 1963 and her portrayal of comedian Fanny Brice (Harold and Anya's old friend) in *Funny Girl* on Broadway in 1964, she sang a new Arlen and Charnin song at this concert. It was "That's a Fine Kind o' Freedom," a rouser that went over so well—"it tore the house down,"[17] remembers Charnin, who was present with Arlen—that the audience wouldn't let her off stage until she sang it again.

It was a political period for Arlen; in 1963 he and Harburg wrote "The Silent Spring" based on the title of the best-selling book by environmentalist Rachel Carson. Lena Horne recorded that song and also sang Arlen and

Ira Gershwin's "It's a New World" at a Carnegie Hall concert, Harold accompanying her at the piano. Ira had reworked that lyric to make it about civil rights.

None of these efforts, however honorable, did much for Harold's flagging career, but a new opportunity presented itself when Arnold Saint-Subber—the man who'd launched *House of Flowers*—approached him and Charnin with an idea for a Broadway show. Saint-Subber had become fascinated with postwar Japanese society and was convinced it could provide the backdrop for a successful musical. When he read *Softly*, a short novel by Indian writer Santha Rama Rau, he thought he'd found the right story. It was about a young Japanese woman who falls in love with an American soldier during the occupation. He purchased the rights, got Arlen and Charnin to agree to write the score, and hired Hugh Wheeler to draft the script.

The problems—there were always problems with Arlen shows—began when Wheeler, a British writer of mystery novels who was as yet inexperienced in musical theater,[18] got stuck as he tried to shape the story. It seemed too reminiscent of Puccini's *Madama Butterfly*. Then came money troubles. Arlen made a demo of his and Charnin's songs and sent it to Goddard Lieberson at Columbia Records, hoping they'd finance the project. When Lieberson declined, the composer had to go through the demeaning process of playing and singing for prospective backers. He thought he had long since moved beyond that sort of thing; it was like going back to the 1920s when he'd auditioned for Jake Shubert while the producer ignored him and read his mail. Still, he did it.

At this point Charnin came up with an idea that appeared to be a breakthrough: make the leading man older, an American colonel. That unblocked Wheeler, who began to fashion a more interesting and original character. It also led Arlen to ask Fred Astaire to play the part. A return by Astaire to Broadway after thirty years in Hollywood would certainly interest investors. Also, writing for Astaire gave Arlen and Charnin a focus. "Harold and I loved the idea of Astaire," wrote Charnin. "Who wouldn't? And we churned out a lot of Astaire-type songs." One was a rewrite of "I Could Be Good for You" to make it, in Charnin's words, "a Fred song." As published, it remains so—playful and mischievous, based on a catchy Arlen riff—and it's fun to imagine what Astaire might have done with it had he not backed out of the venture. Charnin recalls: "It was when Saint [Subber] heard from Fred that he was not sure about leaving Hollywood to do a run in New York that things began to really fall apart, and we all became so disheartened that we abandoned the project."[19] *Softly* was never produced, and few of its more than twenty songs have been published. One unpublished Arlen–Charnin number is "You're Never Fully Dressed without a Smile," whose title Charnin used again thirteen years later when he and composer Charles Strouse wrote the hit musical *Annie*. As for the rest of the score, it can be found in the Library of Congress, where it resides along with the manuscript of *Blues Opera*.

All of these professional and personal troubles were countered, at least somewhat, by the tributes to Arlen that had begun in the early 1960s and continued throughout the decade. In 1965 *Cue*, a magazine that covered New York cultural events, celebrated its thirtieth anniversary with a concert of his music at Philharmonic Hall (now Avery Fisher Hall) at Lincoln Center. It featured soprano Eileen Farrell of the Metropolitan Opera. She had already recorded several Arlen songs, including "Where Is Dis Road A-leadin' Me To?" from *Americanegro Suite*. Also on the program were Sammy Davis Jr., composer-arranger Stan Freeman, pianist Cy Walter, Lisa Kirk, and Bert Lahr. Arlen and Jablonski prepared a written statement for the program that thanked all the participants and ended with the line, "Most sincerely and with deepest affection, Genuflectingly yours, Harold Arlen."[20] This had to have been a nod to Lahr and his great moment in *The Wizard of Oz* when he sang, "the chipmunks genuflect to me" in "If I Were King of the Forest."

Goddard Lieberson and Columbia Records, who'd refused to finance *Softly*, paid tribute to Arlen by asking him to record an LP of his songs. The album was entitled *Harold Sings Arlen (with friend)* and came out in 1966. The friend was Barbra Streisand, with whom he sang a duet—a quasi-rock-and-roll version of "Ding-Dong! The Witch Is Dead." The back of the album jacket showed them recording it, he wearing a white wig and holding a fake guitar. Streisand also sang a solo rendition of "House of Flowers," which Arlen, in the liner notes, called "the most moving, exciting rendition imaginable." He sang the ten other songs, including his and Mercer's "Blues in the Night" and "My Shining Hour" and lesser-known songs such as his and Harburg's "Little Biscuit" from *Jamaica* and his and Charnin's "That's a Find Kind o' Freedom."

On the evening of November 17, 1968, ASCAP saluted Arlen, the late Vincent Youmans, and Noël Coward with a concert at Lincoln Center. The main attraction, kept secret until she actually appeared onstage, was Judy Garland. The plan was to devote the second half of the program to Arlen's songs and to have Garland come out and perform the final four. The orchestra would back her for the first three. Then, on "Over the Rainbow," the composer would accompany her at the piano.

By late 1968 Garland could still command high concert fees, but bad business decisions, dishonest managers, and profligate spending had rendered her all but penniless. Friends (including Arlen) paid her medical bills, incurred from frequent hospital stays, as she often fell while inebriated. Two days before she and Harold met to discuss the concert, she slipped and hit her face on the edge of a coffee table. Their meeting took place on November 1 at the Park Avenue home of the parents of her current lover, songwriter-pianist John Meyer. Also present were Lincoln Center producer Henry Guettel and musical director Jay Blackton, who'd conducted the original production of *Oklahoma!* Harold arrived at the Meyers' home with two red roses for Judy, one from him, the other from Anya. There was a long wait before she entered the living room, because she couldn't decide what to wear for him. Finally, she came out in a shirt and pantyhose, went to Harold, and embraced him. She inquired after Anya's health and began to reminisce, ignoring everyone else in the room. Meyers had to remind her that others were present and that work needed to be done—keys had to be set for the songs so the orchestrations could be made. Arlen declined Meyer's invitation to go to the piano, then sighed when it was decided that Judy would sing "Over the Rainbow" in A-flat—he knew it in F. "I'll just have to practice," he said.[21] As he and the others were leaving, she remarked that the song of his she liked best was "Last Night When We Were Young." It wasn't one of the four she was to sing at Lincoln Center, but as soon as Harold heard her say this, he turned and went to the piano, where he and Judy performed it, he humming, she singing.

On the night of the concert she was in her dressing room, worried about losing her voice. A doctor sprayed her throat with a cocaine analgesic, but that did nothing for her nerves. Her agitation was growing when Meyer responded to a knock on the door and there, standing in the threshold, was the president of Lincoln Center, Richard Rodgers. "'Dick!' she cried happily."[22] He gave her a hug and, seeing how anxious she was, tried to calm her by sitting with her and reminiscing. He spoke of an evening some twenty-five years earlier, during the war, when they were at the piano in the New York home of Cartier executive Jules Glaenzer. Two inebriated soldiers and their girlfriends walked past the building, overheard them, and rang the bell to ask if they could join the party. Glaenzer ushered them in, sat them on the sofa, and Garland and Rodgers gave them an impromptu concert. Rodgers laughed as he recalled the evening, remembering that the foursome had no idea who was singing and playing for them. He hadn't expected them to recognize *him*, he said, but the whole world knew Judy Garland. As she relaxed, Meyer told Rodgers that he and Judy had been singing some of his songs the night before and he mentioned one she particularly liked: "Boys and Girls Like You and Me," written with Oscar Hammerstein. Rodgers went to the piano and played it as Judy sang, warming up her voice. Then, at her request, they did his and Hart's "With a Song in My Heart." With that, she was ready to take the stage

She sang "The Man That Got Away," "It's a New World," and "Get Happy" to the orchestra's accompaniment. Then Arlen entered and sat at the piano. "Now what would you like to do, darling?" she joked. The audience had no doubt what song they'd do. "And when they did it," Meyer remembered, "Judy kneeled by the piano bench and sang it directly to Harold." At "If happy little bluebirds fly beyond the rainbow why, oh, why," she paused and said "Thank you, Harold" before the concluding two notes, "can't I?" "Harold's tears were dropping on the ivory," wrote Meyer, "his fingers literally slipped off the keys. There was a surge of tumultuous applause, as Harold fairly leaped from the stage in acute embarrassment. You can imagine how this very private man felt with fifteen hundred people watching him cry. I was the first person he bumped into offstage (I literally don't think he could see where he was going). He hung on to my shoulder. 'She'll say any goddam thing,' he said."[23]

She died seven months later in London at age forty-seven from an accidental overdose of barbiturates.

CHAPTER 26

Waiting

In the late 1960s, Harold hired a housekeeper, Mrs. Geri Owens, a stout, middle-aged African American woman whose presence made him feel better about all the time he was spending outside the house. He didn't go to bars or golf courses this time; instead, he took long walks, usually from Central Park West to the Midtown theater district. There he would chat with Abe Berman and whoever happened to be in the lawyer/agent's office. Another stop was his barber's for a shave—a luxury he loved because it gave him another place to shoot the breeze. Also on his itinerary was publisher Buddy Morris's office, where he'd get more news and gossip. Evenings often found him at Kay Swift's little apartment. She'd been married and divorced three times, never to George Gershwin, but they'd had a ten-year romance and she still carried the torch for him. Others from Gershwin's circle were often present: his sister Frances Godowsky, Leonore Gershwin's sister Emily Strunsky, and George's longtime friend Mabel Schirmer. Ed Jablonski was often there as well, as was one of Swift's grandchildren, Katharine Weber. She remembers seeing Harold and Kay sitting together at the piano. "I have a strong memory of lying on the rug under my grandmother's piano when I was really young," she writes, "watching her feet and his as they played together. I could see their shoes nudging each other on the sustain pedal."[1]

Mrs. Owens's kindly and sympathetic presence eased Anya's troubled loneliness but couldn't make up for Harold's absences. Anya wanted him with her all the time. For him that meant enduring her sudden angry outbursts. Sometimes her mother would visit and she, too, would suffer Anya's rages. According to Jablonski, she "could not fathom her daughter's peculiar behavior," and visits at the San Remo "often ended stormily with Mary's indignant exit."[2] When Harold had guests Anya didn't know or like, she'd take refuge at her mother's Greenwich Village apartment—Rita Arlen remembers it as a "tiny, stark room"³—and wait there until the coast was clear.

Anya also began to distrust Jablonski's wife, Edith. She suspected that Edith had learned things about Harold from Ed that she needed to know. Ed, in his biographies, always referred to himself and everyone in his family in the third person, never by name. He is always "a friend" or "a neighbor"—and so is Edith. In his second Arlen biography he wrote: "Anya would sometimes call on a trusted neighbor to keep her company while Harold was absent. One woman arrived with two children in tow. Their noisy presence led to a screaming outburst, and the young mother and little girls fled the apartment." This was certainly a reference to Edith and two of the Jablonski children. "On another day, with Mrs. Owens out marketing, Anya called another friend"—presumably Ed.

> It was a bright summer day, but when he arrived he found Anya sitting in the den with the shades drawn. After an affectionate greeting, Anya and her friend sat on a sofa opposite the bookcase and television set. There was no conversation as the two sat side by side and Anya clutched his hand. She started at the sound of the freight elevator, staring in the direction of the sound as if she had never heard it before. The man and the speechless woman sat. Her involuntary movements, a contorted neck, a sudden facial spasm were disturbing. A shaken friend left the apartment when Harold returned. Neither said anything of consequence and nothing about Anya, still in the darkened den.⁴

By early 1969, Arlen and Dr. Schachtel knew the problem was physical. Yet they did nothing. Seventeen years earlier, Harold had asked his brother to drive an unwilling Anya to the sanitarium. He would not insist that she see a neurologist. It wasn't until the summer of 1969, when headaches and nausea became additional symptoms, that she finally agreed to be seen by a specialist. That was when her condition was at last diagnosed as a brain tumor. On August 26, 1969, as she was being readied for surgery, Harold handed her a note—just as he'd done thirty-two years earlier to ask her to marry him. This one said, "Dear Dear Annie. So little time and such sorrow."

But the surgery was successful—or so it seemed. She appeared to have been magically transformed into the woman she'd been during their courtship days. If she was no longer a beautiful seventeen-year-old chorine but a fifty-four-year-old woman undergoing radiation therapy who wore a helmet-like turban—always white, like her other clothing—to hide her scars and hair loss, she was sweet and loving again and they were happy. But it was only a six-month interlude. Jablonski described his and Edith's birthday call to Harold in February 1970: "When friends called on the fifteenth to wish him a happy birthday—his sixty-fifth—Arlen sounded subdued, even sad. He had no interest in the significance of the day. He put Anya on the phone; her voice was weak, and the two or three words she managed were unintelligible."[5] Three weeks later, while Harold was out for a walk, Mary Taranda arrived for a visit. Out of the blue, her daughter screamed at her and ordered her out of the house. It was the last time they saw each other. Anya died the next day, March 9, 1970.

Her funeral service took place at a mortuary on the Upper East Side. That morning Mary phoned Harold in hysterics. He told Jerry and Rita to go downtown and pick her up—he sent them a car and a driver. When they got to her apartment she was so distraught they took her to Dr. Schachtel to, in Rita Arlen's words, "kind of settle her down a little bit."[6] Then they brought her to the Russian Orthodox ceremony, which was, Jablonski wrote, "interminable."[7] Lynn Lane estimated it at four hours. Rita and Jerry flanked Harold. Mary, despite her sedation, screamed with grief all the way through. Anya's father, Frank Taranda, sat grim-faced next to his second wife. William Taranda, Anya's forty-eight-year-old brother, was there too, having flown in from California. According to Rita, he and Anya had remained close over the years. He was also, she says, "a little rough" in personality.[8] An alcoholic who'd been cited numerous times for drunken driving and arrested for a hit-and-run, he was not someone Harold looked forward to spending time with, but William and his mother were to spend the night with him at the San Remo.

Anya was buried at Ferncliff Cemetery in Hartsdale, twenty-five miles north of New York City. Arlen didn't say a word as Jablonski drove him there. He remained silent at the gravesite. He knew it would be his final resting place, too, and that the remains of Judy Garland and Jerome Kern were just a few feet away. His silence continued on the trip back to New York.

That night Harold phoned his brother. When Rita answered, he told her he was afraid of William and asked if Jerry could come over and spend the night. It isn't known why he found William threatening. Perhaps Taranda was angry with him for leaving Anya in a rest home for so many years. Or maybe he'd heard about Harold's affairs with high-profile women while Anya was institutionalized. Or his mother told him that during his sister's final days, Harold often left her to take long walks. Or it could have been about money. Whatever the cause, Jerry's forceful presence was the solution.

A few weeks after the funeral, with Mrs. Owens away, Harold, alone and unobserved, took an overdose of Valium and other pills—he had a bowl of them on hand, mixed like candies. When Jerry and Rita came by to check on him, they found him comatose on his bed. It was a cold March day, yet the air conditioner was on high, creating icicles in the room. When they brought him to, he gave them a surprised and sheepish grin.

After that he holed up in his apartment, refusing to see anyone except Jablonski, Rita, and Jerry. He didn't compose, make jots, or play the piano—a retirement from music that had begun while Anya was still alive. During her final days, he'd gotten a call from Cantor Harold Lerner of Temple Adath Yeshurun in Syracuse. Lerner, a successor to his father, had asked him to compose a piece in his father's memory for the dedication of a new wing of the synagogue. Arlen, weeping, thanked him "profusely" for the honor of the request and the kind words about his father but said he had to refuse due to his wife's illness.[9]

It was not until half a year after Anya's passing that he showed some renewed energy. One of the first signs was a visit to the Jablonskis. He'd heard that Ed's mother had come from Michigan to see her son, so he went to their apartment on West 75th Street with a big bouquet for her. In November of 1970, he was at the 92nd Street Y for a celebration of the work of Dorothy Fields. The next month he attended a celebration of his own music at the Lincoln Center Library Auditorium. Shortly after that, he was back at the 92nd Street Y for a tribute to Yip Harburg. As Christmas approached, he decided to continue his and Anya's Christmas–Chanukah tradition and invited the Jablonskis and their children, as well as Jerry, Rita, and Sam. Sam had a cold and stayed home, but the others were there, as were Robert and Wilva Breen—the couple who'd persuaded him to do *Blues Opera/Free and Easy.*

With that opera's failure, the Breens' interest in big musical productions ended. Still, they loved theater and had grown fond of experimental works in small off-Broadway venues like La Mama, a basement playhouse on the Lower East Side. One of the playwrights who caught their attention was Leonard Melfi, a man in his late thirties who'd written several well-received one-acts. Melfi had never written a musical—the closest he'd come was his contribution of a few sketches to the all-nude revue *Oh! Calcutta!* If Arlen was still interested in Rodgers and Hammerstein–style success, Melfi was hardly the partner to get him there. But he liked the young man, whom he called "Curly" because of his frizzy 1970s hairstyle. Like Capote and Charnin before him, Melfi brought the energy of the younger generation to Harold. He also introduced him to a world he hadn't known—absurdist plays in small Greenwich Village and Lower Manhattan theaters. Once again Arlen was out hitting the nightspots, this time with Melfi and the Breens.

They decided to create a musical for television. Arlen would write the words and music, and Melfi the script. He came up with a story about a

Mr. Clop, nicknamed Clippety by his friends, who drops out of Columbia University to drive a hansom cab in Central Park. His name thus takes on meaning. Toward the end of the play he falls in love with Clementine, who sells organic produce. Their relationship falters when he refuses to abandon his more conventional diet. That was it—the whole play, except for the fact that Clop is African American and Clementine white, a circumstance that has no bearing on the story, which was probably the point.

No one much liked *Clippety-Clop and Clementine*—not even Robert and Wilva Breen. Television executives passed on it and it died a quick death. The score did, however, contain one memorable ballad, "I Had a Love Once," written in Anya's memory. In it Arlen gives the piano its own theme—a bar of tolling major-seventh chords; they are like a funereal version of the major sevenths in "Hit the Road to Dreamland." Harold wrote the lyric himself:

> One moment was good,
> Next moment was sad
> A most peculiar love I had
> I had a love once
> I too was strong once
> Strong as a mighty oak
> Tall as a mountain
> Touched by a silver stream
> Soothed by a silver stream
> Bathed by a silver stream
> So roll on you rivers
> Wind on you valleys
> Gone is my loved one
> Gone, gone this day

With this beautiful song he said goodbye to her and to songwriting.

Irving Berlin urged him to continue his career. He suggested that Harold go on the road with a one-man show singing and playing his own work, as Jule Styne had done and as Sammy Cahn was doing. Arlen's reply was, "I've shot my wad."[10] He had no desire to play the piano anymore, certainly not in public. In April 1974 there was a special ASCAP board meeting to celebrate the issuance of a George Gershwin postage stamp, Eubie Blake's ninetieth birthday, and a new show by Alan Jay Lerner. Arlen attended—he'd been a board member for a number of years—but when someone expressed the hope that some of the songwriters on hand "be prevailed on to play their songs" he, according to the *New York Times*, which covered the event, quietly "slipped out of the room."[11]

Berlin also suggested that he marry again or at least find himself a girl-friend. But Harold was just as uninterested in this as in music. He still allowed himself to be cajoled into attending dinner parties, and when he did he was invariably seated next to an eligible woman, but nothing ever came of it. He often dined at Lynn and Burton Lane's apartment—they, too, lived in the San Remo—and on one occasion June Levant, widow of Oscar, was present. Afterward she told Lynn, "I really like him, could you have us over another time?"[12] But Harold let Lynn know he wasn't interested. It was the same when Dorothy Fields, also widowed, expressed her interest.[13] He was almost seventy now, and when it came to women, he preferred the past. "In the closets were Anya's clothes," Rita told John Lahr of *The New Yorker*. "In the dressing room he had her perfume tray with her makeup and cologne covered with a silk scarf."[14] Sometimes he'd take a dress from her closet and go back to his chair in the den and hold it.

For much of his life he'd been a voracious reader, but no more. He had an extensive record collection but rarely listened to music. Instead, he watched television. He continued going to Jerry and Rita's for Friday-night Sabbath dinners but preferred visiting them on Sundays to watch televised sports, especially with Rita. She'd sit on the sofa, and he'd get comfortable in a recliner. An open box of chocolates was always nearby, and he'd eat them as he smoked cigars. They watched golf, football, baseball, and tennis and wagered on the games. He and Ira, who was reclusive now in Beverly Hills, had for decades bet on the Rose Bowl, and when Arlen won he'd frame Ira's uncashed check and hang it on the wall of his guest bathroom. It made him laugh to think he'd made it difficult for Gershwin to balance his checkbook.

His walks continued to be a source of pleasure. Sometimes Irving Berlin accompanied him and they occasionally ended up at the movies. But with advancing age Berlin spent less time outside his Beekman Place townhouse, a few miles from Harold. And Harold, too, was gradually becoming house-bound. He'd become unsteady on his feet—a problem that sometimes went away, allowing him to believe it was only a consequence of aging. But it always returned and was eventually accompanied by slurred speech, watery eyes, a rheumy nose. When Jerry took him to see Dr. Schachtel the diagnosis was Parkinson's disease, but only Jerry was told, not Harold. The doctor prescribed L-dopa, which Mrs. Owens, against her better judgment, agreed to give him without letting him know what it was or what it was for.

The medicine was beneficial; his hands shook less and his legs weren't so wobbly. Now, however, came hallucinations—attributable, at least in part, to the L-dopa. Jablonski told Jerry that Harold ought to know what his illness was and be informed of the medication's side effects. Jerry contended that the important thing was to keep Harold's depression at bay. He was still able to come to Jerry and Rita's for Sabbath diner and on Sundays for sports broadcasts—although he hated having to be helped into and out of a cab.

In 1976 Harburg called him about a proposed revival of *Bloomer Girl*. Efforts to make a movie of it had failed, but the Goodspeed Opera House in East Haddam, Connecticut, was considering a production, and Yip, eighty years old now, wanted to work with his old collaborator on a couple of new songs for the occasion. Arlen said no. Not only did he refuse to work with him, he refused to see him. Hurt and perplexed, Harburg got in touch with Jablonski to find out what was going on, and Ed told him that Harold had Parkinson's and didn't want to be seen suffering from its symptoms. When Yip said Harold hadn't told him about his illness, Ed replied that Harold didn't know about it, either, that he was being kept in the dark. Yip insisted that Harold be told. Ed's reply was, "When I asked Jerry about that a couple of days ago he damn near chewed my ear off."[15]

By this time, a lot of people knew that Harold had Parkinson's disease. Kay Swift knew. Her twenty-year-old granddaughter, Katharine Weber, knew. To Yip it was ridiculous and unfair that Harold didn't know. He made an appointment for Arlen to see a neurologist and came by with Jablonski to take him there. This doctor didn't hesitate to tell Harold what was wrong with him, and the result was as Jerry had feared. Arlen returned to his apartment, took to his chair in the den, and sat there in a "disturbing silence"[16] day and night, apparently waiting to die. Mrs. Owens, alarmed, alerted Jablonski, who came over to explain the disease—with a little sugar coating. It wasn't a death sentence, he said. The medication was effective. Pain would be minimal. Relieved, Harold joked that if all this were true he might as well get back to work. But he didn't. The Goodspeed Opera House had to make do with two previously unpublished Arlen–Harburg songs: "Looks Like the End of a Beautiful Friendship" and "Promise Me Not to Love Me."

Toward the end of the 1970s, two strange events affected Arlen's home and family life. One was the firing of Mrs. Owens. She was let go by Jerry and Rita on the advice of Jeanne Matalon. Matalon was a secretary to Abe Berman, who sent her over to straighten out Harold's financial affairs, which were in disarray. It has never been explained why she wanted Geri Owens dismissed. This was certainly not Harold's wish, since she'd always treated him with kindness, and he'd developed a great affection for her. Carla Jablonski remembers how she would watch over him as he made his way from the dining table to the hallway under his own power, and then take over and help him the rest of the way to his room.[17] According to Ed

Jablonski, she was discharged because she'd get into heated arguments with nurses brought in to care for Harold. True to form, Harold offered no resistance. He agreed "reluctantly," wrote Jablonski, "for she had been more than a housekeeper and a good often fiercely protective friend."[18]

A small dining room became Matalon's office, where she managed Harold's checkbook and expenses as well as his business and legal affairs. As his condition worsened, she grew concerned about his estate and helped him draw up his will. She and Berman knew that his heir would receive a substantial income from his copyrights. Because he had no children of his own, the money would eventually go to Jerry's son, Sam, who was now in his twenties and no longer living at home. Matalon told Harold he needed to adopt Sam as his own son in order to make sure the money didn't end up going elsewhere. She told him that someone else might take the royalties when the copyrights came up for renewal. It was a fallacious argument, since Sam would be able to renew them when the time came. But Harold accepted Matalon's reasoning and adopted his nephew. It was a moment that seemed to sum up the relationship between him and Jerry. He'd had the career, the hit songs, the glamour, and the money, and now he had the son, too. According to Rita, Jerry went along with the arrangement because it promised Sam a better life. But in truth, she says, he "was upset about this—it *did* bother him."[19] And it bothered her, too. As for Harold, it may be that he took this step thinking back to the day in 1946 when the *shames* at the Pine Street Synagogue in Buffalo, upon hearing that he and Anya were childless, said, "What good are you?"

The will gave Jerry and Rita Harold's piano and personal effects, including George Gershwin's portrait of Jerome Kern—his most prized possession—which Rita eventually donated to the Library of Congress. It also gave them a George Gershwin self-portrait and a painting of Harold and Anya by Irving Berlin. Harold had already given Jerry, as a birthday gift, a painting he'd made of their father on the synagogue bimah. Matalon's final touch, presumably with Harold's consent, was to leave Jablonski out of the will. It is hard to imagine a better or more selfless friend than Jablonski. He certainly wasn't looking for money. He was, if anything, overly generous—constantly giving away valuable items that had come to him from his friendships with Ira Gershwin, Al Hirschfeld, Arlen, Berlin, and others. "Ed Jablonski was a lovely man," says Lynn Lane. "He was a gentle man, in love with the composers, music, lyrics. He was scholarly, kind. He had a lovely sense of humor. He did everything for Harold. He took him to the doctor, waited there, took him home. He picked the shoes up at the shoemaker. Then Harold didn't leave him one penny. Ed really needed the money."[20] It was as this will was being drawn up—Jablonski didn't learn of it until years later—that Edith died suddenly of a cerebral hemorrhage leaving him and their three children bereft in their small apartment.

As Harold's disease progressed, his public appearances became rare and arduous. On November 7, 1977, he attended a revue called *Sweet and Hot*, created by two musical theater experts and aficionados, Berthe Schuchat and Ken Bloom. The title came from the song Lyda Roberti had sung with her entertaining Polish accent in *You Said It*, Arlen's first Broadway effort, written in 1932 with Jack Yellen. *Sweet and Hot* presented a broad selection of his songs, many obscure, and the composer attended, accompanied by Yip Harburg and Robert Breen. Three years later, against the advice of Jablonski and Breen, who didn't think him up to it, he decided to attend an event at the New York Hilton honoring Frank Sinatra. As he exited the cab one of his legs buckled, and his two friends caught him before he landed on the pavement. The hotel ballroom was filled with friends and acquaintances, and they looked on with concern as he sat at his table with a fixed, dazed stare. Two years later he ventured out again, this time to accept the Johnny Mercer Award, established by the Songwriters Hall of Fame after the death in 1976 of his old friend and partner. He managed to get through the dinner—Rita helped him with his utensils—and through the speeches made in honor of the new inductees, Paul Simon, Bob Dylan, and Meredith Willson among them. He determinedly rose to his feet to accept the award bearing Mercer's image. That done, he headed for the exit, Rita clearing a path for him through a crowd of well-wishers. One did reach him, however. This was Willson—the man who'd commissioned *American Minuet* forty-three years earlier and who was now, as he embraced Harold, in tears.

One by one, death was claiming his generation of songwriters. Ted Koehler passed in 1973, Dorothy Fields followed him the next year, and Richard Rodgers in 1979—Broadway theaters dimmed their lights in his memory. Ira Gershwin died quietly in 1983 at eighty-six as he sat in a chair watching television. Mercer didn't have it so easy. After suffering balance and coordination problems, he grudgingly went to a doctor and was told he had an inoperable brain tumor. Against his better judgment, he gave in to an overconfident surgeon who thought he could remove it. The result was a botch that left him in a vegetative state for the final eight months of his life.

Harburg had tried without success through the 1960s and 1970s to connect with the new generation of political activists. Michael Feinstein remembers him as "extraordinarily compassionate but sometimes hard to take. He was the kind of person who wouldn't take 'yes' for an answer. I saw him give a lecture at UCLA to a group of young hopeful songwriters who were thrilled to be in his presence. And then he immediately began haranguing them about how horrible their music was and how people didn't know how to write anymore. He completely lost all the students. It was tragic and a true missed opportunity to build a bridge."[21] His death came in March 1981, a month before his eighty-fifth birthday, at the wheel of his car on Sunset Boulevard in Los Angeles. Initial reports were that he'd died in a fiery crash. Actually he'd stopped for a red light when a fatal heart attack caused his foot to slip off the gas pedal and his car to roll into the vehicle in front. He'd been on his way to a meeting about a musical version of *Treasure Island*.

Harry Warren's life also ended in 1981. He was eighty-seven. In 1980 David Merrick produced a musical that used the songs Warren had written with Al Dubin for the groundbreaking 1933 movie *42nd Street*. Because Warner Bros. owned the copyrights, Merrick paid no attention to Warren. He called the show *David Merrick's Song and Dance Extravaganza 42nd Street*. It was a huge success—bigger than *Oklahoma!* or any Rodgers and Hammerstein show. Not only was Warren's name missing from the title and the marquee, it wasn't even on the cover of the best-selling original cast album. "The night I went to the show," wrote Michael Feinstein, who had befriended Warren in his final years, "shortly after it opened, I stood in the lobby and asked people at random if they knew who had written all those great songs. Not one person could tell me. Some thought it was David Merrick."[22]

Through all this, Arlen hung on by a thread. He was diagnosed with prostate cancer, operated on, and survived. He continued his phone chats with Irving Berlin, who called whenever he heard an Arlen song on the radio or television. During one of those calls, Berlin was surprised when Arlen said he was busy and would have to call him back. Jablonski had brought a treat: a young piano prodigy named Kevin Cole who knew just about every piece Arlen had ever written and could also play Gershwin the way Gershwin had played Gershwin—so said Kay Swift. Harold had been primed for this moment several days earlier when Jablonski came by with a concert tape of Cole playing and discussing two obscure piano pieces: Gershwin's *Rialto Ripples*, written when he was nineteen, and Arlen's *Rhythmic Moments*, written at twenty-three. After hearing this tape, Arlen rose to his feet and gave it a standing ovation. Now Cole was in his den at the Martha Washington spinet, sight-reading from stacks of unpublished works. He played the *Clippety-Clop and Clementine* songs and then one little-known Arlen piece after another. Arlen enjoyed this so much he turned it into a game, trying to stump Cole by requesting pieces he couldn't possibly know. But he knew them all.

Another pleasure was the publication of *The Harold Arlen Songbook* by Paul McCartney's company, MPL Communications. McCartney had taken the advice of his father-in-law, Lee Eastman—a friend of Arlen's—and invested his money in music, purchasing the song catalogs of many composers, Arlen among them. Sam Arlen would get the composer's royalties; McCartney, the publisher's royalties. It was a big moment for Arlen when he saw this folio take its place alongside bound volumes of songs by Gershwin, Rodgers, Porter, and Kern.

He was also pleased when National Public Radio honored him with a fifteen-minute segment on its evening news program *All Things Considered*. "Today Harold Arlen celebrates his eightieth birthday," said host Susan Stamberg, "and if the name doesn't ring a bell, well, just listen. Maybe you'll want to celebrate, too." She followed this with recordings of Judy Garland singing "Over the Rainbow," Ella Fitzgerald's version of "It's Only a Paper Moon," Sinatra's "I've Got the World on a String," Mel Tormé's "My Shining Hour," and Streisand singing "Right as the Rain." The versatility, complexity, and beauty of his music were discussed in an interview with Jablonski, who said,

> So many of the songs are of such varying lengths and have such interesting contrasting sections. I said, "What's going on?" and he said, "Well, I get into trouble and try to figure out some way of getting out of it" . . . A couple of days ago I was telling him about how musicians and everyone admire him. Gloria Vanderbilt gave Al Hirschfeld a Harold Arlen cassette on which Arlen sang every song. Hirschfeld was so delighted he called Harold and then Harold called me and said, "I didn't know Al Hirschfeld was a fan of mine." I said, "Harold, a lot of people are . . . you're considered one of the greats." He said, "Aww, come on."

The NPR tribute ended with a rarity: Arlen's demo of "Such Unusual Weather," a gem written for but not used in the 1942 film *Rio Rita*, lyrics by Harburg.

Another radio tribute occurred on March 2, 1985, this one on New York station WNEW. The host was Jonathan Schwartz, who as a boy had gone with his father, composer Arthur Schwartz, to a Beverly Hills party and, while sitting on the carpet next to Anya, her arm across his shoulders, listened to Harold sing and play. Now, forty years later, he played a recording of an interview he'd conducted with Arlen two weeks earlier on the composer's eightieth birthday. Harold's speech was halting and slurred, his words occasionally garbled, but he was obviously in command of his thoughts. About writing "Ac-cent-tchu-ate the Positive": "He [Mercer] asked me while he was driving, he touched on the making of a song out of a little spiritual that I had. He remembered it. And by the time I got home the song was finished." On the genesis of "Stormy Weather": "I was up at Frances Williams's, who was a star then for George White's Scandals. In her apartment with some friends. And I was worried, troubled . . . I started it there. I had the first phrase. Luckily I put it down." Schwartz then asked,

"Of all of your men friends through the years, who would you like to see come through your door right now? Yip Harburg?"

Arlen: "Wouldn't mind."

Schwartz: "Johnny Mercer?"

Arlen: "Likewise."

Schwartz: "Of all of the songs that you did not write, what would you have liked to have written?"

Arlen: "Kern."

Schwartz: "All the Things You Are?"

Arlen: "No, not necessarily."

Schwartz: "Does that mean you don't favor 'All the Things You Are'?"

Arlen: "No, I do favor it, but it's not at the top of my list."

Schwartz: "Harold, who in your life have you been closest to of all of the other composers through the years? Not your collaborators. But just as a friend?"

Arlen: "Berlin is a friend of mine. Kern was. George was."

Schwartz: "George was really an astonishing fellow, wasn't he?"

Arlen: "Yeah."

Schwartz: "His songs, the ones that haunt you—what would they be?"

Arlen: "Well, I take a fancy to all of them."

Schwartz: "Anything in particular?"

Arlen: "Yes, *Porgy and Bess.*"

Schwartz: "If you had to pick one man or woman through the years, one person to sing a song of yours who would it be?"

Arlen: "Well, right now . . . I would give Lena the nod . . . I saw her show. It was dynamite."

Early on the morning of April 23, 1986, two months past Arlen's eighty-first birthday and during Passover, Rita arrived at his apartment with some homemade matzo ball soup and gefilte fish. Harold was in his den, sitting at a card table. He was looking forward to this meal, and when Rita offered to warm it up he said no, he wanted it cold and with horseradish. He made a breakfast of it and had it again for lunch. Shortly after lunch, early in the afternoon, he asked his nurse to help him to his bedroom. This was unusual, because he liked to sit in his chair afternoons and evenings and watch television. The nurse saw that something was very wrong and, worried, phoned Rita, Jerry, and Ed Jablonski, who came over and were with him when he died.

There were several unusual, even bizarre events in connection with his funeral at Ferncliff Cemetery. Jerry learned that Harold had not purchased a separate plot for himself and was told by the funeral directors that the ground next to Anya was unavailable. All they could suggest was that Harold be buried with her, which is what happened. Not many people were present for the internment, but one who was, Lisa Kirk, suddenly broke away from the others and had to be kept from throwing herself into the open grave.[23] Perhaps the strangest moment was a meteorological one, described a few days later by Ron Alexander in his "Metropolitan Diary" column in the *New York Times*. It read:

> Department of Away Above the Chimney Tops in Northern New Jersey: Jacqueline Beusse and Ray Seery were the first two of a number of New Jersey residents to tell us about the spectacular rainbow that appeared in the sky over the northwestern part of that state in the late afternoon–early evening of April 25. Mr. Seery and his wife caught it in Morris Plains; Miss Caldwell [*sic*] saw the rainbow—a double one—arcing over the towns of Caldwell and Essex Falls.
>
> All the rainbow reporters mentioned two facts: that they hadn't seen a rainbow in a long, long time and that April 25th was also the day Harold Arlen was buried. Mr. Arlen, of course, was the composer of "Over the Rainbow" (lyrics by E. Y. Harburg). There was also some mention of lemon drops and happy little bluebirds, but enough is enough.[24]

Not long ago, there was another interesting outdoor scene, this one on Shattuck Avenue in Berkeley, California. It was rush hour at twilight on a winter workday, and an elderly man stood outside the busy BART subway station playing "Blues in the Night" on his saxophone, hoping that commuters and students would drop a coin or a bill into the upturned hat he'd set down on the pavement. His choice of songs was appropriate to the moment, given the darkening skies. But when a mother and her little girl—she couldn't have been more than five—stopped to listen to him, he switched to "We're Off to See the Wizard" and the girl launched into an impromptu, joyous dance. Onlookers, who probably didn't know who Arlen was, were witnesses to the breadth of his achievement. A tune he'd written for a girl to dance to in 1939 was being danced to now by a child of the twenty-first century.

Great songs break free of time and carry energy and emotion with them from the past. They come from composers and lyricists whose names ought to be timeless, too. Given the enduring vitality of Arlen's music, it's a good bet that one day his songs will evoke not just the names of the greats who sang them, but his name as well. It's appropriate to think of Sinatra when we hear "One for My Baby," but we should, as he always did, credit Arlen and Mercer, who wrote the song. It's fitting to think of Judy Garland when we hear "Over the Rainbow," but we ought to say, as she did that night in Lincoln Center, "Thank you, Harold"—and add, "Thank you, Yip."

As for the rainbows that filled the sky the day he was buried and whether Mr. Seery, his wife, and the others witnessed a cosmic display in Arlen's honor: what we do know is that the melody of "Over the Rainbow" came to him from out of the blue—an occurrence that seems just as unlikely and inexplicable. Who's to say what is or isn't "imposerous"?[25]

ACKNOWLEDGMENTS

I've learned about Harold Arlen from the writings of the late Edward Jablonski and by speaking to people who knew the composer. Lynn Lane was especially generous not only with her memories, but with introductions to those I needed to talk to. Her daughter, Peggy Kaye, provided me with the photo of Burton Lane that appears in this book. Rita Arlen granted me access to letters, photos, and other documents and, in many hours of conversation, displayed an affection for Harold Arlen that proved to be universal among all who knew him. My gratitude also goes to Irving Berlin's daughter, Mary Ellin Barrett, who discussed her memories of Arlen and her father's friendship with him and their reaction to the music of the 1960s.

I also want to thank the following people for allowing me to interview them and for the information they generously shared: Edward Jablonski's daughter Carla Jablonski, lyricist Martin Charnin, theater historian Miles Kreuger, singer-pianist-archivist Michael Feinstein, composer-conductor-pianist André Previn, Michael Kerker of ASCAP, Jim Steinblatt of ASCAP, Maryann Chach of the Shubert Archive, pianist Kevin Cole, novelist Katharine Weber, Dr. Rod Gorney, Marge Harburg, Ernie Harburg, Joan Arlen, Norman Booth, Chris Cuppula, Sharon Fischer, R. Bobby Ducharme, Debi Whiting, Dr. Gary Abrams, Aljean Harmetz, Nick Markovich, Cantor Harold Lerner, Susan Stamberg, Edward Comstock, Phyllis Cole Braunlich, Sondra Gorney, George K. Arthur, Larry Weinstein, Dick Riederer, and Jeff Lunden.

Mark Horowitz of the Music Division of the Library of Congress was especially helpful, pointing me to document collections that I might otherwise have missed. Thanks also to Kevin S. Fleming of the Georgia State University Library for his help with and knowledge about their collection of Johnny Mercer's papers. Sam Arlen was kind enough to provide a photo of

Harold and Anya Arlen from his collection and allow me to quote Arlen's final song, "I Had a Love Once."

Thank you to Laurie Matheson, editor-in-chief at the University of Illinois Press, for encouraging this project from the beginning, to assistant acquisitions editor Marika Christofides and assistant managing editor Jennifer Clark for their know-how and good humor, and to Angela Arcese for her expert copyediting.

I was lucky to be able to rely on the expertise of many good friends. Dr. Elizabeth F. Thomas helped me understand Anya Arlen's medical prescriptions. Estelle Eisenberg translated Yiddish words and expressions. Theatrical Producer Berthe Schuchat shared her memories of Arlen as well as an extensive collection of Arlen sheet music. Joe Spampinato allowed me access to his correspondence with Ed Jablonski. Pianist-raconteur Richard Glazier shared his knowledge of and thoughts about Arlen and treated me to exciting performances of his works. I had enjoyable and valuable discussions with Joan Alexander and Jonathan Thomas about Arlen and the people in his life. Another close friend, Vivian Wills, read the manuscript and suggested needed corrections. Blair Kilpatrick, Margit Stange, Randy Kasten, Anna Fonte, and Barbara Yoder of the Ada Street Writers Group consistently provided valuable critiques in a friendly and supportive atmosphere. Equally important were the suggestions—and patience—of my wife, Peg Rimler, our sons Jacob and Jesse, and our daughter, Rose.

NOTES

INTRODUCTION

1. Harold Arlen, letter to Paul McCartney, October 14, 1984, Edward Jablonski Collection, Library of Congress.

2. Paul McCartney, letter to Harold Arlen, October 16, 1984, courtesy of Rita Arlen.

3. Max Wilk, *They're Playing Our Song* (Westport, Conn.: Easton Studio Press, 2008), 178. This word translates into "crappy."

4. Jack O'Brien, *New York Journal American*, February 18, 1962.

5. Charles Hamm, *Yesterdays: Popular Song in America* (New York: Norton, 1979), 357–63. The Tin Pan Alley format, which became standard in popular songs in the 1920s, uses a conversational or recitative verse to set up a situation that becomes the subject of the more melodic refrain. These verses are often dispensed with in performances. For instance, it's rare to hear the verse to "Over the Rainbow" ("When all the world is a hopeless jumble") although everyone knows the refrain ("Somewhere over the rainbow"). Prior to the 1920s songs were more typically like Stephen Foster's "Oh Susanna," in which verses with different words use the same music ("Oh, I come from Alabama") and alternate with a refrain ("Oh, Susannah") that doesn't change musically or lyrically.

CHAPTER 1. BUFFALO, NY

1. Although Arlen is usually said to have been born on February 15, the date February 14 is on his birth certificate.

2. George K. Arthur, telephone interview with the author, July 25, 2012.

3. Max Wilk, *They're Playing Our Song* (Westport, Conn.: Easton Studio Press, 2008), 166.

4. Edward Jablonski, *Harold Arlen: Happy with the Blues* (New York: Doubleday, 1961), 32.

5. Ibid., 32.

6. Samuel Arluck, letter to Harold Arlen, April 19, 1940, courtesy of Rita Arlen.

7. This anecdote was told to the author by Sharon Fischer during a January 16, 2012, telephone interview. Ms. Fischer was a close friend of the youngest Sandler son, Bernie, who told the story to her.

8. Dick Riederer, president of the Buffalo Musicians' Union Local 92 AFM, telephone interview, July 30, 2012.

9. The lyricist, Hyman Cheiffetz, may have been considering a name change, too. On the cover it is Hymon Cheiffetz and on the inside Hymon Cheiffets.

10. Edward Jablonski, *Harold Arlen: Rhythm, Rainbows, and Blues* (Boston: Northeastern University Press, 1996), 17.

11. Ibid., 10.

CHAPTER 2. NEW YORK, NY

1. Aljean Harmetz, *The Making of the Wizard of Oz* (New York: Hyperion, 1977), 114. Bolger was born in 1904, two years after Stone appeared as the scarecrow in the first stage production of *The Wizard of Oz*.

2. Edward Jablonski, *Harold Arlen: Rhythm, Rainbows, and Blues*, 18.

3. Max Wilk, *They're Playing Our Song* (Westport, Conn.: Easton Studio Press, 2008), 165.

4. Will Friedwald, *A Biographical Guide to the Great Jazz and Pop Singers* (New York: Pantheon, 2010), 624–25.

5. Bing Crosby, letter to Bob Wachsman, December 15, 1947, courtesy of Rita Arlen.

6. Harold Arluck, undated letter titled "Happening's [*sic*] of the Day," to "Boots" (Norman Booth). This letter was provided to the author by Booth's son and namesake, Norman Booth.

7. Yip Harburg interview by the Canadian Broadcasting Company, November 26, 1979.

8. Philip Furia, *Skylark: The Life and Times of Johnny Mercer* (New York: St. Martin's, 2003), 73.

9. Vernon Duke, *Passport to Paris* (Boston: Little, Brown, 1955), 278.

10. Wilfrid Sheed, *The House That George Built* (New York: Random House, 2008), 83.

CHAPTER 3. "GET HAPPY"

1. Max Wilk, *They're Playing Our Song* (Westport, Conn.: Easton Studio Press, 2008), 167.

2. John Lahr, "Come Rain or Come Shine: The Bittersweet Life of Harold Arlen," *The New Yorker*, September 19, 2005.

3. Edward Jablonski, *Harold Arlen: Happy with the Blues* (New York: Doubleday, 1961), 89.

4. Gene Lees, *Portrait of Johnny: The Life of John Herndon Mercer* (Milwaukee: Hal Leonard, 2004), 249.

5. Lahr, "Come Rain or Come Shine."

6. Access to Arlen's journal was granted to the author by Rita Arlen.

7. "Mrs. Selwyn Learns an Old Truth," *New York Times*, February 16, 1930.

8. Jablonski, *Harold Arlen: Happy with the Blues*, 46.

9. Mayme Peak, "Reel Life in Hollywood," *Daily Boston Globe*, February 5, 1934.

10. In 1930, Earl Carroll was using the New Amsterdam Theatre while his eponymous new theater was under construction. He chose the opulent New Amsterdam because it was famous for hosting musicals put on by his rival, Florenz Ziegfeld. Ziegfeld, in the meantime, had opened the Ziegfeld Theatre.

Chapter 4. The Cotton Club

1. Richard Rodgers, *Musical Stages: An Autobiography* (Cambridge, Mass.: Da Capo Press, 2002), 20.

2. Meryl Secrest, *Somewhere for Me: A Biography of Richard Rodgers* (New York: Knopf, 2001), 22.

3. Alyn Shipton, *I Feel a Song Coming On: The Life of Jimmy McHugh* (Urbana: University of Illinois Press, 2009), 72.

4. Alyn Shipton, *Hi-De-Ho: The Life of Cab Calloway* (New York: Oxford University Press, 2010), 37. The quote is by Calloway.

5. In his manuscript for this song, Koehler calls the following the "catch line": "Don't you treat my pussy rough / You've got to be discreet / Without it how the devil / Would I make ends meet." This manuscript is in the Edward Jablonski Collection at the Library of Congress.

6. Ken Bloom, *Broadway: Its History, People and Places* (New York: Routledge, 2012), 300.

7. Edward Jablonski, *Harold Arlen: Happy with the Blues* (New York: Doubleday, 1961), 79.

8. Brooks Atkinson, "The Play: Collegiate," *New York Times*, January 20, 1931.

9. Jablonski, *Harold Arlen: Happy with the Blues*, 80–81.

10. Harold Arlen, "To Dorothy Kilgallen: From Harlem to the Land of Oz and Beyond," June 6, 1958, courtesy of Rita Arlen.

11. Edward Jablonski, *Harold Arlen: Rhythm, Rainbows, and Blues* (Boston: Northeastern University Press, 1996), 48.

12. Ibid.

13. Ibid., 69.

14. Harold Arlen, interview by Walter Cronkite for the February 9, 1964, episode of the CBS television program *The Twentieth Century*. This part of the interview was not broadcast.

15. Will Friedwald, *A Biographical Guide to the Great Jazz and Pop Singers* (New York: Pantheon Books, 2010), 625.

CHAPTER 5. ANYA

1. Studs Terkel, *Hard Times: An Oral History of the Great Depression* (New York: The New Press, 2005), 20.

2. Harburg recounted this story to his son, Ernie Harburg, who related it to the author in an in-person interview on October 13, 2011. "When he said something," Ernie cautioned, "you had to take it with a grain of salt."

3. Harold Myerson and Ernie Harburg, *Who Put the Rainbow in the Wizard of Oz?* (Ann Arbor: University of Michigan Press, 1993), 16.

4. Ibid., 25.

5. Ibid., 65.

6. Michael Feinstein, telephone interview with the author, July 3, 2012.

7. Ibid.

8. Philip Furia, *Skylark: The Life and Times of Johnny Mercer*, 73.

CHAPTER 6. "STORMY WEATHER"

1. Max Wilk, *They're Playing Our Song* (Westport, Conn.: Easton Studio Press, 2008), 295.

2. Ethel Waters, *His Eye Is on the Sparrow* (Cambridge, Mass.: Da Capo Press, 1992), ix.

3. Alec Wilder, *American Popular Song* (New York: Oxford University Press, 1972), 272.

4. Ibid.

5. This was pointed out to the author by Laurie Matheson of the University of Illinois Press.

6. Edward Jablonski, *Harold Arlen: Happy with the Blues* (New York: Doubleday, 1961), 37.

7. Edward Jablonski, *Harold Arlen: Rhythm, Rainbows, and Blues* (Boston: Northeastern University Press, 1996), 51.

8. Burton Lane, eulogy for Harold Arlen, April 25, 1986.

9. Wilfrid Sheed, *The House That George Built* (New York: Random House, 2008), 93.

10. Laurence Bergreen, *As Thousands Cheer: The Life of Irving Berlin* (New York: Penguin, 1990), 6.

11. John Corry, "Graybeard Arlen Recalls Birth of Career," *Sarasota Herald Tribune*, June 10, 1971.

12. Tony Thomas, *Harry Warren and the Hollywood Musical* (Secaucus, N.J.: Citadel Press, 1975), 21.

13. Ted Libbey, *The NPR Listener's Encyclopedia of Classical Music* (New York: Workman, 2006), 903.

14. Mayme Peak, "Reel Life in Hollywood," *Daily Boston Globe*, February 5, 1934.

15. Margaret Talbot, *The Entertainer* (New York: Riverhead Books, 2012), 133.

CHAPTER 7. ON BROADWAY WITH IRA AND YIP

1. Edward Jablonski, *Harold Arlen: Happy with the Blues* (New York: Doubleday, 1961), 88.

2. Ibid.

3. Comment by jmacleve on a YouTube video called "Slapstick Song and Dance Man."

4. John Lahr, "The Lion and Me," *The New Yorker,* November 16, 1998, 64.

5. John Lahr, *Notes on a Cowardly Lion* (New York: Knopf, 1969), 138.

CHAPTER 8. "LAST NIGHT WHEN WE WERE YOUNG"

1. John Lahr, "Come Rain or Come Shine: The Bittersweet Life of Harold Arlen," *The New Yorker*, September 19, 2005, 91.

2. Edward Jablonski, *Harold Arlen: Rhythm, Rainbows, and Blues* (Boston: Northeastern University Press, 1996), 96.

3. Harold Arlen, interviewed by Walter Cronkite for the February 9, 1964, episode of the CBS television program *The Twentieth Century.* This part of the interview was not broadcast.

4. Ibid.

5. Edward Jablonski, *Harold Arlen: Happy with the Blues* (New York: Doubleday, 1961), 157.

6. Harriet Hyman Alonso, *Yip Harburg: Legendary Lyricist and Human Rights Activist* (Middletown, Conn.: Wesleyan University Press, 2012), 60.

7. Ibid., 60.

8. Ibid., 62.

9. Christopher Finch, *Rainbow: The Stormy Life of Judy Garland* (New York: Grosset and Dunlap, 1975), 178.

CHAPTER 9. MARRIAGE

1. Cab Calloway, *Minnie the Moocher and Me* (New York: Thomas Y. Crowell, 1976), 131.

2. Michel Rogin, *Blackface, White Noise: Jewish Immigrants in the Hollywood Melting Pot* (Berkeley: University of California Press, 1998), 6.

3. Arthur Knight, *Disintegrating the Musical: Black Performance and American Musical Film* (Durham, N.C.: Duke University Press, 2002), 74–75.

4. This and other examples of Harburg's early writing, as well as a discussion of his art and career, can be found in Harold Meyerson and Ernie Harburg's *Who Put the Rainbow in the Wizard of Oz?* (Ann Arbor: University of Michigan Press, 1993).

5. Harriet Hyman Alonso, *Yip Harburg: Legendary Lyricist and Human Rights Activist* (Middletown, Conn.: Wesleyan University Press, 2012), 73.

6. Max Wilk, *They're Playing Our Song* (Westport, Conn.: Easton Studio Press, 2008), 170.

7. Edward Jablonski, *Harold Arlen: Rhythm, Rainbows, and Blues* (Boston: Northeastern University Press, 1996), 107.

8. Jerry Arlen, letter to Harold Arlen, undated, courtesy of Rita Arlen.

9. Samuel Arluck, letter to "Dear Son," January 10, 1936, courtesy of Rita Arlen.

10. Jablonski, *Harold Arlen: Rhythm, Rainbows, and Blues*, 107.

11. Ibid., 108.

12. On p. 108 of *Harold Arlen: Rhythm, Rainbows, and Blues*, Edward Jablonski writes that Abe Berman and Jerry Arlen were the two witnesses. However, the marriage license has the names of Berman and his wife.

13. "Harold Arlen Married, 'Asserts Dame Rumor,'" Sunday, April 18, 1937, Syracuse *American*, p. 16. The newspaper was published on Sundays as the *American* and on weekdays as the *Journal*. On p. 110 of *Harold Arlen: Rhythm, Rainbows, and Blues*, Edward Jablonski writes that Harold and Anya went to Syracuse not long after the wedding to inform the Arlucks and "face the music" and that the reception they received was "reserved but cordial." This may be true, but if so, it is hard to understand why there was so much secrecy about the wedding and for so long.

14. This anecdote was told to the author by Sharon Fischer during a January 16, 2012, interview. Ms. Fischer was a close friend of the youngest Sandler son, Bernie, who told the story to her.

CHAPTER 10. DEATH OF GERSHWIN

1. Entering someone's house without knocking was apparently commonplace in Hollywood in those days. Arlen once popped in on William Powell and Carole Lombard only to find them having sex on their living room rug. Powell, nonplussed, sat up and said, "So, *you* wrote 'Stormy Weather.'" The incident is described in Edward Jablonski, *Harold Arlen: Rhythm, Rainbows, and Blues* (Boston: Northeastern University Press, 1996), 125.

2. Robert Kimball and Alfred Simon, *The Gershwins* (New York: Atheneum, 1973), 204.

3. Joan Peyser, *The Memory of All That: The Life of George Gershwin* (New York: Simon and Schuster, 1993), 263.

4. Dr. Rod Gorney, email to the author, August 25, 2014.

5. "In later years Ira would feel guilty about not having defended his fatally ill brother from his wife," wrote Jablonski in *Harold Arlen: Rhythm, Rainbows, and Blues*, 113.

6. Her hatred for him continued long after his death. In a September 26, 2011, interview with the author, theater historian Miles Kreuger spoke about an incident

recounted to him by Michael Feinstein. Feinstein was working as Ira Gershwin's archivist in the late 1970s and early 1980s and had found in one of Ira's closets some papers of George long thought to have been lost. He set them on a chair. When Leonore came into the room and was told of the discovery, she went to the chair and sat on the papers.

7. "Gershwin at Eighty," a September 26, 1978, radio program by Miles Kreuger, featuring interviews with Gershwin's friends and family members.

8. Gerald Bordman, *Days to Be Happy, Years to Be Sad: The Life and Music of Vincent Youmans* (New York: Oxford University Press, 1982), 177–78.

CHAPTER 11. *HOORAY FOR WHAT!*

1. Edward Jablonski, *Harold Arlen: Happy with the Blues* (New York: Doubleday, 1961), 82.

2. After Blane's death, Martin revealed that he had written "Have Yourself a Merry Little Christmas" on his own, with no input from Blane. They worked in separate rooms, writing separate songs, but every song bore both names.

3. Agnes de Mille, *Portrait Gallery* (Boston: Houghton Mifflin, 1990), 99–100.

4. Sam Irvin, *Kay Thompson: From* Funny Face *to* Eloise (New York: Simon and Schuster, 2010), 64–65.

5. Edward Jablonski, *Harold Arlen: Rhythm, Rainbows, and Blues* (New York: Doubleday, 1961), 118.

6. In a November 26, 1979, Canadian Broadcasting interview, Yip Harburg said, "Harold had a lot of tunes that he's thrown away that were great that I'd love to resuscitate some time."

7. Aljean Harmetz, *The Making of the Wizard of Oz* (New York: Hyperion, 1977), 7–8.

8. MGM producer Mervyn LeRoy claimed that he was the one who persuaded Mayer to buy the rights.

CHAPTER 12. *THE WIZARD OF OZ*

1. Aljean Harmetz, *The Making of the Wizard of Oz* (New York: Hyperion, 1977), 21.

2. Ibid., 34.

3. Michael Feinstein, telephone interview with the author, July 3, 2012.

4. Meinhardt Raabe played the coroner in the film, but his singing was done by Rad Robinson, whose voice was electronically altered. Arlen sang the coroner part on the July 1939 Decca studio album.

5. Harold Arlen, interview by Walter Cronkite for the February 9, 1964, episode of the CBS television program *The Twentieth Century*.

6. Harriet Hyman Alonso, *Yip Harburg: Legendary Lyricist and Human Rights Activist* (Middletown, Conn.: Wesleyan University Press, 2012), 83.

7. Harold Arlen, interview by Walter Cronkite for the February 9, 1964, episode of the CBS television program *The Twentieth Century*.

8. Edward Jablonski, *Harold Arlen: Rhythm, Rainbows, and Blues* (Boston: Northeastern University Press, 1996), 131.

9. In 1970, when Harburg gave a lecture at the 92nd Street Y in New York, he said that Arlen had gotten stuck when it came to the song's bridge (or release) and that he had solved the problem by suggesting Harold use the melody made by his whistle when he called his dog Pan. Arlen was in the audience and called out, "Not true." As for the tag, Michael Feinstein said that Ira Gershwin told him he provided Yip with the concluding line, "If happy little bluebirds fly / beyond the rainbow why, oh why, can't I?" When Feinstein asked Ira how this came about, Ira replied, "They'd been working at the piano for a long, long time and I wanted to make it a short evening." Michael Feinstein, *Nice Work If You Can Get It: My Life in Rhythm and Rhyme* (New York: Hyperion, 1995), 284–85.

10. In 1970, when Harburg gave a lecture at the 92nd Street Y in New York, he said that Arlen had phoned him at midnight.

11. Arlen was an habitué at the Hillcrest Country Club on Pico Boulevard in Los Angeles, across the street from Fox Studios, where he would he often play two complete rounds of golf a day.

12. Harold Myerson and Ernie Harburg, *Who Put the Rainbow in the Wizard of Oz?* (Ann Arbor: University of Michigan Press, 1993), 131.

13. "The Songs of Harold Arlen," Canadian Broadcasting Company broadcast, November 26, 1979.

14. Myerson and Harburg, *Who Put the Rainbow in the Wizard of Oz?*, 132.

15. Dr. Rod Gorney, email to the author, August 25, 2014.

16. When Walter Cronkite interviewed Arlen in 1964 for the CBS television program *The Twentieth Century*, Arlen, talking about his music for this song, said, "I don't think it would have meant anything with another lyric. Now, of course, you can't divorce the lyric from it. But if you'd hear that cold or with another lyric I'm sure it wouldn't mean anything." This part of the interview was not broadcast.

17. This may well have occurred to Cantor Arluck, as it became his tradition to sing "Over the Rainbow" in Hebrew during the afternoon service on Yom Kippur. Cantor Harold Lerner, a successor to Cantor Arluck, provided the author with this information in a telephone interview on August 10, 2011.

18. Hugh Martin, *Hugh Martin: The Boy Next Door* (Encinitas, Calif.: The Trolley Press, 2010), 291.

19. Jablonski, *Harold Arlen: Rhythm, Rainbows, and Blues*, 127.

CHAPTER 13. AN ITINERANT SONGWRITER

1. Harold Myerson and Ernie Harburg, *Who Put the Rainbow in the Wizard of Oz?* (Ann Arbor: University of Michigan Press, 1993), 169.

2. Edward Jablonski, *Harold Arlen: Rhythm, Rainbows, and Blues* (Boston: Northeastern University Press, 1996), 160.

3. "Day-to-Dayer," *The New Yorker*, January 29, 1955, 19.

4. The author is grateful to Michael Feinstein for providing him with this recording.

5. Jablonski, *Harold Arlen: Rhythm, Rainbows, and Blues*, 148.

Chapter 14. Writing with Johnny Mercer

1. Philip Furia, *Skylark: The Life and Times of Johnny Mercer* (New York: St. Martin's, 2003), 271.

2. "Arluck" letter to "Dear Son," January 2, 1939, courtesy of Rita Arlen.

3. Ginger did come up with at least one good line. Mercer quoted her as saying that the motto of their tiny New York pied-à-terre should be "I'll be loving you sideways." Max Wilk, *They're Playing Our Song* (Westport, Conn.: Easton Studio Press, 2008), 144.

4. Gene Lees, *Portrait of Johnny: The Life of John Herndon Mercer* (New York: Pantheon, 2004), 183.

5. Furia, *Skylark: The Life and Times of Johnny Mercer*, 123.

6. Ibid., 127.

7. Wilk, *They're Playing Our Song*, 171–72.

8. Ibid., 172.

9. Ibid., 152.

10. Alec Wilder, *American Popular Song* (New York: Oxford University Press, 1972), 272.

Chapter 15. "One for My Baby"

1. Edward Jablonski, *Harold Arlen: Rhythm, Rainbows, and Blues* (Boston: Northeastern University Press, 1996), 164.

2. Money from the sale of a recording was shared by the retail outlet, record company, recording artist, music publisher, and songwriters.

3. Meryle Secrest, *Somewhere for Me: A Biography of Richard Rodgers* (New York: Applause, 2001), 217.

4. Richard Rodgers, *Musical Stages: An Autobiography* (New York: Random House, 1975), 243.

5. Secrest, *Somewhere for Me*, 227.

6. Vernon Duke, *Passport to Paris* (Boston: Little, Brown, 1955), 384.

7. Ibid., 383.

8. John Lahr, "Come Rain or Come Shine: The Bittersweet Life of Harold Arlen," *The New Yorker*, September 19, 2005.

9. Harold Myerson and Ernie Harburg, *Who Put the Rainbow in the Wizard of Oz?* (Ann Arbor: University of Michigan Press, 1993), 179.

10. According to Edward Jablonski, Arlen told him that the song began when Harburg saw the phrase "Happiness is a thing called" (he couldn't remember the name), and that he and Harburg wanted to add the name of the film's main character, Joe, to the phrase but hesitated out of fear they'd be accused of plagiarism. They went ahead

and there was no such accusation. "Despite Harburg's flair for a good story," wrote Jablonski, "it is more likely that the melody was crafted to Harburg's final lyric—this was not a trunk tune." *Harold Arlen: Rhythm, Rainbows, and Blues*, 178.

11. Myerson and Harburg, *Who Put the Rainbow in the Wizard of Oz?*, 179.

12. Jablonski, *Harold Arlen: Rhythm, Rainbows, and Blues*, 165.

13. Edward Jablonski, *Harold Arlen: Happy with the Blues* (New York: Doubleday, 1961), 146.

CHAPTER 16. "AC-CENT-TCHU-ATE THE POSITIVE"

1. Agnes de Mille, *And Promenade Home* (Boston: Little, Brown, 1956), 195.

2. Trude Rittmann (her last name is sometimes spelled Ritman) had a remarkable career on Broadway, working not only with Arlen, but with Richard Rodgers, Irving Berlin, Lerner and Loewe, and many others. As the *New York Times* stated in their March 10, 2005, obituary for her: "Ms. Rittmann's was an unsung art, performed mostly behind the scenes, with no Tonys and little public notice until fairly recent years. It was her forte to take a composer's theme or melody and mold it into ballet or the incidental music woven in for dramatic effect."

3. Agnes de Mille, *And Promenade Home*, 194.

4. Ibid., 196.

5. Lisa Jo Sagolla, *The Girl Who Fell Down: A Biography of Joan McCracken* (Boston: Northeastern University Press, 2003), 103.

6. Ibid., 104.

7. Martin Charnin, telephone interview with the author, May 31, 2011.

8. Philip Furia, *Skylark: The Life and Times of Johnny Mercer* (New York: St. Martin's, 2003), 143.

CHAPTER 17. ST. LOUIS WOMAN

1. Hammerstein sweetened the ending by making the last encounter between father and daughter a happy one, followed by her high school graduation.

2. Edward Jablonski, *Harold Arlen: Rhythm, Rainbows, and Blues* (Boston: Northeastern University Press, 1996), 181.

3. James Gavin, *Stormy Weather: The Life of Lena Horne* (New York: Atria Books, 2009), 174.

4. Ibid., 174.

5. Lena Horne and Richard Schickel, *Lena* (Garden City, N.Y.: Doubleday, 1965), 187.

6. Gavin, *Stormy Weather*, 175.

7. Philip Furia, *Skylark: The Life and Times of Johnny Mercer* (New York: St. Martin's, 2003), 159.

8. Jablonski, *Harold Arlen: Rhythm, Rainbows, and Blues*, 204.

9. In saying "this man," she used the singular because she was being interviewed about Mercer. Arlen and Mercer both demonstrated the music.

10. Furia, *Skylark*, 159.

11. Ibid., 161.

12. Margaret Whiting and Will Holt, *It Might as Well Be Spring* (New York: William Morrow, 1987), 89.

13. Bob Dylan, *Chronicles* (New York: Simon & Schuster, 2004), 49. Dylan might have picked up this phrase from Alec Wilder, who wrote of Arlen's "emotional kinship with the jazz musician and his bittersweet, witty, lonely, intense, world." Alec Wilder, *American Popular Song* (New York: Oxford University Press, 1972), 255.

Chapter 18. Descent into Misery

1. Lynn Lane, in-person interview with the author, October 14, 2011.

2. Harold Meyerson and Ernie Harburg, *Who Put the Rainbow in the Wizard of Oz?* (Ann Arbor: University of Michigan Press, 1993), 219.

3. Harold Arlen, letter to Irving Berlin, April 20, 1948, Library of Congress, Irving Berlin Collection, Box 305, Folder 8.

4. Irving Berlin, letter to Harold Arlen, April 22, 1948, Library of Congress Irving Berlin Collection, Box 305, Folder 8.

5. Jonathan Schwartz, *All In Good Time* (New York: Random House, 2004), 29.

6. Mary Ellin Barrett, telephone interview with the author, February 9, 2012.

Chapter 19. "She Was Sweet and Adorable and Then She Went Mad"

1. Edward Jablonski, *Harold Arlen: Rhythm, Rainbows, and Blues* (Boston: Northeastern University Press, 1996), 206.

2. Ibid., 206.

3. Harold Meyerson and Ernie Harburg, *Who Put the Rainbow in the Wizard of Oz?* (Ann Arbor: University of Michigan Press, 1993), 272.

4. Phyllis Cole Braunlich, *Ralph Blane: Oklahoma's Hall of Fame Songwriter From Hollywood's Golden Age* (Tulsa: TCS, 2008), 39.

5. Jablonski, *Harold Arlen: Rhythm, Rainbows, and Blues*, 226.

6. Ibid., 227.

7. Edward Jablonski, "A brief, if not illuminating, lecture on Anya Arlen's Illness," Jablonski Collection, Library of Congress.

8. Michael Feinstein, telephone interview with the author, July 3, 2012.

Chapter 20. *A Star Is Born*

1. Gerald Clarke, *Get Happy: The Life of Judy Garland* (New York: Delta, 2000), 238.

2. Ibid., 266.

3. Lawrence D. Stewart, "Ira Gershwin and 'The Man That Got Away'," an unpublished paper, University of California, Los Angeles.

4. Philip Furia, *Skylark: The Life and Times of Johnny Mercer* (New York: St. Martin's, 2003), 202.

5. Ibid., 202.

6. Max Wilk, *They're Playing Our Song* (Westport, Conn.: Easton Studio Press, 2008), 173.

7. Stewart, "Ira Gershwin and 'The Man That Got Away.'"

8. Edward Jablonski, *Harold Arlen: Rhythm, Rainbows, and Blues* (Boston: Northeastern University Press, 1996), 236.

9. Ira Gershwin, *Lyrics on Several Occasions* (New York: Knopf, 1959), 242.

10. Wilk, *They're Playing Our Song*, 173.

11. Unless otherwise noted, the quotes in this paragraph come from Ronald Haver, *A Star Is Born: The Making of the 1954 Movie and Its 1983 Restoration* (New York: Knopf, 2002), 55.

12. Hugh Martin, *Hugh Martin: The Boy Next Door* (Encinitas, Calif.: Trolley Press, 2010), 305.

13. Ibid.

14. Ibid., 309.

15. Clarke, *Get Happy: The Life of Judy Garland*, 319.

16. Ibid., 319.

17. Jablonski, *Harold Arlen: Rhythm, Rainbows, and Blues*, 240.

18. Courtesy of Rita Arlen.

CHAPTER 21. *HOUSE OF FLOWERS*

1. Yipper, letter to Harold Arlen, March 27, 1952, courtesy of Rita Arlen.

2. Yipper, letter to "Dear Chaim," August 1, 1952, courtesy of Rita Arlen.

3. There is nothing to indicate that Harburg and Arlen had worked together since 1944, which was eight years before this letter, not five.

4. Yipper, letter to "Dear Chaim," August 1, 1952, courtesy of Rita Arlen.

5. E. Y. Harburg, letter to Harold Arlen, February 12, 1953, courtesy of Rita Arlen.

6. Gerald Clarke, *Capote: A Biography* (New York: Simon and Schuster, 1988), 69.

7. According to Edward Jablonski, the melody for "A Sleepin' Bee" predated *A Star Is Born* (*Happy with the Blues* [New York: Doubleday, 1961], 192).

8. William K. Zinsser, "Harold Arlen: The Secret Music Maker," *Harper's Magazine*, May 1960.

9. Maria Riva, *Marlene Dietrich by Her Daughter* (New York: Knopf, 1993), 639.

10. William K. Zinsser, "Harold Arlen: The Secret Music Maker."

11. Riva, *Marlene Dietrich by Her Daughter*, 639.

12. Ibid.

13. Edward Jablonski, *Harold Arlen: Rhythm, Rainbows, and Blues* (Boston: Northeastern University Press, 1996), 249.

14. Ibid., 254–55.

15. Gerald Clarke, *Capote: A Biography* (New York: Simon and Schuster, 1988), 261.

16. Jablonski, *Harold Arlen: Rhythm, Rainbows, and Blues*, 253.

17. Clarke, *Capote*, 262.

18. John Malcolm Brinnin, *Truman Capote: Dear Heart, Old Buddy* (New York: Delacorte, 1981), 106.

19. Clarke, *Capote*, 262.

20. Brooks Atkinson, "Truman Capote's Musical," *New York Times*, December 31, 1954, 11.

21. Lehman Engel, *Words with Music* (New York: Macmillan, 1972), 271.

CHAPTER 22. IN SEARCH OF FAME

1. Edward Jablonski, *Harold Arlen: Rhythm, Rainbows, and Blues* (Boston: Northeastern University Press, 1996), 262.

CHAPTER 23. AN OPERA

1. Stanley Green, *The World of Musical Comedy* (San Diego: Da Capo Press, 1980), 182.

2. Edward Jablonski, *Harold Arlen: Rhythm, Rainbows, and Blues* (Boston: Northeastern University Press, 1996), 288.

3. Ibid., 271.

4. Ibid., 275.

5. Dr. Steinman's note and prescription are in the Jablonski Collection at the Library of Congress, Box 4, Folder 19.

6. Information about these medications and their dosages was provided to the author by Elizabeth F. Thomas, M.D., in a November 13, 2012, email.

7. Jablonski, *Harold Arlen: Rhythm, Rainbows, and Blues*, 279.

8. Ernie Harburg, in-person interview with the author, October 13, 2011.

9. The quotations from this conversation come from Harriet Hyman Alonso's *Yip Harburg: Legendary Lyricist and Human Rights Activist* (Middletown, Conn.: Wesleyan University Press, 2012), 197–98.

10. Jablonski, *Harold Arlen: Rhythm, Rainbows, and Blues*, 279.

11. Ibid., 279.

12. Lena Horne and Richard Schickel, *Lena* (Garden City, N.Y.: Doubleday, 1965), 258.

13. Jablonski, *Harold Arlen: Rhythm, Rainbows, and Blues*, 280.

14. Horne and Schickel, *Lena*, 194.

15. James Gavin, *Stormy Weather: The Life of Lena Horne* (New York: Atria Books, 2009), 267.

16. Jablonski, *Harold Arlen: Rhythm, Rainbows, and Blues*, 282.

17. Ibid., 286.

18. Ibid., 292.

19. Ibid., 292.

CHAPTER 24. TWO DEBACLES

1. Julie Goldsmith Gilbert, *Edna Ferber and Her Circle: A Biography* (New York: Applause Books, 1978), 123.

2. In an October 14, 2011, in-person interview with the author, Lynn Lane recalled dining at Ira and Leonore Gershwin's house when Levant, too, was a dinner guest. During the conversation he said that Edna Ferber was America's greatest writer. Lane, who'd been an English major and favors F. Scott Fitzgerald, couldn't let that go by without questioning Levant's judgment. As they left the dining room, Ira told her, "You are so lucky that Oscar decided not to attack you. If he had it would have been terrible. I like him. But no one disagrees with him. And you did. And he didn't lash out at you."

3. Gene Lees, *Portrait of Johnny: The Life of John Herndon Mercer* (New York: Pantheon, 2004), 244.

4. Philip Furia, *Skylark: The Life and Times of Johnny Mercer* (New York: St. Martin's, 2003), 212.

5. Edward Jablonski, *Harold Arlen: Rhythm, Rainbows, and Blues* (Boston: Northeastern University Press, 1996), 296.

CHAPTER 25. THE 1960S

1. Edward Jablonski, *Harold Arlen: Rhythm, Rainbows, and Blues* (Boston: Northeastern University Press, 1996), 315.

2. Ibid., 316.

3. Dr. Rod Gorney, telephone interview with the author, April 4, 2012.

4. André Previn, telephone interview with the author, June 7, 2012.

5. Lynn Lane, in-person interview with the author, October 14, 2011.

6. Jablonski, *Harold Arlen: Rhythm, Rainbows, and Blues*, 331.

7. Ibid., 331.

8. Lynn Lane, in-person interview with the author, October 14, 2011.

9. Carla Jablonski, telephone interview with the author, April 10, 2012.

10. Irving Berlin Collection, Library of Congress.

11. In an article titled "A Salute to Arlen," by Emory Lewis in the March 20, 1965, edition of *Cue*, Harburg was at least as generous to Arlen when it came to credit for "Over the Rainbow." Addressing him in absentia, he said: "You have built yourself a monument better than all the bronze statues in Central Park . . . As for me, I was indeed a lucky hitch-hiker—having negotiated a ride on the tail of this meteoric melody by waving a few adjectives at you. Thanks for the lift."

12. Jablonski, *Harold Arlen: Rhythm, Rainbows, and Blues*, 330.

13. Ibid., 316.

14. In 1962 Warren wrote "Mass in Honor of St. Anthony," a Roman Catholic Mass to a Latin text. It was performed once (he was there) but has never been recorded.

15. There were exceptions: producer Martin wrote the string quartet backing for "Yesterday" as well as the string octet arrangement for "Eleanor Rigby." The strings and harp arrangement for "She's Leaving Home" was by Mike Leander.

16. In a July 10, 2014, email to the author Martin Charnin wrote: "The note I slipped into Harold's pocket read, 'I can be good for you.' He liked the phrase, but we both felt that 'could' was more interesting and less pompous when I suggested that we write a song using my presumptuous note to him as a title."

17. Martin Charnin, email to the author, July 10, 2014.

18. He would later write the books for several of Stephen Sondheim's most notable musicals, including *A Little Night Music*, *Pacific Overtures*, and *Sweeney Todd*.

19. Martin Charnin, email to the author, July 10, 2014.

20. Jablonski, *Harold Arlen: Rhythm, Rainbows, and Blues*, 330.

21. John Meyer, *Heartbreaker* (Garden City, N.Y.: Doubleday, 1983), 69.

22. Ibid., 105.

23. Ibid., 109–10.

Chapter 26. Waiting

1. Katharine Weber, email to the author, October 16, 2012.

2. Edward Jablonski, *Harold Arlen: Rhythm, Rainbows, and Blues* (Boston: Northeastern University Press, 1996), 336.

3. Rita Arlen, in-person interview with the author, October 12, 2011.

4. Jablonski, *Harold Arlen: Rhythm, Rainbows, and Blues*, 336.

5. Ibid., 340.

6. Rita Arlen, in-person interview with the author, October 12, 2011.

7. Jablonski, *Harold Arlen: Rhythm, Rainbows, and Blues*, 341.

8. Rita Arlen, telephone interview with the author, July 5, 2011.

9. Cantor Harold Lerner, telephone interview with the author, August 10, 2011.

10. Jablonski, *Harold Arlen: Rhythm, Rainbows, and Blues*, 349.

11. John Corry, "About New York: O for the Songs of Yesteryear," *New York Times*, April 3, 1974.

12. Lynn Lane, in-person interview with the author, October 14, 2011.

13. Laurence Bergreen, *As Thousands Cheer* (New York: Penguin, 1990), 569.

14. John Lahr, "Come Rain or Come Shine: The Bittersweet Life of Harold Arlen," *The New Yorker*, September 19, 2005.

15. Jablonski, *Harold Arlen: Rhythm, Rainbows, and Blues*, 348.

16. Ibid., 348.

17. Carla Jablonski, telephone interview with the author, April 10, 2012.

18. Jablonski, *Harold Arlen: Rhythm, Rainbows, and Blues*, 360.

19. Rita Arlen, in-person interview with the author, October 12, 2011.

20. Lynn Lane, in-person interview with the author, October 14, 2011.

21. Michael Feinstein, telephone interview with the author, July 3, 2012.

22. Michael Feinstein, *Nice Work If You Can Get It: My Life in Rhythm and Rhyme* (New York: Hyperion, 1995), 248.

23. Lynn Lane, in-person interview with the author, October 14, 2011.

24. Ron Alexander, "Metropolitan Diary," *New York Times*, May 7, 1986.

25. The Cowardly Lion, courtesy of E. Y. Harburg.

INDEX

Robin, Leo, 2, 112–14, 116
Robinson, Bill "Bojangles," 21, 24
Rodeo (Copland), 98
Rodgers, Mary, 159
Rodgers, Richard, 14, 25, 37, 38, 41, 52, 108, 111, 116, 135, 148, 152, 156, 159, 172; *Carousel*, 102, 106; final years, 157; Judy Garland and, 162–63; as a musical theater innovator, 20–21, 64–65, 76, 89, 90–92, 98, 100, 114
Rogers, Ginger, 37, 50, 58, 94
Rogin, Michael, 50
Rollini, Adrian, 54
Romberg, Sigmund, 25
Rome, Harold, 187
Ronell, Ann, 14, 111
Rooney, Mickey, 75, 84, 86
Roosevelt, Franklin D., 29, 39, 65, 144
Rose, Billy, 15, 32, 110
Rose, David, 85, 88
Ross, Herbert, 133
Royal, Ted, 151
Russell, Connie, 138
Ryerson, Florence, 70–71

Saidy, Fred, 98, 100, 105, 145, 146
Saint-Subber, Arnold, 128, 133–34, 160
Sandler, Bernie, 230n12, 232n98
Sandler, Hymie, 6, 8
Saratoga (Arlen-Mercer), 148–50, 151
Saratoga Trunk (Ferber), 148
"Satan's Li'l Lamb" (Arlen-Harburg-Mercer), 29, 30, 82
"Says Who? Says You, Says I!" (Arlen-Mercer), 85
Schachtel, Maurice, 154–55, 165, 166, 169
Schirmer, Mabel, 164
Schuchat, Berthe, 172
Schwartz, Arthur, 14, 94, 110, 174
Schwartz, Jonathan, 110, 174–75
Searle, Ronald, 148
Sedaka, Neil, 137
Seidel, Leon, 202
Selwyn, Edgar, 18
Selwyn, Ruth, 18
Se-More Jazz Band, 8
"Shakin' the African" (Arlen-Koehler), 21
Shall We Dance (Gershwin-Gershwin), 57, 58, 70

Sheed, Wilfrid, 34
Show Boat (Kern-Hammerstein), 14, 18, 149
Show Is On (revue), 54
Shubert brothers, 12, 28, 40, 59, 63, 64, 77, 160
Siegel, Sol, 116
Signorelli, Frank, 9
"Silent Spring" (Arlen-Harburg), 159
Silvers, Phil, 84
Silvers, Sid, 23
Silver Slipper, 11, 21
Simon, Paul, 29, 158, 172
Sinatra, Frank, 88, 90, 95, 121, 138, 158, 172, 174, 176
Singing Kid, (Arlen-Harburg), 50–51
"Sing My Heart" (Arlen-Koehler), 78
Skeleton Dance (Stalling), 37
Skolsky, Sidney, 55, 111
Sky's the Limit (Arlen-Meercer), 94
Slaughter on Tenth Avenue (Rodgers), 97
"Sleepin' Bee, A" (Arlen-Capote), 130, 135, 146, 156, 159
Snappy Trio, 8
Snow White and the Seven Dwarfs, 66, 72
Softly (Arlen-Charnin), 160–61
"Soliloquy" (Rodgers-Hammerstein), 106
"So Long, Big Time!" (Arlen-Langdon), 156
"Someday My Prince Will Come" (Churchill-Morey), 66, 72
Sondheim, Stephen, 100
Song of Norway (Grieg), 102
Song of the Woodman" (Arlen-Harburg), 54
Songs by Arlen, Stories by Skolsky, 111
Sound of Music (Rodgers-Hammerstein), 60, 157
Southbound Shufflers, 8, 11
South Pacific (Rodgers-Hammerstein), 114, 117
Spector, Phil, 158
Stage Struck (Arlen-Harburg), 52
Stalling, Carl, 37
Stamberg, Susan, 174
"Stand By Me" (King-Leiber-Stoller), 137
Star Is Born, A, 121–22, 129, 141
Stark, Herman, 33
Star Spangled Rhythm (Arlen-Mercer), 92
Steiner, Max, 37
Steinman, Morris, 122, 143

WALTER RIMLER is the author of *George Gershwin: An Intimate Portrait* and *A Cole Porter Discography*.

Louis Prima   *Garry Boulard*
Marian McPartland's Jazz World: All in Good Time   *Marian McPartland*
Robert Johnson: Lost and Found   *Barry Lee Pearson and Bill McCulloch*
Bound for America: Three British Composers   *Nicholas Temperley*
Lost Sounds: Blacks and the Birth of the Recording Industry,
    1890–1919   *Tim Brooks*
Burn, Baby! BURN! The Autobiography of Magnificent
    Montague   *Magnificent Montague with Bob Baker*
Way Up North in Dixie: A Black Family's Claim to the
    Confederate Anthem   *Howard L. Sacks and Judith Rose Sacks*
The Bluegrass Reader   *Edited by Thomas Goldsmith*
Colin McPhee: Composer in Two Worlds   *Carol J. Oja*
Robert Johnson, Mythmaking, and Contemporary American
    Culture   *Patricia R. Schroeder*
Composing a World: Lou Harrison, Musical Wayfarer
    Leta E. Miller and Fredric Lieberman
Fritz Reiner, Maestro and Martinet   *Kenneth Morgan*
That Toddlin' Town: Chicago's White Dance Bands and Orchestras,
    1900–1950   *Charles A. Sengstock Jr.*
Dewey and Elvis: The Life and Times of a Rock 'n' Roll Deejay
    Louis Cantor
Come Hither to Go Yonder: Playing Bluegrass with Bill Monroe
    Bob Black
Chicago Blues: Portraits and Stories   *David Whiteis*
The Incredible Band of John Philip Sousa   *Paul E. Bierley*
"Maximum Clarity" and Other Writings on Music   *Ben Johnston, e
    dited by Bob Gilmore*
Staging Tradition: John Lair and Sarah Gertrude Knott
    Michael Ann Williams
Homegrown Music: Discovering Bluegrass   *Stephanie P. Ledgin*
Tales of a Theatrical Guru   *Danny Newman*
The Music of Bill Monroe   *Neil V. Rosenberg and Charles K. Wolfe*
Pressing On: The Roni Stoneman Story   *Roni Stoneman,
    as told to Ellen Wright*
Together Let Us Sweetly Live   *Jonathan C. David,
    with photographs by Richard Holloway*
Live Fast, Love Hard: The Faron Young Story   *Diane Diekman*
Air Castle of the South: WSM Radio and the Making of Music City
    Craig P. Havighurst
Traveling Home: Sacred Harp Singing and American Pluralism   *Kiri Miller*
Where Did Our Love Go? The Rise and Fall of the
    Motown Sound   *Nelson George*

The University of Illinois Press
is a founding member of the
Association of American University Presses.

_____

Composed in 10/13 Sabon
by Lisa Connery
at the University of Illinois Press
Designed by Dennis Roberts
Manufactured by Cushing-Malloy, Inc.

University of Illinois Press
1325 South Oak Street
Champaign, IL 61820-6903
www.press.uillinois.edu